BREAKING THE NEWS

For Joan Mason
In memory of Nan Sellors
Jackie

For Ben, Sam and Josh
Luke

Published in 2022 by
The British Library
96 Euston Road
London NW1 2DB

www.bl.uk/publishing
ISBN 978 0 7123 5441 7

British Library Cataloguing-in-Publication Data
A catalogue record for this publication is available from the British Library

Designed and typeset by Ocky Murray
Picture research by Sally Nicholls
Project edited by Abbie Day
Printed and bound in the Czech Republic by Finidr

This publication accompanies the British Library exhibition
Breaking the News (April–August 2022).

BREAKING
THE NEWS

500 Years of
News in Britain

Supported by

Newsworks
Because journalism matters

Edited by Jackie Harrison and Luke McKernan

Contents

Foreword

When this book and the exhibition it accompanies were conceived in mid-2019, the COVID-19 pandemic lay unknown in the future – a horrifying reminder of the magnitude of news events that can engulf us without warning.

Some of us were taught in school of the six ingredients of a news story: what, when, where, who, why and how. In the many objects and stories brought together in these pages you will find evidence that the 'what' of news has mostly remained the same: war, natural disaster, crime, politics and celebrity scandal. All that has changed is the speed and the medium of transmission; sometimes news is unfiltered, sometimes deliberately manipulated, and it has circulated via media ranging from seventeenth-century pamphlets to daily newspapers and live feeds from a smartphone, viewable around the world and quickly shared.

A positive part of the story of news emerges in the enduring drive of individual journalists and campaigning institutions to speak truth to power: from the challenging pamphleteer spirit of the Reformation and the English Civil War, to the campaigning investigative journalism of W.T. Stead, who exposed the scale of child sexual trafficking in Victorian London, to Harold Evans and the *Sunday Times* Insight Team, who uncovered the thalidomide scandal, and the persistence of Carole Cadwalladr in exposing Cambridge Analytica.

A positive part of the story of news emerges in the enduring drive of individual journalists and campaigning institutions to speak truth to power.

Fifty years ago an exhibition called *Breaking the News* might well have had an extended section on totalitarian propaganda. It seemed reasonable to believe that the more media voices there were, the better. Instead, while curating the exhibition and writing this book, we have found that the new technology of social media has enabled not just a huge democratised citizen journalism, but also a proliferation of fake news and groupthink. Who anticipated groups of anti-vaxxers launching angry protests and attacks on news journalists and once widely respected news organisations such as the BBC and ITN? We've also discovered how authoritarian regimes endure in societies with pluralised modern media, from Russia and the so-called Arab Spring to crackdowns in Myanmar, Belarus and Hong Kong, and learned sobering lessons about the speed with which supposedly model democracies such as the US and the UK can be sucked by unscrupulous politicians into an endless news cycle of claim and counter-claim, while fact-checking journalism struggles to keep up.

In these pages lies the strange contradiction of news itself: it is contained within the flimsy physicality of newsprint, film reels, photographs and computer hard drives that can be smashed with hammers. By contemplating these objects and the stories they conveyed we can see the enduring human desire to share events, uniting in joy, shock, outrage or compassion, and to learn lessons by putting them on the record. Who knew that, in the supposedly heartless business of news, there lay so much emotion and desire to make a better world?

Acknowledgements

This book was produced to accompany the 2022 British Library exhibition *Breaking the News*. Grateful thanks go to the exhibition's advisory panel for their wise guidance and enthusiasm. The panel, several of whom were able to contribute to the book, were Samira Ahmed (chair), Kurt Barling, George Brock, Jo Fox, Kathryn Geels, David Dunkley Gyimah, Jackie Harrison and Joad Raymond. Grateful thanks are likewise due to the others who have written so knowledgeably for the book: Adrian Bingham, Laurel Brake, Beth Gaskell, Tony Harcup, Linda Kaye, Matthew Parris, Maddy Smith, Tamara Tubb, James Whitworth and Brian Winston.

Thanks go to all those behind the *Breaking the News* exhibition, particularly the Head of Culture Programmes at the British Library, Conrad Bodman, and to the organising team of Howard Batho, Caroline Brown and Cleo Laskarin. The curatorial team were Beth Gaskell, Stephen Lester, Luke McKernan, Maddy Smith and Tamara Tubb, each of whom contributed much to the development of this book. Thanks also to other curators at the British Library for their support, notably Neil McCowlen and Paul Wilson; to Ed King, former Head of Newspaper Collections, for his advice; to Stewart Gillies and the British Library news reference team; and to those members of a news curatorial group who, some years ago, thought that an exhibition to mark 500 years of British news might be a good idea.

Final thanks are due to Abbie Day and John Lee at British Library Publishing for commissioning the book and showing such faith in it.

Conventions

Newspaper titles are cited as they were at the date referred to in the text (e.g. *The Manchester Guardian* for 1821–1959, *The Guardian* thereafter). Titles are taken from the mastheads, as recorded in the British Library catalogue (http://explore.bl.uk), with definite articles except where these might lead to an ungrammatical construction e.g. *The Times*, but a *Times* journalist, or as a short reference after the full title has been cited earlier e.g. *Mirror* instead of *Daily Mirror*.

The dates for all significant people mentioned are given in parentheses after the first mention of their name in any one chapter, except where this might make for awkward reading.

Contributors

Award-winning journalist and broadcaster **Samira Ahmed** presents *Front Row* on Radio 4, *Newswatch* on BBC1 and made the BBC4 documentary series *Art of Persia*. Previously a presenter and reporter on Channel 4 News, she began her career as a BBC News Trainee, working as a News Correspondent and for Deutsche Welle TV in Berlin.

Kurt Barling is Professor of Journalism at Middlesex University. He was an award-winning BBC investigative journalist and film-maker until 2015. Over a twenty-five-year journalism career Kurt won five national awards for his reporting of race in Britain, the US, Africa and the Caribbean. He is the author and editor of books on German history, terrorism and economic development, as well as the polemic *The R Word: Racism* (2015).

Adrian Bingham is Professor of Modern British History at the University of Sheffield. He has written extensively on the history of British journalism, including *Family Newspapers? Sex, Private Life, and the British Popular Press 1918–1978* (2009), and, with Martin Conboy, *Tabloid Century: The Popular Press in Britain, 1896 to the Present* (2015).

Laurel Brake is Professor Emerita of Literature and Print Culture, Birkbeck, University of London. She is the author of *Subjugated Knowledges* (1994) and *Print in Transition, 1850–1910* (2001), and many articles on nineteenth-century press and media history. She has co-edited *Dictionary of Nineteenth-Century Journalism* (2009; 2018), *The Lure of Illustration* (2009), *W.T. Stead: Newspaper Revolutionary* (2012), *The News of the World and the British Press* (2016) and *Nineteenth-Century Serials Edition* (https://ncse.ac.uk).

George Brock is a former journalist on *The Times* and *The Observer* and Professor of Journalism at City, University of London. He published *Out of Print: Newspapers, Journalism and the Business of News in the Digital Age* in 2013.

Professor Jo Fox is Pro Vice Chancellor (Research and Engagement) and Dean of the School of Advanced Study, University of London. She has published widely on propaganda and disinformation from 1914 to the present.

Beth Gaskell is the British Library's Curator of Newspaper Digitisation. Her work focuses on nineteenth-century newspapers, as part of the Library's Heritage Made Digital project. Her research interests include newspaper and periodical history, the development of the 'professional' press and military–media relations. She has a chapter in the Colby Award-winning *Researching the Nineteenth-Century Press: Case Studies* (2018).

David Dunkley Gyimah is Senior Lecturer at the School of Journalism, Media and Culture, Cardiff University. He has worked for Channel 4 News, ABC News and BBC radio and television. He created Viewmagazine. tv, an international award-winning hybrid digital publication and agency, and is co-founder of *Reprezentology*, a journal for research and best practice in how to make UK media more representative of all sections of society.

Tony Harcup is an Emeritus Fellow in Journalism Studies at the University of Sheffield, having spent decades working as a journalist within mainstream and alternative media before becoming a journalism educator. His books include the *Oxford Dictionary of Journalism* (2014) and *What's the Point of News?* (2020).

Jackie Harrison is Professor of Public Communication, UNESCO Chair on Media Freedom, Journalism Safety and the Issue of Impunity and Chair of the interdisciplinary Centre for Freedom of the Media (CFOM) at the University of Sheffield. Her most recent book is *The Civil Power of the News* (2019).

Linda Kaye is a film historian and archivist. Her research interest is in government communications, specifically through film in the era of the Central Office of Information, newsreels and cinemagazines. She has co-edited *Projecting Britain: The Guide to British Cinemagazines* (2008).

Luke McKernan is Lead Curator, News and Moving Image at the British Library. His publications include *Topical Budget: The Great British News Film* (1992) and *Yesterday's Witness: The British Cinema Newsreel Reader* (2002). He has also written on early cinema and audiovisual Shakespeare. He is lead curator for the British Library's exhibition *Breaking the News*.

Matthew Parris is a former MP and a prize-winning author, columnist and broadcaster. He currently writes columns for *The Times* and *The Spectator* as well as presenting the BBC Radio 4 biographical programme *Great Lives*. He was named Political Journalist of the Year at the Press Awards 2015.

Joad Raymond is a Welsh academic and writer based in London, where he is Professor of Renaissance Studies at Queen Mary University of London. He is the author and editor of twelve books, especially on the history of news in Europe, and releases and performs music under the name 'The Unattached'.

Maddy Smith is a curator in the British Library's Printed Heritage Collections department, which is responsible for Western printed books, periodicals, prints and ephemera from the fifteenth century through to the year 2000. She specialises in seventeenth- and eighteenth-century material. She is part of the curatorial team for the British Library's exhibition *Breaking the News*.

Tamara Tubb is Project Curator in the British Library's News, Radio and Moving Image team, and is one of the curators for the British Library's *Breaking the News* exhibition. Prior to joining the Library in 2016, she worked as a teacher, researcher and digital media executive.

James Whitworth teaches at the University of Sheffield, where his main area of research is the British newspaper cartoon in the twentieth century. He has published widely and is currently writing a book on the pocket cartoon. He is also a nationally syndicated cartoonist with work appearing in magazines including *Private Eye*.

Brian Winston's latest book on the press is *The Roots of Fake News: Objecting to Objective Journalism* (with Mathew Winston, 2020). He has worked on both sides of the Atlantic as a journalist since 1963 and as a media academic since 1974.

Jackie Harrison

Introduction

The chapters that follow tell a story about the last 500 years of news in Britain. This is not a historical timeline, but rather a collection of contributions which together reveal the evolving nature of news, its changing formats and the many different circumstances it has found itself operating in – circumstances that have ranged from suppression and censorship on one end of the spectrum, to an abundance of opportunities for relatively free expression and publication on the other.

These contributions show its serious side through the reporting of war and conflict, crime and disasters, and its responses to the misuses and abuses of power through campaigns and the use of satire. They also show the less serious side of news by pointing out its fascination with celebrities, 'human interest' stories, celebrations, the strange and the bizarre. And they discuss the things news should do, such as hold power to account and serve the public interest, and the things it should not do: distort, lie, mislead or deceive. Supporting these chapters are a series of short biographical sketches of people who were central in breaking news of significance and, on a more speculative note, there is a chapter on the future of the news. In their various ways all chapters point to the immutable fact that the news is an important and constant commentary on how people choose and struggle to live together, past and present.

From the inception of the UK press, those individuals responsible for the development and expansion of the publication of news saw the appeal of news journalism in terms of its connectedness to the cultural and social experiences of the public. Importantly, this was not a public understood as a homogeneous entity exclusively concerned with reasoning and deliberation. On the contrary, it was a collection of publics understood as having different opinions and concerns – based on their knowledge (or what they thought they knew) as well as their thoughts and feelings about things that mattered to them immediately and directly. Combined, these views constitute what we can call public sentiment.

The news is an important and constant commentary on how people choose and struggle to live together.

Public sentiment may be expressed passionately, angrily, reasonably or rationally; it may exemplify hospitality, decency, generosity and openness, or display hatred, bigotry and closed-mindedness; it has long been communicated in letters and more recently appears in many digital formulations. In whatever way it is manifest, it was and still is something that those selecting and producing the news have responded to and sought to influence. Competition between news providers in responding to and engaging with public sentiment means that they have needed to understand how different groups of people – their audiences – have formed different interest groups with diverse views and beliefs. Given that news audiences cohere around their own particular priorities, which are based on their own cultural and social experiences, news providers have always needed (for commercial and ideological reasons) to find the most effective and attractive ways to engage 'their own' audience and to keep it 'interested'. Finding one's audience and engaging with its changing priorities, views and tastes has been a driving concern for news providers for over 500 years, first through the printed news medium, followed by film, broadcast and digital formats in a ceaseless competition for attention. What this means is that for centuries we have been able to observe a fundamental feature of news journalism, which is its circular relationship with its own audience. We see it in the way in which public sentiment influences news selection when particular audiences express what is newsworthy for them by choosing particular news products, and how news providers, in turn, engage with public sentiment through specific types of reporting.

This leads us to the interesting question of why different news providers, which are all concerned with news journalism for different kinds of audiences, find more or less the same events newsworthy. Why is it the case that, if public sentiment coheres around different conceptions of self-interest, or different versions of what is in the best interest for all, and news journalism consists of responding to and reporting on these different outlooks, many of the same events are judged to be of universal and common interest? The answer is straightforward: where publics are part of a common culture and society they also share overlapping concerns, ideas and beliefs about the fundamental nature of that civil society. Here civil society simply refers to social life configured around versions of citizenship, solidarity and associative life, established norms

Events that are judged to impinge upon our invariant civil concerns are newsworthy.

and laws of behaviour, institutions of representation and rights. Even here, though, it is still the case that different publics have different versions of how we should all co-exist within civil society. These are naturally contested and disagreed upon, and it is this contestation that is constantly reflected in the news. However, and importantly, despite these disagreements there are still timeless concerns that are shared by all the various publics that make up any society. This means there is a consensus that events that are judged to impinge upon our invariant civil concerns are newsworthy, and it is through the telling of these events as stories that the news exhibits its civil power.

What are these invariant civil concerns that are shared by all and yet interpreted so differently? The first is a concern about *identity* and the way in which we are able to define 'ourselves', to say who 'we' are and to say openly what it is that 'we' belong to. The second is a concern about *legitimacy* and is focused on the extent to which we agree with the justifications for the rules, regulations and laws we must all follow. The third is our ongoing concern about *risk* and the assessments and calculations about threats that we all make in relation to our safety and also about risks to 'our' way of life. Discussions about our invariant civil concerns of identity, legitimacy and risk are constantly playing out in stories ranging from disagreements about immigration, criticism of the handling of health crises, judgements of criminal wrongdoing, the reporting of different sides of conflicts and the handling of disasters to contested elections, the appropriateness of welfare benefits, criticism of the actions of politicians and political parties and disagreements about the need to enforce rules on the public during a pandemic. Stories like these – that is, stories that engage with our invariant civil concerns, both rationally expressed or emotionally felt – have characterised news over the last 500 years and will continue to do so.

More specifically, in the news concerns about identity guide us in terms of who we should be hospitable towards and who 'we' should not, who is like 'us' and who is not. While we are free to disagree with particular judgements and assumptions about this and change to another news provider, in the news there is always an 'us' which is both inclusive and contrastive, carrying with it a notion of shared citizenship (and with that an abstract equality). The contrastive 'us' tells us about the boundaries 'we' already place around ourselves or wish to see imposed and about whom we wish to exclude. News stories that deal with matters of civil identity do so in the way they identify and compare individuals and groups against some perceived standard of civility. Crucially, these comparisons in news often relate to gender, sexuality, race, ethnicity, age, nationality and occupation.

Stories that engage with our invariant civil concerns have characterised news over the last 500 years.

In the chapters that follow we can see how news about scandal charts taboos and changing attitudes, scandalising its audience with tales of cover-ups, hypocrisy and what is deemed at any given time to be inappropriate behaviour. When actions are cast as being outside expected norms or as undertaken by people who should know better, it is all too easy to label them as being uncivil and mark them as outsiders. Here we see the demonisation of some victims of murder (women who were classed as immoral), condemning them to be portrayed as less worthy of our empathy, as a means to exclude them from civil life. The same occurs whenever the

Concerns about risk can be both real and exaggerated (and in some cases manufactured).

news coverage of peaceful protests focuses mainly on the theme of violence, serving only to distort and exclude. We can also see how in stories of conflict and battle the civil 'we' of the British Empire was cast in heroic terms, something that itself would be highly contested today; and yet national identity has long been played out in celebratory statements about 'our' national victories in sport, in international politics, wars and conflicts and in the celebratory coverage of British pageantry around coronations, jubilees and royal weddings.

In the news, concerns about legitimacy focus on why some beliefs and actions are justified and some are not, why some forms of behaviour, beliefs, norms, codes and laws are justified and need preserving, or are deemed unjustified and need changing or discarding. We see in the following chapters how justifications are always contested and beliefs about what is legitimate or not vary and span all forms of editorial beliefs and arguments. Sometimes the news engages in its own crusades and public campaigns about such things as the efficacy of vaccinations, injustice against minority groups or the need for a law to protect children. The news may support state action to ensure a greater sense of security or wellbeing at times of national crisis, but at other times actions by the state, such as taking the country to war, may be seen to be illegitimate and is questioned, satirised or openly contested. Sometimes such an attack on the authority of governments and states may engender doubt, suspicion, fear or anger about formal, legalised or institutionalised legitimacy and authority, especially if news specifically seeks to excite public sentiment on weighty matters.

Concerns about risk can be both real and exaggerated (and in some cases manufactured), and stories in the news about risk span from catastrophic disaster, threat of war or conflict and fear of violence from within society to personal uncertainty. Risk is both global and local. It may even be reported in the news that life is more or less dangerous than at some time in the past, so that risk and fearfulness are linked together in the news with security and insecurity. This can lead to a sense of loss of control that must somehow be restored. We see in the chapters that follow that the news may be reported in a highly sensational way that increases the sense of insecurity and fear. The fear of the unknown serial

From Rome the 21. of August. 1621.

THere is aduice from Naples, that certaine Ambassadours of Messina are arriued there and from thence are to go into Spaine, to congratulate the king, and to giue him a present of 150000. crownes, as also that in Naples a contention falling out betweene the Spaniards and Neopolitans, there were many on both sides slaine and wounded, so that if the Cardinall the *Vice Roy* had not stept in amongst them, there would haue bene a great slaughter.

The Popes galleyes are gone to Gaeta and Messina, but the gally Saint *Peter* stayes at Gaeta.

On tuesday Prince *Philibert* with 15. gallyes sayled along by Ciuita Vechia towards Sicilia.

Here by commandement of the Pope there are costly swadling bands, mantles, and other blankets made, they are embroidered with gold siluer, and other costly workes, to present vnto the queene of Spaine against she is brought to bed of her first child, amounting to the vallew of 10000. crownes.

From Venice the 27 of August. 1621.

BY letters of the 21. from Genua it is certified, that *Petro de Liens* is arriued there with two gallyes from Spaine, and that the rest stay still at Vado. The next day the Generall followed him, and in a ship richly laden went from Genua to Spaine, and passing by Nizza refused to pay the Tole, whereupon certaine vessels were sent out against them, and ouertaking the in the Prouince Sea, tooke them and brought them to Nizza from Grieckisckwisenburg. It is certified that the bridges that are made ouer the riuer Donaw by the Turkes, are now ready, and that the Turke hath left an army of 50000. men by Cameniz to defend the bridges, after whom there followed 15000. waggons laden with victuals and munition for the Army, in the meane time the Turks sent 10000. Turkes to forrage the country, who being met with all by 15000. Polonians fought together, the Polanders at last hauing the victory.

From Vienna the 25 of August. 1621.

AFter the Hungarians had burnt & destroyed about 200. castles, villages, and market townes, and spoyled a great quantity of corne standing vpon the ground, they went backe againe and planted a siege before Presburge, & vpon the 19.20 21. & 22. of August shot fiercely against it, and still continue their battery, the Emperours souldiers defend themselues valiantly therein, notwithstanding that they are shut vp therein, and are determined to fight as long as any of them are aliue, if they bee not forced to yeeld for want of ayde and prouision of victuals.

There are 8000. men of Morauia, Bohemia and many souldiers of Sylesia gathered together in Marble, that are to go withall speede to releeue Presburge.

On this side the riuer, Donaw the Budianers in great numbers ouer-runne and ransacke the countrey, doing great hurt by burning and spoyling the same, and haue come within foure miles of this towne, and burnt the countrey: whereupon the poore people in great feare run away, and by that means the corne in the countrey is all spoyled. The Earle of Colalto, hath commission to defend Newstadt, and to let the, from making incursio. After that the Emperor had proclaymed a generall pardon in Morania, and the prisoners set at libertie, they began to defend themselues, and are determined to defend their countrey from further inuasions. There are more men expected to come hither from Inn. Captain *Beeker*, that had bin 3. weekes prisoner with the Hungarians is now released and come hither.

The Ducket is yet 3. Florins and a halfe, and the Rex Doller 2. Florins and 30. Crutzers. The gold Doller 2. Florins, which sort of mony shall be raysed to 4.3. and 2. and a halfe.

The Duke of Saxons, and the English Ambassadors are yet here.

The Earle of Colalto, 8 dayes since, meeting with the Hungarians that came to Newstadt, and there in the suburbs tooke certaine childre and carryed them prisoners, whereof some of them were Turkes.

The Budianers with who there are 6000. Turks ioyned are gone with their army towards the borders of the Steirmarke.

From Presburge the 21. of August. 1621.

THe 16.17. and 18. of this month the enemy planted his siege in Hohemery winegardens, on both sides about this towne, in such manner that all the ground is couered with the which done vpon the 19.20. 21. they began to batter the towne and presently entred the suburbs, and began to ensconce themselues against the towne, against whom our souldiers are not idle, and ceased not 3. dayes together to shoot out of the towne and castle against them, and they in like maner against vs, whereby many are slaine on both sides: the last night the enemy brought his great ordinace to the Schadtorfer street, and planted a great peece ouer against St. *Michaels* tower, to batter the bulwark and sconce, but to little end, for that not onely the wals in that place are very strong, but also the vttermost Bulwarke, for that they cannot speedily make any bretch; and as soone as any hurt is done, presently it is repayred and ramperd killer and other random events both scares and titillates, in stories of crime and disaster that stir the emotions and amplify the drama. Sometimes, as a counter-force, there is a mobilisation of expertise, definitive arguments, conclusive proofs and categorical assertions about what needs to be done to reduce fearfulness and improve feelings of security, evident for example in celebratory stories about our military and those who serve the public, who, through their brave and heroic acts, protect us.

News can either support openness and inclusivity, or it can contribute to prejudice and exclusion.

All three invariant civil concerns – identity, legitimacy and risk – are often accompanied by various codes and symbolic and cultural expressions that resonate with the language and priorities of the particular audience being addressed. Those who write the news headlines are well practised at drawing us in. News stories may endorse civil values; they may push for the restoration of something lost, seek to correct injustice or orchestrate a more solidarising public sentiment when public sentiment is polarised. The news can of course also endorse anti-civil values through a more instrumental use of its civil power actively to promote political or other vested interests, leading to a narrower, more excluding and partisan news. News can either support and help define a vibrant civil sphere of openness and inclusivity, or it can contribute to a minimalist civil sphere of prejudice and exclusion. The extent to which there is freedom of publication and expression relates to the extent to which news providers can and do resist those forces of suppression and distortion that would diminish the exercise of the civil power of the news to verify facts, to report truthfully and, importantly, to contribute to the quality of life in civil society.

Corante, or, Newes from Italy, Germany, Hungarie, Spaine and France, the first newspaper to be published in Britain, 24 September 1621.

1

WHAT MAKES A NEWS EVENT?

Jackie Harrison

INTRODUCTION

The news and those involved in its production cannot by themselves determine its relevance. Far from it: the news resides in a deep relationship with events that are deemed to be of interest and are relevant to particular audiences and also to the sentiments each audience holds about itself. Clearly not all events are newsworthy, so how events come to be considered newsworthy, and who the relevant agents are in determining their newsworthiness, is down to an event having particular aspects. Stories that include conflict, sensationalism, scandal, celebrity, disaster, politics and celebration, with their ability to draw audiences in and keep them engaged, have long been the staple of news journalism. The authors in this section treat each of these aspects of newsworthiness as historical constants, showing how they have been seen to be newsworthy for the last 500 years. Whether this says something more about human nature or about journalism itself is moot, but it is clear that whatever the motive for covering a particular event (and this too is examined here), stories told then and now are remarkably similar.

Brian Winston

The trewe encountre: Conflict and the press

Hereafter enſue the trewe encountre or...
Batayle lately done, betwene Englâde and:
Scotlande. In which batayle the Scottſſhe
Kynge was ſlayne

Ⅰ f it bleeds, it leads' was noted as a tabloid newspaper editorial injunction in the 1950s, but four and a half centuries earlier, the oldest surviving news report printed in English concerned a bloody event: the Battle of Flodden Field, 9 September 1513. England won and, wow!, the 'splash' was that James IV, the Scottish king, had been 'ſlayne'.[1]

It is no wonder that this four-page pamphlet dealt with conflict. Printers, such as Richard Faques who produced it, were insatiable in their search for 'vendible' content, and their publics eagerly consumed whatever they sent to market. Not only bound volumes but also more ephemeral matter of all kinds were printed. Indeed, a few years after Flodden, Martin Luther's protest against the pope was initially triggered by the pre-printed indulgences – buy one, write in your name and have your sins remitted – published by the thousand. Raucous pamphlets helped fan the war of words Luther started into open violence. The conflict over the Reformation of the Church became so bloody that before it ended, in a climatic Thirty Years' War (1618–48), it had taken one-third of Europe's population. Religious and civil strife, among much else, stimulated the appearance of the first newspapers in the form that is, essentially, still with us.

News – 'trewe', 'warrented tidings', 'full true and particular accounts', 'true relations', *véritable contes* – certainly sold before the Reformation in the form of sheets, and as slim 'newsbooks'; but given the draconian censorship of both Church and state, the selling of news was fraught. The presses themselves were licensed and what came off them was closely monitored. Prison for transgressing printers was common. But *Strange Newes* of wonders, witches and miracles or *horrid cruel* crimes and monsters sold well and, moreover, worried the heavy-handed censors less than did more sober reports. For publishers in such an environment, 'truth', from the off, was as much a branding device as a guarantee of actual veracity. Pivoting from such entertaining sensationalism to the sobriety that was to become a given of journalism as a serious social enterprise (in so far as it has ever done) did not happen until the early seventeenth century.

Given the draconian censorship of both Church and state, the selling of news was fraught.

Seventeenth-century newspapers are unbound, dated, numbered periodicals using a consistent title and containing a variety of reports, independently edited. In effect, they offer – usually, at first, weekly – compendiums of the single-story news publications that preceded them; and, as the Thirty Years' War was getting under way, they were soon being issued across Europe in a number of languages. They were entitled *Tydings* or *Coranto* or *Mercurius* (honouring the Roman messenger god).

And war was the big story, just as it had been for Richard Faques. Conflict loosened – or even removed – the constraints of censorship. Political reporting became possible, but war was not only as serious a subject as politics, it was also as sensationally bloody (and therefore as popular) as any newsbook's account of peacetime horrors. Newspapers began very much marching to the drumbeat of battle, but truth, a main selling point of the news, was already thought to be war reporting's first casualty. But print journalism had played fast and loose with it from the founding of the Gutenberg press (1450) on, so its absence, distortion or minimisation during the Thirty Years' War did not now inhibit development or reduce the news-printers' claim on seriousness.

'Hereafter ensue the trewe encountre or ... batayle lately don betwene. Engla[n] de and: Scotlande.' (England: R. Faques, 1513). The earliest surviving example of printed news in Britain, on the Battle of Flodden.

¶ Hereafter ensue the trewe encountre or
Bataple lately don betwene .Englāde and.
Scotlande. In whiche bataple the .Scottis-
he .Kynge was flayne. ◄◄◄◄◄◄◄

¶ The maner of thaduaūcesynge of mylord of
Surrey tresourier and .Marshall of .Englande
and leutenūte generall of the north pties of th
e same with .xxvi .M. men towardes the kynge of .Scottȝ and his .Armye vewed and nom/
bred to an/hundred thousande men at/theleest.

Printed news of the first great encounter of the Thirty Years' War arrived in England on 2 December 1620:

> Letters out of Nuremberg make mention that they had advice from the borders of Bohemia, that there had been a very great Battle by Prage, between the King and the Duke of Beyeren and many 1000 slaine on both sides, but that the Duke of Beyeren should have any folks with him in Prage is yet uncertaine.[2]

Needham was an innovator. He tried headlines, run as single words or de facto 'stand-firsts' set beside the body of the reports he carried.

This report of the defeat of the Protestant Duke of Bavaria (Beyeren) by the forces of the Catholic Holy Roman Emperor at the Battle of White Mountain took twenty-four days to reach London. Despite being pretty much a month out of date, the publication was nevertheless branded as being current. It had been printed, in English, in Amsterdam, and over the next ten months, fourteen further issues, in English, crossed the Channel. The commercial success of this enterprise demanded local emulation, and in 1621, a *Corante*, carrying 'news from Italy, Germany, Hungarie, Spaine and France out of the Hie Dutch Coppy printed at Franckford', was translated and printed in London.[3]

The Thirty Years' War finally came to Protestant England in 1642 when its religiously uncertain but firmly autocratic king, Charles I, determined to test his authority over his staunchly Protestant Parliament by passage of arms. In January 1643, from his headquarters in Oxford, the first edition of a newspaper appeared arguing his case: the *Mercurius Aulicus ... Communicating Intelligence from all Parts, to all parts of the Kingdome, touching all Affaires, Conditions, Humours and Defigns*. It was ostentatiously printed on Sundays to infuriate the Puritans in Westminster. Parliament took until the summer to unleash a reply: the *Mercurius Britanicus*.

In the hands of Marchmont Needham (1620–1678), in modern terms Oliver Cromwell's PR man, the *Britanicus* took on the *Aulicus* point by point until the tide of war undid the king and silenced the paper. Needham was an innovator. He tried headlines, run as single words or de facto 'stand-firsts' set beside the body of the reports he carried. He produced a very early 'scoop', publishing the king's private letters captured in his horse's panniers after the Royalists' disastrous defeat at the Battle of Naseby, 14 June 1645: 'I mean to anatomize every Paper ... keeping still to my old Motto, "For the better Information of the People".[4]

It took him eight weeks. Marchmont was, for good or ill, the very model of the English journalist. His pen was wicked, witty and astute. Importing into the news pages opinionated pamphleteering, he could write persuasive arguments for republicanism, but his loyalties were flexible – he changed sides more than once and was never overly troubled by the truth, however defined. But his work speaks to the critical function of the press in times of war. Newspapers emerged not just as sources of information, factual or fanciful, but also as moulders of public opinion and sustainers of morale. Conflict and journalism were to be forever in symbiotic embrace.

In the eighteenth century, for the English press, wars were a matter of empire building and foreign entanglement and the papers, still blatantly partisan, covered them essentially by reprinting the reports of others. In the absence of eyewitnesses, provenance (e.g. 'Letters from Nuremberg … advice … from Bohemia') remained essential to establishing authenticity, even after the appearance of paid reporters. How the story got to the paper could itself become the story. *The Morning Post*, 22 June 1815:

> *The honourable Major Percy arrived between 11 and 12 o'clock last night, in post-chaise and four, with two of Napoleon's eagles captured in battle, which were displayed from the windows of his carriage. He was the bearer of dispatches from the Duke of Wellington dated Waterloo, the nineteenth instant …*[5]

Later in the nineteenth century, news from the front, witnessed by reporters, came to be a commonplace. In 1837, Charles Gruneisen (1806–1879) was assigned by *The Morning Post* to cover a Spanish civil war over succession to the throne. 'Activated', he was to recall, 'by youthful curiosity [he was thirty-one at the time] to see something of the realities of war', he made a pathbreaking journey to San Sebastián to become the first war correspondent – 'Travelling Gentlemen', or 'TGs', they were to be called.[6]

How the story got to the paper could itself become the story.

A report from another TG in *The Times*, 14 November 1854, read:

> *Heights Before Sebastopol, October 25th*
>
> *They swept proudly past, glittering in the morning sun in all the pride and splendour of war. We could hardly believe the evidence of our senses! Surely that handful of men were not going to charge an army in position? Alas! it was but too true ...* [7]

This, one of English journalism's most famous reports, was written by William Russell and communicated to London 'by Submarine and British Telegraph'. In the 234 years between the Battle of White Mountain (1620) and the Charge of the Light Brigade at Balaclava (1854), the speed at which the news could travel had increased from under 2 to over 5.5 kilometres per hour. Train and telegraph were beginning to render information perishable, like fresh fruit. But technology was to have effects apart from ever-increasingly making instantaneity journalism's *sine qua non*.

Putting the public in the position of first-hand witness also became possible with twentieth-century technology. It too became an essential component in the newsreels, for example:

> *As dawn breaks [announces the commentator] Pathé Gazette's cameraman is on a tiny merchant ship. He is risking his life to bring you the pictures. He is on his way to Dunkirk ... Now you are off burning Dunkirk ... You will see the calm waters dotted with hundreds of men ... Here in pictures is the triumph that turned a major military disaster into a miracle of deliverance.* [8]

The inevitable echo of propaganda – 'triumph', 'miracle' – is muted by the vividness of the imagery and legitimated by the inherent slanting of war reporting. Stridency and the big lie favoured by Goebbels and his ilk were never in play in Britain. Sobriety conditioned reporting, whatever the medium. D-Day, 6 June 1944, on the wireless:

> For: The British Broadcasting Corporation, London
>
> From: Robert Dunner, aboard an American Headquarters Ship
>
> *We are in the ships. The next time our feet touch dry land it will be the soil of Europe. For the moment ... England behind, yet visible, and a certain beach on the continent as yet undisturbed by the thunder of our attack ...* [9]

In this century, the moral ambiguities involved in witnessing horror, ideally without emotion, have become ever more vexed. Wars have been increasingly seen as controversial as to cause and reprehensible in execution. Negative reporting of wars has become something of a norm but, given the principle of a free press, it is not easily prevented by authority. The military nevertheless has tried. A system of embedding reporters with the frontline troops on an individual basis, for instance, assumes camaraderie might do the trick. But conflicts were becoming too confused and the coverage too intrusive for any control to work effectively. State involvements were murky and non-state players utterly unpredictable, to the point where Needham's 'old Motto, "For the better Information of the People"', clearly remains a necessity.

A civil war began in Syria in the spring of 2011, multi-sided, with unrestrained proxy forces brutally acting for other proxy forces, atrocities everywhere. An American, Marie Colvin (1956–2012), whose personal bravery as a war correspondent out-matched any TG's, was there for *The Sunday Times* – 'the only British newspaper reporter in Syria', in the

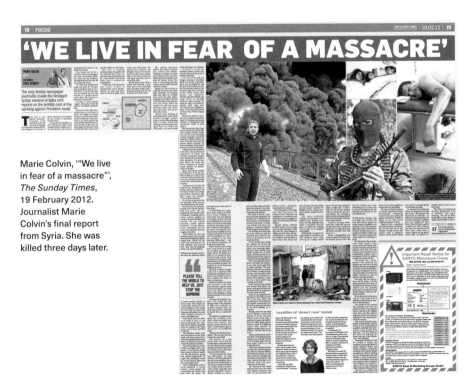

Marie Colvin, '"We live in fear of a massacre"', *The Sunday Times*, 19 February 2012. Journalist Marie Colvin's final report from Syria. She was killed three days later.

Baba Amr enclave besieged by the Assad government's most brutal forces.[10] In an operating theatre which was actually a room in an apartment, Colvin found victims of the relentless attacks:

Ali the dentist was cutting the cloths off 24-year-old Ahmed al-Irini on one of the make-shift clinic's two operating tables. Shrapnel had gashed huge bloody chunks out of Irini's thighs. Blood poured out as Ali used tweezers to draw a piece of metal from beneath his left eye.

Irini's legs spasmed and he died on the table.[11]

As of December 2020, thirteen British media workers' deaths covering wars have been noted since 2000.

The 'better Information of the People' extracts its price from journalists like Colvin who risk all to gather it. As of December 2020, thirteen British media workers' deaths covering wars have been noted since 2000. Globally the figure is 1,174.[12] Marie Colvin's story appeared on *The Sunday Times* front page and across two inside pages on 19 February 2012. On 22 February, the Syrians targeted the building they knew to be a temporary media centre in Baba Amr. On 2 March, they handed over bodies of journalists killed in the bombardment ten days earlier. One was Marie Colvin – slain.

William Howard Russell

by Beth Gaskell

William Howard Russell (1820–1907) became famous for his reporting of the Crimean War (1853–6) on behalf of *The Times*. He provided eyewitness coverage of the war, including his famous account of the Charge of the Light Brigade. His reporting helped uncover the organisational failings of the military, which had resulted in large-scale suffering of British troops.

Born in County Dublin, Ireland, Russell studied for a career in the law, but never pursued it. He gained freelance reporting experience covering Irish politics for *The Times*, before receiving his first overseas posting, accompanying British forces to Malta. Those forces would shortly set sail for the Crimea, and Russell would go with them.

The Crimean War was a defining moment for newspaper war reporting. It was the first time that civilian war correspondents reported from the seat of war in an organised fashion and in significant numbers. Russell covered the war for *The Times*, acting as their frontline correspondent. His ground-breaking reporting focused on the experiences of the officers and men fighting the war. Combined with powerful descriptive writing, Russell's accounts caught the imagination of a public who had never heard the realities of war told with such frankness, while horrifying the military establishment. He was instrumental in raising public awareness of the privations that the British troops suffered, which in turn helped to inspire Florence Nightingale to take up wartime nursing. The public outrage caused by Russell's reports helped bring down the government of the day.

Russell continued as a special correspondent for *The Times* for many years. He covered a wide range of events including the American Civil War (1861–5), the Franco-Prussian War (1870–1) and the Zulu War of 1879. Yet he never recreated his success from the Crimea. Russell struggled to adapt to the faster pace of reporting during later conflicts, and the increasing importance of new technologies such as the telegraph.

From 1860 Russell owned and edited his own newspaper, the *Army and Navy Gazette*. The success and influence of the publication rested on Russell's reputation, and his ability to network with servicemen, politicians and even royalty. He was knighted in 1895, now feted by an establishment that had once feared him.

Maddy Smith

Sensationalism's shocking secrets

Who can resist a sensational news story about a juicy sex scandal or a gory murder? Nobody can, and that's the point. Sensationalism is a centuries-old editorial tactic in which particular types of news stories are selected and reported in such a way as to excite the greatest number of readers.

Crime is one of the most popular sensational news categories. Lurid and provocative stories are sold to us ostensibly to warn of the consequences of transgressive behaviour, alert us to dangerous criminals or expose the moral failings of others. However, in reality, they exist to thrill, titillate and stir our emotions.

Sensationalism and printed news have a backstory that dates to the sixteenth century. Violence, sex, witchcraft, disasters, wonders and other strange events were the fodder of sensational news pamphlets and broadside ballads. These formats reached their heyday in the seventeenth century, but continued in some shape or form for the following two centuries. They predate the often-cited markers in the development of English printed news: the arrival of single-sheet corantos in the 1620s, the first printed report of parliamentary proceedings in 1641 and the explosion of partisan newsbooks during the English Civil War.

Sensational news pamphlets were cheap and perennially popular. They were apparently regarded by the upper echelons of society as unreliable, trashy and profligate, but 'there is plenty of evidence that the readership of ballads and sensational news pamphlets was not limited to the uneducated' and that, to readers, there was no real distinction between so-called serious and sensational news.[1] After all, news is 'a coarse, unrefined substance, made up of events selected for their strangeness as much as their significance, their emotional appeal as much as their import'.[2]

Crime is an essential ingredient of sensation news, but it is only the most violent and unusual of crimes that get reported. In the seventeenth century these were primarily murder and witchcraft. News pamphlets transformed these crimes into sensational news stories dripping with blood and gore. Their attention-grabbing titles were heavy on superlatives and emotive adjectives such as 'cruel', 'bloody' and 'horrible'.

Sensational crime news pamphlets customarily began with a didactic message to the reader and ended with the repentant criminal confessing to their crimes. This framed the pamphlet as a warning against sinful behaviour. *The Burning of Margaret Ferne-Seede,* for example, begins with the following:

The grossest part of folly, and the most repugnant … is to thinke that our hidden abhominations can be concealed from the eie of the Almightie, or that hee seeing our bloodie and crying sinnes, will not … power downe sharpe vengeance for such presumptuous and rebellious offences.[3]

Why did sensational news pamphlets have this didactic element? This was a period in which 'the activities of a criminal were offensive first to God and then to the common law'.[4] Religious beliefs were central to the way in which crime was understood and therefore reported. However, it was sensationalism, not didacticism, that really sold these pamphlets. Sensational stories 'of extreme violence, sexual license, outlandish and disgusting acts were presented to the reader ostensibly for his or her moral instruction, but, in fact, in order not merely to edify but also to shock, titillate and engender that frisson of horror laced with disapproval'.[5] The didacticism made the consumption and enjoyment of this sensational material socially acceptable.

The report of the crime itself was always embellished with sensationalism to make it as

It is only the most violent and unusual of crimes that get reported.

People cannot resist 'click-bait' sensationalism, but it can have a negative effect on us.

thrilling and emotive as possible. Two pamphlets survive about a sensational case of child murder in 1606.

Innkeeper Annis Dell was hanged for her involvement in the crime. One of the pamphlets, *The Most Cruel and Bloody Murder*, is more sensational than the other. The language is particularly lurid and the bare bones of the crime are fleshed out with an invented, melodramatic backstory. This is typical of the way in which sensationalism shapes news as entertainment. As if one murder was not enough, the family of the child who is later murdered are themselves killed by a violent gang of outlaws. The gang has a female member who kills the pregnant mother. She 'rips' open the woman's stomach with a knife and is described as 'a monstrous female', 'a devilish devil', a 'whore' and a 'she-wolf'.[6]

The author of this pamphlet knew what they were doing: in the early modern period, female murderers were highly sensational. They were rare and seen as transgressing their traditional gender role. Women who commit murder are always figures of fascination and often generate a sensationalised media response. Then as now, people cannot resist 'click-bait' sensationalism, but it can have a negative effect on us. The media's choice of language, phrasing and accompanying photographs can easily provoke unwarranted and disproportionate responses of alarm and fear in all of us.

Between 1788 and 1790, this panic focused on an individual who was dubbed 'the Monster' by the press. Women in London reported attacks by an assailant who had the signature behaviour of piquerism – the pricking or stabbing of victims with a knife, pin or needle. Some claimed to have been stabbed in the buttocks. Others reported that the attacker invited victims to smell a fake nosegay before stabbing them in the face with a hidden spike. The attacker always escaped before help arrived. London newspapers such as *The Oracle*, *The World* and *The Argus* reported on each incident. Broadsides, satirical prints and even a play were produced about the attacks.

Sarah Sophia Banks (1744–1818), antiquarian collector and sister of the botanist Sir Joseph Banks, was as caught up in the Monster hysteria as anyone. Banks collected newspaper cuttings, prints and other ephemera about the attacks, including some unique broadside notices written by John Julius Angerstein (1735–1823), a merchant and underwriter for Lloyd's of London who was heavily

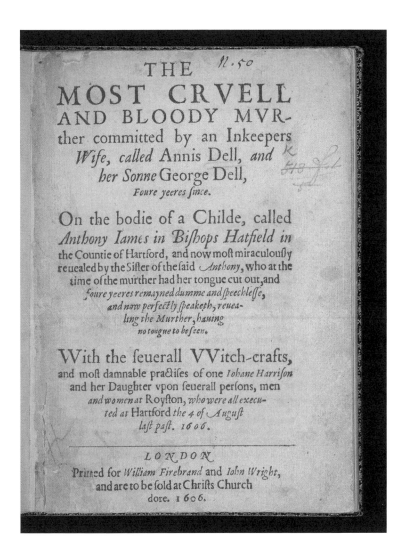

THE $n.50$

MOST CRVELL
AND BLOODY MVR-
ther committed by an Inkeepers
Wife, called Annis Dell, *and*
her Sonne George Dell,
Foure yeeres fince.

On the bodie of a Childe, called
Anthony Iames in Bifhops Hatfield in
the Countie of Hartford, and now moft miraculoufly
reuealed by the Sifter of the faid *Anthony*, who at the
time of the murther had her tongue cut out, and
foure yeeres remayned dumme and fpeechleffe,
and now perfectly fpeaketh, reuea-
ling the Murther, hauing
no tongue to be feen.

With the feuerall VVitch-crafts,
and moft damnable practifes of one *Iohane Harrifon*
and her Daughter vpon feuerall perfons, men
and women at Royfton, *who were all execu-*
ted at Hartford *the 4 of August*
laft paft. 1606.

LONDON
Printed for *William Firebrand* and *Iohn Wright*,
and are to be fold at Chrifts Church
dore. 1606.

The Most Cruell and Bloody Murther Committed by an Inkeepers Wife, Called Annis Dell [...] (London: Printed by T. Purfoot for William Firebrand and Iohn Wright, 1606). It offered a lurid account of a 1606 child murder case for which innkeeper Annis Dell was hanged.

involved in the transatlantic slave trade. Angerstein promised a £100 reward for the Monster's capture. The sensational language of these notices frames the unidentified assailant(s) as an outsider, reiterating theories already voiced in newspapers that the Monster was a dangerous foreigner – perhaps a Russian.[7] One such notice reads:

Mr Angerstein informs the public, that from the information he has received of the person who since Friday last, has assaulted and wounded several women, there is great reason to fear that more than one of those wretches infest the streets.[8]

These broadsides were so hysterical that satirical versions were produced. One uses hyperbolic language to make its point, claiming that the attacker 'has attempted to cut up his own children' and is back in London to 'devour all editors of newspapers, book-sellers, engravers and publishers of satiric prints'.[9]

Sarah Sophia Banks also collected a broadside issued by the Bow Street Runners, an early version of the police force. Printed in red for maximum impact, it encourages all servants 'to take notice if any man has staid at home without apparent cause, within these few days, during day light. All washerwomen and servants should take notice of any blood on a man's handkerchief.'[10] These sensational broadsides trod a fine line between encouraging the public to stay alert and tipping over the edge into mass hysteria. Coupled with the unrelenting coverage of the attacks in the newspapers, they undoubtedly fuelled the flames of the panic. Vigilante 'Monster hunters' roamed the streets, but the attacks continued for months. In June a suspect was finally arrested: a young unemployed Welshman named Rhynwick Williams. When questioned at Bow Street, the mob threatened to lynch him. Williams was eventually charged – although the judges struggled with what exactly he should be charged with – and he was sentenced to six years in Newgate Prison. Coincidentally or not, the attacks stopped. Today, historians are sceptical about Williams being the Monster; descriptions of the culprit varied wildly and Williams had an alibi for at least one of the attacks. Additionally, some reports were falsified and it was suggested that the attacks may have been carried out by more than one person. Some historians go even further, asking whether there ever was a Monster at all or was the entire scare a case of mass hysteria? We will likely never know.

Was there ever a Monster at all or was the entire scare a case of mass hysteria?

The nineteenth century brought technological and social developments that transformed sensationalism into its own distinct, marketable journalistic approach. Printing technology was made more efficient by mechanised processes, allowing mass circulation of newspapers. The capacity for illustration expanded dramatically. As reading material became increasingly available and affordable, literacy rates also improved.

The Illustrated Police News (IPN) was a weekly illustrated newspaper, first published in 1864, that was built wholly on sensation. Its speciality was melodramatic reports of murder and other violent crime. It used large-scale, front-page illustrations to gain a readership, tapping into the public's appetite for sensational crime to drive sales. Despite its popularity, it was deemed lowbrow and morbid by a small minority. Its founder George Purkess (1840–1892) acknowledged it as a sensational newspaper, but argued that it warned of the dangers and consequences of crime, rather than glorifying it.[11]

He was not England's first serial killer but he became the most famous serial killer in English history.

In 1888 an unidentified assailant murdered at least five women in Whitechapel, East London. He was not England's first serial killer, nor was he the first to target destitute women, which raises the question of how he became the most famous serial killer in English history. The sensationalist newspaper press certainly helped by splashing the murders across their front pages for months on end. Coupled with the lack of an arrest, this amplified public fear.

The press focused heavily on the female murder victims, using grisly illustrations and salacious language to describe them. The IPN depicted the discovery of each victim's body on its front pages. Mary Ann Nichols's body was exposed in the 8 September 1888 issue, her cut throat emphasised. She is presented as an object or, at best, a piece of evidence. The description of her body is similarly gruesome: her 'livid face was stained with blood and her throat cut from ear to ear'.[12] Catherine Eddowes was only identified as 'the mutilated body' or as belonging 'to an immoral class' when there was not and still is not any evidence that she was a sex worker.[13] All the victims were assumed to be sex workers when in fact most were not. The IPN devalued the women while giving readers a tour of the crime scene from their living room.

Why were the victims depicted in this way? A crucial element of sensationalism is the otherisation of the subject, keeping the reader at a distance. It frames the news story not only as entertainment but also as a lamentation of the failings of others, reassuring the reader that this could not possibly happen to them. In reality, the victims in Whitechapel were poor and vulnerable women. In the sensationalist press, they were immoral sex workers who got what was coming for them. The victims were

POLICE *THE ILLUSTRATED* NEWS
LAW COURTS AND WEEKLY RECORD

No. 1,284. SATURDAY, SEPTEMBER 22, 1888. Price One Penny.

"IS HE THE WHITECHAPEL MURDERER?"

READY FOR THE WHITECHAPEL FIEND. WOMEN SECRETLY ARMED.

LATEST DETAILS OF THE WHITECHAPEL MURDERS

FOREMAN OF JURY

DR. PHILLIPS

BROTHER OF VICTIM

CHEAP LODGING HOUSE

THE VICTIM LAST SEEN ALIVE

ANNIE CHAPMAN BEFORE AND AFTER DEATH

I HAVEN'T THE MONEY FOR MY LODGING

SCOTLAND YARD OFFICIALS WATCH THE CASE

CORONER

DETECTIVE THICKE

A WHITECHAPEL SLAUGHTER YARD.

PAPER ON WHICH MURDERER WIPED HIS HANDS

LODGING HOUSE KEEPER

HANDKERCHIEF WORN BY VICTIM

BLOOD STAINS HANBURY ST

EXCITING SCENE IN BOSTOCK AND WOMBWELL'S MENAGERIE

MORE HORRIBLE MYSTERIES.

The victims were brutalised once by the murderer and then by the press and its readers.

brutalised once by the murderer and then by the press and its readers.

By this time sensationalist journalism was an overtly commercial enterprise. As the murders continued, the *IPN* devoted more and more space to their coverage. Illustrations brought news stories to life in a more dramatic way than ever before. Advertisements increased because many were keen to cash in on the hysteria. However, the commercialisation of the Whitechapel murders did not sit well with everybody. W.T. Stead, himself no stranger to sensationalism, editorialised in *The Pall Mall Gazette*:

> *What is the right thing to do? … The paying thing is to go in for sensation, to bring out a sheet which drips with gore and is almost as 'creepy' and revolting as the gashed and mangled corpse of the murderer's victim. To work up the sensation by every means known to journalism … that is the plain path set before the journal by considerations of profit and loss.*[14]

The relationship between sensationalism and printed news stretches back to the late sixteenth century. Of course, many things have changed in this time. The news industry has become for some a monster in a way scarcely imaginable to people of the seventeenth century, although they would probably recognise elements of modern-day tabloid journalism. Social attitudes have also gone through many transformations in the last five centuries, yet despite these changes, the constants of sensationalism remain.

'Latest Details of the Whitechapel Murders', *The Illustrated Police News*, 22 September 1888. Characteristic front page of *The Illustrated Police News*, on the 'Jack the Ripper' murders.

Greta Thunberg

by Beth Gaskell

Greta Thunberg (born 2003) is a Swedish environmental activist who started the 'School Strike for Climate' movement. She became well known for her straight-talking approach and her social media engagement.

Thunberg was first taught about climate change at school when she was eight years old. What she learned had a huge impact on her mental health, and she stopped talking and eating. She was subsequently diagnosed with Asperger syndrome, OCD (obsessive compulsive disorder) and selective mutism. She does not see these disorders as debilitating illnesses, but rather as tools that allow her to focus all of her energy into campaigning against climate change.

For two years Thunberg concentrated on making a difference at home, cutting her family's carbon emissions by giving up meat and air travel. In August 2018 she turned her attention to the wider world, beginning her 'School Strike for Climate', skipping school to protest outside the Swedish parliament building. From the beginning Thunberg exploited social media, posting a picture from her first protest on Instagram and Twitter. Her cause was quickly picked up by others, and by her second strike she was joined by other activists.

She was soon involved in demonstrations throughout Europe, making high-profile speeches and gaining a large social media following. Thousands of students around the world began to follow her example, skipping school on Fridays to protest. In November 2018 she was invited to give a TED talk and was soon speaking at international events including the United Nations Climate Change Conference (2018), the World Economic Forum (2019) and the United Nations Climate Action Summit (2019).

Thunberg's message has spread around the world, thanks in large part to her social media engagement. Her activism has led to the 'Greta Effect', with world leaders acknowledging climate change, and also the impact of youth activism. Greta Thunberg was named as one of *Time* magazine's twenty-five most influential teenagers in 2019 and was nominated for the Nobel Peace Prize in both 2019 and 2020. She has helped put climate change at the forefront of the world's news agenda.

Devouring scandal

As England entered the eighteenth century and memories of the Civil War and political crises of the previous century faded, new publications sprouted to meet deepening demand for news, opinion and gossip.

One journalist founded the aptly named *Female Tatler* (1709); her *nom de plume* was 'Mrs Crackenthorpe, a Lady that knows everything'. Her rivals called her 'Scandalosissima Scoundrelia'. Why is it that scandal has a permanent place in news? Why is 'scandal' the word that has most haunted and terrified politicians for centuries?

Scandal sells subscriptions and copies, of course. However reluctant people are to admit it, the reporting of hidden failings or invisible underworlds is perpetually fascinating. Scandal dramatises moral disagreements, tells us why people actually read and buy news, occasionally changes the political weather and charts changing attitudes to sex. What constitutes a top-flight scandal may alter across centuries, but its public impact seems timeless.

A really good scandal resembles a large slice of fruit cake. You feel a little guilty devouring it, many different ingredients are included and each bite is delicious. What goes into that recipe? We can assemble a checklist. The more elements from our list that are present, the larger the resonance of the scandal.

Start with *shock*. Scandals begin with a detonation: something explodes. In old Fleet Street slang, a 'marmalade-dropper' must be astonishing enough to make the reader drop something at breakfast. That is often the revelation that triggers the scandal, but it can also be the unexpected twist in the narrative. Scandal drags a public event into uncharted territory full of traps for the unwary or over-confident. Public figures famous for their achievements or talents are suddenly tarnished. 'For greatest scandal waits on greatest state,' wrote Shakespeare.[1]

In 1895 Oscar Wilde (1854–1900) was at the height of his fame: his most popular play, *The Importance of Being Earnest*, was enjoying a long run. He was gay at a time when homosexuality was a crime, but thought that his fame and mocking wit would protect him from the punitive media culture and public attitudes of the time. He was caught in a vicious family quarrel between his lover Lord Alfred Douglas (1870–1945) and Douglas's father the Marquess of Queensberry (1844–1900), who was determined to destroy the relationship and, if possible, Wilde.

In old Fleet Street slang, a 'marmalade-dropper' must be astonishing enough to make the reader drop something at breakfast.

Frustrated in an attempt to insult Wilde in public by throwing a bouquet of rotting vegetables onto the stage of the theatre where Wilde's hit play was running, Queensberry left a card at Wilde's club. It read: 'For Oscar Wilde, posing somdomite [sic]'. Wilde, against advice from all his friends except Douglas, sued Queensberry for criminal libel. Queensberry's lawyers hired private detectives to interview young uneducated men who had been paid for sex by Wilde. Later Wilde described these encounters as thrilling gambles: 'It was like feasting with panthers; the danger was half the excitement.'[2]

The trial was a media sensation: details of the Victorian gay underground were revealed which would have appalled many who read them. The trial was also a catastrophe for Wilde: he stopped the prosecution when it became obvious that it could not succeed and that he had all but admitted homosexual activity. He was arrested and eventually imprisoned; his gilded and admired performance was over. Wilde's fall revealed three facets of scandal to add to our list: his inability to *control his image* as he thought he could, his *dicing with disaster* in his sexual life and his fast, steep *fall from grace*.

Many political scandals show us gamblers playing games of chance which excite them. They are convinced that they will get away with adultery, cheating, fraud or plain old lying. They are often wrong and find that the odds against them are worse than they think. But scandal does not always dole out punishments which fit the failure. One politician can walk away unharmed from a scandal that would sink another. Not only did Boris Johnson (born 1964) rise to be prime minister of the United Kingdom despite episodes in his past that might have terminated other careers, but his talents as a cheerful escapologist were part of the appeal that saw him elected as Conservative leader.

Politicians who wake up to grisly headlines about them in black capitals accompanied by blurry long-lens pictures have two possible protections against the scandal already gaining momentum and running out of control: how much they are liked or disliked and how supportive are their party's leaders and whips. In 1992, the then leader of the Liberal Democrats Paddy Ashdown (1941–2018) heard that *The News of the World* was likely to expose an extra-marital affair. He decided to pre-empt the exposure and made his own statement, reported by *The Sun* under the headline 'It's Paddy Pantsdown' – wording which Ashdown himself described as 'dreadful but brilliant'.[3] The leaders of both major parties at the time, John Major (born 1943) and Neil Kinnock (born 1942), were sympathetic, Ashdown was popular, his wife stood by him and his lover refused to sell her story. He survived.

> *Politicians who wake up to grisly headlines about them in black capitals accompanied by blurry long-lens pictures have two possible protections: how much they are liked or disliked and how supportive are their party's leaders and whips.*

When the Conservative Party chairman Cecil Parkinson (1931–2016) was forced in 1983 by accumulating rumours and an item in *Private Eye* to admit that he was the father of a child expected by his secretary Sara Keays (born 1947), Margaret Thatcher (1925–2013) and her colleagues wanted to protect his political career. Parkinson was tipped as a future Tory leader. For some days, the rescue efforts appeared to be succeeding. Keays, who believed that her reputation was being trashed by anonymous briefings, then issued a long and furious statement to *The Times* describing how Parkinson had reneged on offers of marriage.[4] That torpedo sank

The Daily Telegraph

Thursday, May 21, 2009 · ·   **BRITAIN'S BEST-SELLING QUALITY DAILY**   No 47,888   90p

The phantom mortgage, the insurance mystery and a £1,600 duck house

● Serious questions over three more MPs   ● Cameron forced to act over £30,000 claim

An £11,000 'mistake': Bill Wiggin claimed for a mortgage on a home he owned outright   Mopping up: Ruth Kelly used her expenses, not her insurance, to claim for flood damage   Looking after his feathered friends: Tory grandee spent £30,000 on gardening

THE EXPENSES FILES DAY 14

By Robert Winnett, Martin Beckford and Nick Allen

A CONSERVATIVE whip can today be uncovered as the most senior MP to have claimed interest payments for a property which had no mortgage.

Bill Wiggin, a contemporary of David Cameron at Eton, received more than £11,000 in parliamentary expenses to cover interest payments after declaring that his Herefordshire property was his "second home".

Last night, another senior Tory, Sir Peter Viggers, was forced to announce his retirement at the next election, after claiming tens of thousands of pounds for gardening. He is expected to repay more than £10,000.

Mr Wiggin, who has been a whip since January, joins two Labour MPs, Elliot Morley and David Chaytor, who could face a police investigation into "phantom mortgage" expenses. Lawyers believe such claims may be a criminal offence under the 2007 Fraud Act and the 1968 Theft Act.

Last night, Mr Wiggin said that the claims had been in error and he had issued them to relate to his London property, which he had previously designated as his second home.

The sums matched those paid for the London house. However, he completed and signed 23 statements for parliamentary officials declaring that his second home was in Herefordshire.

In 2007, he switched his claim back to the London property. Mr Wiggin insisted he was not profited. "It was purely an administrative error, and it was of absolutely no financial advantage to me," he said.

The disclosures come on the 14th day of *The Daily Telegraph's* investigation into the MPs' expenses system.

This newspaper has now exposed claims made by more than 170 MPs from the main parties in England, Scotland and Northern Ireland.

MANDRAKE

What the Queen and Baroness Thatcher made of the Speaker's demise p12

'If you put a copy of the Telegraph in the window it keeps the politicians away'

Although Gordon Brown has announced new rules to overhaul the system, there is still pressure on the Prime Minister and Mr Cameron to act against individual MPs found to have abused expenses.

Anthony Steen, the Tory MP, announced last night that he would stand down at the next election, after disclosures that he claimed £90,000 for his second home, including tree work.

A Labour official said that up to 50 of the party's MPs could be deselected as a result of the expenses scandal.

However, many constituency associations are fighting to protect their MPs, frustrating voters' attempts to discover details of their representative's expense claims.

As *The Telegraph* continues to release information on MPs' expenses, some of the questionable claims made by both Conservative and Labour MPs are disclosed today:

☐ Sir Peter Viggers claimed for a £1,645 floating "duck island" in the garden pond at his Hampshire house. In a statement, the Conservative Party said: "Sir Peter Viggers has confirmed that he will retire as MP for Gosport at the next election. He will do so at the direct request of David Cameron";

☐ Ruth Kelly, the former Cabinet minister, claimed thousands of pounds of taxpayers' money for flood damage to her second house, although she had a building insurance policy at the time;

☐ Natascha Engel, a back-bench Labour MP, claimed thousands of pounds for furniture, champagne flutes and other household items, including a £2,000 sofa. She disclosed her own claims after deciding that some constituents would find them unacceptable and had organised a series of meetings for her constituents to judge whether she should stand down. She explains her reasons in an article for telegraph.co.uk.

The latest disclosures come after Mr Cameron challenged Mr Brown to call a general election and the Prime Minister conceded for the first time that he feared the Conservatives could win.

All the political parties have now agreed immediate restrictions on what can be claimed on expenses, banning furniture, household items and food and capping mortgage interest or rent at £1,250 per month.

Two more Cabinet ministers avoided tax on home sales

By Holly Watt

JAMES PURNELL, the Work and Pensions Secretary, avoided paying capital gains tax on the sale of his London flat after claiming taxpayer-funded expenses for advice from an accountant, *The Daily Telegraph* can disclose.

The Cabinet minister saved thousands of pounds after informing the parliamentary authorities that Manchester was his "main" home while the tax authorities considered London to be his "primary" residence. Mr Purnell claimed for a £385 accountant's bill that included "tax advice provided in October 2004 regarding sale of flat" on parliamentary expenses which are not intended to cover the costs of running an MP's office.

It can also be disclosed that Geoff Hoon, the Transport Secretary, did not pay capital gains tax on the sale of his London home in 2006. Earlier this week, Gordon Brown criticised Hazel Blears's similar failure to pay capital gains tax as "totally unacceptable". Miss Blears, the Communities Secretary, wrote a cheque for £13,000 to cover the tax last week. She said yesterday that acting within the rules "doesn't cut it with the public".

Accountants have compared the behaviour of Mr Purnell and Mr Hoon to that of Miss Blears. The ministers are not accused of breaking the law but their behaviour is unlikely to be regarded as ethical by many voters. Capital gains tax of 40 per cent of profits is usually only avoided when selling a main or family home.

Mr Purnell bought a flat in a central London mansion block in 2000 and a house in his Manchester constituency in June 2002. He told the parliamentary authorities that his main home was in Manchester and claimed the "second home" allowance in London. In October 2004, Mr Purnell sold the London flat. He did not pay capital gains tax on the sale as the property was regarded by HM Revenue and Customs as his "principal" residence. It is not known how much profit Mr Purnell made from the transaction. It appears that Mr Purnell received specialist tax advice over the sale of the property and took advantage of a loophole in the rules. This is available to everyone and allows sellers to claim that a property is a main residence for capital gains tax purposes provided they lived there less than three years before the sale.

Mr Hoon is believed to have made a profit of around £300,000 on the London house he sold in 2006. The property had been rented out for four years before it was sold. During this time, he had lived in a grace-and-favour house in Whitehall and owned a substantial "family" home in Derbyshire. Within months of

Continued on Page 2

ISSN 0307-1235

Most scandals are about individuals. But the parliamentary expenses scandal of 2009 was about an institution.

attempts to keep Parkinson's career afloat. We must add to our checklist of components for memorable scandals a person *determined to disclose* in the interests of defending their version and reputation.

On the subject of political scandals, two more items for the list: scandals are made by *details* and often magnified by inept *cover-ups*. In 1998, the Labour MP and Secretary of State for Wales Ron Davies (born 1946) was robbed on Clapham Common when seeking gay sex with a stranger; he resigned and confessed to a 'moment of madness'. It was not a one-off. In 2003, he was photographed leaving an outdoor gay sex haunt. He at first claimed ignorance, then 'confusion', then said that he had been there to watch badgers. The last detail rendered the defence ridiculous.

Most scandals are about individuals. But the parliamentary expenses scandal of 2009 was about an institution. The leaking of the records of MPs' expense claims shone a bright light on lifestyles and domestic details which many honest members of the House of Commons thought unfair. *The Daily Telegraph* had a huge scoop and, given that the hard drive the paper had been given contained a few million pieces of information, the revelations continued for weeks. When the information was published in full online, constituents could look up their MP and read their claims in detail.

This deluge of information was encapsulated in public memory by one item alone. Tory MP Sir Peter Viggers (1938–2020) claimed £1,645 for a floating duck house in the pond at his second home (which was itself taxpayer-supported). Viggers was forced to leave the House of Commons. The ducks, he lamented, had never even liked their little home. MPs faced demands for repayment of expenses they should not have received and total voluntary repayments totalled over £500,000. Four MPs were jailed for false accounting; three peers were suspended from the House of Lords.

'The phantom mortgage, the insurance mystery and a £1,600 duck house', *The Daily Telegraph*, 21 May 2009. One of a series of front-page reports on the UK parliamentary expenses scandal, a story broken by *The Daily Telegraph*.

The timing could not have been worse: these stories ran and ran as the world suffered the effects of a financial crash. The prime minister, Gordon Brown (born 1951), apologised 'on behalf of all politicians', rightly recognising that the scandal had done great damage to the reputation of Parliament and politics. The facts exposed to view shifted public opinion. The suspicion and resentment of elites grew markedly after the crash and the parliamentary expenses scandal fed the idea that political decisions were being taken by people 'in it for themselves'. One of the results was the Brexit vote in 2016. Some scandals really do move the dial.

Another item for our checklist: scandals that seem to confirm a growing opinion will be magnified by *confirming an existing perception* (see Chapter 15). In the case of King George IV's (1762–1830) attempt to divorce Queen Caroline (1768–1821), strong public feeling managed to frustrate even a monarch's attempt to control the narrative of a royal scandal. The politics of the early nineteenth century in Britain, as in the rest of Europe, were dominated by the reverberations of the French Revolution and swelling movements for reform. Kings and queens were being forced to notice public opinion and parliaments.

George IV would not have agreed: he behaved as if the political ground was not shifting beneath him. He came to the throne in 1820, succeeding his father George III (1738–1820) after long years as prince regent. As he waited impatiently to become king, he had acquired a public reputation for being idle, drunk, extravagantly fond of luxury and promiscuous.

He had also married one of his mistresses in secret and without his father's permission; the marriage was therefore illegal. In 1795, he had married Princess Caroline of Brunswick despite disliking her on sight. He had been persuaded to marry a suitable aristocrat in the hope that Parliament would increase his allowance and help him clear his enormous debts. The marriage produced a daughter, Charlotte (1796–1817), but the couple were soon living apart and gossip about the estrangement started to appear in the press. The tone of the coverage was strongly sympathetic to Caroline.

A supposedly secret investigation by a quartet of eminent persons, wonderfully named the 'Delicate Investigation', was conducted into claims of Caroline's infidelity.

A supposedly secret investigation by a quartet of eminent persons, wonderfully named the 'Delicate Investigation', was conducted into claims of Caroline's infidelity. News of the inquiry was leaked, but it found no evidence of impropriety. The spin cycle began again as allies of both the prince and princess leaked the parts of the Delicate Investigation evidence that suited their cause.

Caroline's allies were radical Whig politicians who saw agitation against the king as useful to the cause of reform.

But Charlotte died in childbirth and Caroline went abroad, behaving with increasing eccentricity and living openly with an Italian man she had originally employed as a servant. When the prince finally became king, he was determined to divorce Caroline, who was now nominally Queen of England. The government was weak and unstable: it faced rising popular opposition enraged by the recent killing of demonstrators at Peterloo and the Six Acts aimed at suppressing political gatherings. Ministers decided to avoid a divorce hearing (which might have involved disclosures about the behaviour of both king and queen) and instead introduced a bill to strip Caroline of her title and dissolve the marriage. In effect, a parliamentary debate became a public trial of whether the queen had committed adultery.

For months on end in 1820, 'the Queen's business' was the story of the moment. 'It was the only question I have ever known', wrote William Hazlitt (1778–1830), 'that excited a thorough popular feeling. It struck its roots into the heart of the nation; it took possession of every house or cottage in the kingdom.'[5] Queen Caroline was portrayed by her backers as a victim of 'Old Corruption' and appeared on jugs, plates and coins. She became the temporary and improbable heroine of the reform cause.

Petitioners linked what they saw as her persecution to wider arguments. Citizens in Godalming saw the trial as the culmination of 'a long-practised system of corruption given to Ministers of the influence and power almost despotic'.[6] A petition from Cockermouth described its authors as dutiful subjects 'but without any voice in the choice [of] its Representation'.[7] 'No British monarch has ever been portrayed in more ridiculous postures nor in more odious terms than George IV during the Queen Caroline agitation,' wrote the historian E.P. Thompson.[8] Ministers eventually withdrew the bill in light of its unpopularity. Caroline's alliance with the radicals ended; she accepted a large sum to leave the country but died shortly afterwards in London. In the public mind the scandal connected an insensitive king with a decayed, undemocratic electoral system and pushed Britain towards reform a dozen years later.

Scandals *take on a life of their own*. The revelations and debates often leave the original facts behind as journalists and those they talk to

For months on end in 1820, 'the Queen's business' was the story of the moment.

'Profumo Quits: I Lied', *Daily Express*, 6 June 1963. John Profumo admits lying to the House of Commons about his affair with Christine Keeler.

speculate and interpret when they cannot reveal anything new. The most striking example of this remains the scandal that had everything: Profumo. The brief affair between John Profumo (1915–2006), fast-rising Minister of War, and the young Christine Keeler (1942–2017) sped up the end of a long period of Conservative government. An exhausted prime minister, Harold Macmillan (1894–1986), resigned seven months after Profumo admitted to the House

The story had all the hallmarks already noted and others: a government minister, sex, drugs, Soviet espionage, aristocrats, grand houses, orgies and blackmail.

of Commons in 1963 that he had lied about his relationship with Keeler.

Profumo's confession to the Commons was the least of it. The story had all the hallmarks we have already noted and others: a government minister, sex, drugs, Soviet espionage, aristocrats, grand houses, orgies and blackmail. Or at least every one of those things was gossiped about, speculated on or assumed. Much of the outrage and reporting was confected. Profumo, besotted with Keeler, had inadvertently collided with an MI5 attempt to honeytrap a Soviet naval attaché and so the much-hyped 'security risk' of his involvement with Keeler was nonsense from the start. Wild allegations appeared about an unnamed VIP known only as the 'man in the mask'. The story was a feeding frenzy and reached peak absurdity when a senior judge ordered a doctor to inspect the penis of a prominent politician. It is the most memorable British scandal of the late twentieth century, not because it was the most serious but because it ticked every box on our list of possible components for impact.

That long list of ingredients reminds us that these scandalous dramas will not end. No other type of story assembles so many elements that fascinate. Human beings in positions of power and influence will take risks and make mistakes, and some will fall. We will continue to devour the details.

The *Sunday Times* Insight team

Profile by Beth Gaskell

Insight is the investigative journalism team working for *The Sunday Times*. It has investigated some of the biggest news stories in recent decades, including the Profumo affair, the Cambridge spy ring and the thalidomide scandal.

Insight was founded in 1963 by Clive Irving, Ron Hall and Jeremy Wallington. It flourished in particular under the regime of Harold Evans, editor of *The Sunday Times* from 1967 to 1981. Insight built up its own style of reporting, with a strong narrative drive and a climactic approach. It benefited from a strong network of contacts and from being given the time necessary to pursue a subject thoroughly. Over the years the team expanded, drawing in and developing the careers of many top investigative journalists, including Bruce Page, Phillip Knightley, Alex Mitchell and Nelson Mews (illustrated L–R), Godfrey Hodgson, Marjorie Wallace, Elaine Potter and Jonathan Calvert.

In its founding year the team would cover its first big story, the Profumo affair, as well as exposing the slum landlord Peter Rachman and his methods of intimidation and vandalism against his tenants. It has gone on to investigate and report on some of the most important stories of the twentieth and twenty-first centuries, including outing Kim Philby as part of the Cambridge spy ring in 1967, uncovering the secret Israeli nuclear weapons programme in 1986 and exposing the FIFA cash for votes scandal in 2010–11. Most famously, the team conducted a prolonged investigation, between 1968 and 1979, to expose the drugs companies behind the thalidomide scandal. Thanks to the Insight investigation and *Sunday Times* campaign, compensation was obtained for the victims from Distillers, which had distributed the drug in the UK.

The team and its members have won numerous awards, including a Paul Foot Award for investigative and campaigning journalism in 2014 for the FIFA scandal coverage, a Journalist of the Year Award at the British Journalism Awards for Jonathan Calvert and a Scoop: Popular Life Award for the team in April 2020 for their exposure of Boris Johnson's relationship with the entrepreneur Jennifer Arcuri.

Tamara Tubb

Celebrity news: The sanctioned and the invasive

Coleen Rooney's claim that fellow WAG Rebekah Vardy (or someone close to her) was selling personal stories from Rooney's private Instagram account to *The Sun* disrupted the news cycle.[1]

or a few hours on 9–10 October 2019 WAG-gate vied for top billing with news reports on deteriorating Brexit negotiations, government in-fighting and Turkey's bombardment of the Kurds in Syria. The posts on Twitter and Instagram caused an instant sensation. Rooney's (born 1986) original tweet was liked more than 300,000 times and quickly went viral alongside the hashtag #WagathaChristie. The hashtag – comparing Rooney's sleuthing skills to that of famous murder mystery author Agatha Christie – generated thousands of responses, memes and videos, and overflowed onto other social media. It also caught the attention of the 'traditional' news media, which translated the story offline into print articles, phone-in discussions on radio news shows and bulletins across multiple TV news broadcasts.

#WagathaChristie became a prominent part of the news agenda for a number of reasons. It provided some much-needed light relief in a long and weighty news season: Brexit, Syria and Tory fragmentation were all well-established and ongoing news events. It captured popular imagination with a dramatic narrative that cast heroes, villains and victims from the familiar worlds of media and showbiz. And, unusually, it lifted the curtain on the news media's relationship with celebrity. Rooney exposed the invasive methods used to collect information about the private lives of celebrities and demonstrated how showbiz news stories often come from betrayals of trust. Nick Robinson got to the heart of the matter on BBC Radio 4's *Today* programme: 'People are having great fun reading the papers and reading the headlines, but in truth does it reveal a kind of private agony?'[2]

The false stories unwittingly published by *The Sun* – including a possible return to TV and a report of a flooded basement – were planted by Rooney on her private Instagram account to catch the close friend who was leaking details of her personal life for money or media clout. The ploy succeeded and, in the process, turned the tables on the informant and the news brand, who were both made to appear foolish and mercenary for their unscrupulous interest in the banal details of Rooney's family life. With one post that spanned social media, Rooney entertained a nation and held up an unflattering mirror to celebrity news journalism.

Before the age of social media, a slower but by no means more sedate relationship existed between individuals in the public eye and the media. As Greg Jenner suggests: 'The relationship between the media, celebrities, and public is full of tension; sometimes it's collaborative, sometimes it's coercive, and sometimes it's combative.'[3] Throughout the twentieth century, TV and radio promotions for upcoming album or film releases and glossy weekend supplement spreads detailing the lifestyles of the rich and famous were common forms of structured publicity willingly provided to celebrities by the media (news and otherwise) in return for increased audience numbers. Alongside this mutually beneficial trade in sanctioned exposure for strengthened sales another, more invasive, form of showbiz news was developed by the red tops and mid-market newspapers of Fleet Street. Subscribing wholeheartedly to the mantra that 'sex sells', it focused on exposing the private lives of famous people through kiss-and-tells and compromising paparazzi pics. Both sanctioned and invasive forms of celebrity news were created and

'The relationship between the media, celebrities, and public is full of tension; sometimes it's collaborative, sometimes it's coercive, and sometimes it's combative.'

Greg Jenner

Regular news titles became ready vehicles for society gossip and cultural news.

sustained by a reliance on popular interest in the personal lives of their well-known subjects.

Modern celebrity journalism has its roots in the eighteenth century, which saw the rise of the literate middle classes, technological improvements in printing and image reproduction, and a boom in the culture industry. Against this backdrop, news publication flourished and settled into a recognisable rhythm of daily or weekly production. Regular news titles became ready vehicles for society gossip and cultural news, serialising the activities of well-known nobles, society belles and beaux, actors and criminals with panache. As Brian Cowan puts it:

The eighteenth-century press generated a commercialized fame market that could make anyone with an interesting story, or even anyone associated with an interesting story, into a figure of public speculation.[4]

Speculation was usually where it ended. Although the news media of the long eighteenth century took an interest in the movements of these notable personages, it usually shied away from in-depth exposés of their private lives. To do so was a matter of public decency, and strict libel law.

Occasionally, particularly outraged news purveyors would breach the unspoken rules and publish stories about the mad, bad or dangerous exploits of star individuals. One such star was George Gordon Byron, 6th Lord Byron (1788–1824). Often credited as being one of the first modern cultural celebrities, Lord Byron was famed not only for his literary talent and aristocratic status, but also for his colourful private life and willingness to publicise the sordid details. Throughout his literary career Byron blurred the lines between fact and fiction. He self-consciously presented much of his poetry as autobiographical: *Childe Harold's Pilgrimage* (1812–18), an early bestseller, was originally to be called *Childe Burun* in a clear reference to his own, already well-known family name. By associating his personal life with his public output Byron made himself accessible to his readers, which fuelled their interest and, as a knock-on effect, legitimised news coverage and commentary on the hitherto deferentially disregarded details of his sex life.

Byron's separation from Annabella Milbanke (1792–1860), his wife of only fifteen months, was unusual and scandalous by the standards of the day.

thus goes out with the light of life; and his name, which but a moment before was caressed and honoured by all, now becomes hourly more and more neglected, till it serves but to feed the vanities and fading recollections of age, by giving momentary gleams of the days of youth and delight. The Dodds, and Hendersons, and Garricks, are still boastingly held forth by all who have seen them, as being very far superior to the Kembles and Keans of our day:—and the time will arrive, when some of us will shake our heads at the actors to come, and, with a glorying energy, talk of Liston, and Young, and Munden, as powers, whom it were vain to expect ever to see equalled. The name of Garrick is, perhaps, an exception to this charge of oblivion,—it still lives in the works of Johnson, and Goldsmith, and Reynolds; but he owed this honour more, we think, to his companionable manners and ready wit than to his acting. Johnson speaks of him with affection and admiration, but not with reference to his performances:—he calls him a puppet on the stage. This short fame is however made welcome to the heart of an actor by its excessive brightness, while it lasts;—it is a perpetual sun-light to his life;—it is the fine flattery of a wondering world;—it procures him gaieties, and luxuries, and lofty society,—things which are deemed most desirable by those who pass their time in indolence, or the personification of greatness. An actor is generally a man of a luxurious and passive turn of mind,—for few become actors, except from their antipathy to business and exertion. The Theatre leaves them most of the day to themselves, and makes them followed and fine at night. With all its faults, however, there is something honourable in the life of an actor,—and we always hear and utter the name with an inward gratitude and gratification:—he reflects life back upon our minds—he makes us familiar with the beauties of our poets—he is the mean of conveying to us the most rational pleasure,—and his name reminds us of the hours of revelry and relaxation. He keeps human nature in perfect harmony, and helps to make life a thing of enjoyment. He is indeed endeared to all parties;—beauty graces him with her presence—the philosopher unbends with him—the soldier finds in him a relief, after fatigue and danger—and the poor and humble, in his presence, become free, happy, and vociferous judges. It is for these reasons that we feel desirous of venturing our opinion of the actors of the present day,—many of whom we look upon to be as excellent as any that have ever existed. We wish posterity could see Kean or Liston—the sight would do it good. The energies of the one, and the apathies of the other, are not to be surpassed.

It is not our intention to commence our critical notices with remarks on the best actor of the day, or to pass regularly through the theatrical companies selecting according to merit;—we shall pitch upon a performer at random, and continue our remarks till we deem our task concluded. Neither shall we descend to observations on what may be called the underlings of the theatres; it would not become us, neither would it be useful, to speak harshly of those, of whom, as *Dennis Bulgruddery* says, "We could say nothing good without telling d——d lies."

Mr. Terry of Covent Garden (the gentleman whom we have chosen for the subject of our first article) is a very excellent actor. His figure is of a middle size and well proportioned, and his features, though hard, are full of strong and silent sensibility,—they are somewhat of the Kemble cast. This gentleman performs a greater variety of parts than any other actor on the stage,—and, strange to say, he pleases in all. He will play *Cassius* and *Megrim* one night, and *Sir Oliver Surface*, and *Gondibert*, and *Sir George Thunder* on the night following. This restlessness will however injure his talents ultimately; no person can be perfect in one thing who attempts all. Perpetual variety wears the mind out. We would recommend Mr. Terry to adhere to comedy, which is more suited to him than tragedy every way. In the former his dry humour tells admirably,—in the latter, he is too stiff,—too laboured,—too monotonous. His voice is indeed a bad one at all times—it seems rooted in his breast, and not to be come at without great exertions. The main fault of his acting, we take to be formality,—he appears to have passed a life of reading and not of observation on life,—books have been his study, it would seem, and not man,—so that he gets human nature but at second hand. This fault is however very creditable to him;—the fault of over-study is not a common one with actors. Mr. Terry has but to acquire a freedom of utterance and manner, to become a very superior performer. He wins the good-will of the audience by his plain air of sound sense,—his merit shines through his unobtrusiveness,—he travels the high-road to public favour. We should be glad if he would forget that such men as Kemble and Young exist;—at present he steps too closely after them,—and they have too much of the *cant* of the stage,—too much artfulness of tone, and tread, and dress, and action. There ought to be no manner peculiar to the Drama:—actors should read the motto over their heads and profit accordingly:—they should walk as men do in Cheapside or Piccadilly,—and talk as they would at a friend's tea-table. What can be more out of character than the eternal, pompous march and look, and the conventicle sort of declamation which have so long kept possession of the stage. Mr. Kemble moves as if he did it by act of parliament,—Mr. Terry is easier, but he too much imitates Mr. Kemble:—he has his time before him, and is possessed of great ability;—we therefore hope to see him adopt a juster system. He has written a play, but we have nothing to do with him as an author.

Salyrane.

MISCELLANEA.

LORD BYRON'S POEMS ON HIS OWN DOMESTIC CIRCUMSTANCES.

FARE THEE WELL.

Fare thee well! and if for ever—
Still for ever, fare *thee well*—
Even though unforgiving, never
'Gainst thee shall my heart rebel.—
Would that breast were bared before thee
Where thy head so oft hath lain,
While that placid sleep came o'er thee
Which thou ne'er can'st know again:
Would that breast by thee glanc'd over,
Every inmost thought could show!
Then, thou would'st at last discover
'Twas not well to spurn it so—
Though the world for this commend thee—
Though it smile upon the blow,
Even its praises must offend thee,
Founded on another's woe—
Though my many faults defaced me;
Could no other arm be found
Than the one which once embraced me
To inflict a cureless wound?
Yet—oh, yet—thyself deceive not—
Love may sink by low decay,
But by sudden wrench, believe not,
Hearts can thus be torn away;
Still thine own its life retaineth—
Still must mine—though bleeding—beat,
And the undying thought which paineth
Is—that we no more may meet.—
These are words of deeper sorrow
Than the wail above the dead,
Both shall live—but every morrow
Wake us from a widowed bed.—
And when thou would'st solace gather—
When our child's first accents flow—
Wilt thou teach her to say,—"Father!"
Though his care she must forego?
When her little hands shall press thee—
When her lip to thine is prest—
Think of him whose prayer shall bless thee—
Think of him thy love had bless'd.
Should her lineaments resemble
Those thou never more may'st see—
Then thy heart will softly tremble
With a pulse yet true to me.—
All my faults—perchance thou knowest—
All my madness—none can know;
All my hopes—where'er thou goest—
Wither—yet with *thee* they go—
Every feeling hath been shaken,
Pride—which not a world could bow—
Bows to thee—by thee forsaken
Even my soul forsakes me now.—
But 'tis done—all words are idle—
Words from me are vainer still;
But the thoughts we cannot bridle
Force their way without the will.—
Fare thee well!—thus disunited—
Torn from every nearer tie—
Seared in heart—and lone—and blighted—
More than this I scarce can die.—

March 30, 1816.

A SKETCH FROM PRIVATE LIFE.

"Honest—Honest Iago!
"If that thou be'st a devil, I cannot kill thee."

Shakspeare.

Born in the garret, in the kitchen bred,
Promoted thence to deck her mistress' head;
Next—for some gracious service unexprest,
And from its wages only to be guess'd—
Rais'd from the toilet to the table,—where
Her wondering betters wait behind her chair,
With eye unmoved, and forehead unabash'd,
She dines from off the plate she lately wash'd,
Quick with the tale, and ready with the lie—
The genial confidante, and general spy—
Who could, ye gods! her next employment guess—
An only infant's earliest governess!
She taught the child to read, and taught so well,
That she herself, by teaching, learn'd to spell.
An adept next in penmanship she grows,
As many a nameless slander deftly shows:
What she had made the pupil of her art,
None know—but that high Soul secured the heart,
And panted for the truth it could not hear,
With longing breast and undeluded ear.

Foil'd was perversion by that youthful mind,
Which Flattery fooled not—Baseness could not blind,
Deceit infect not—near Contagion soil—
Indulgence weaken—nor Example spoil—
Nor master'd Science tempt her to look down
On humbler talents with a pitying frown—
Nor Genius swell—nor Beauty render vain—
Nor Envy ruffle to retaliate pain—
Nor Fortune change—Pride raise—nor Passion bow,
Nor Virtue teach austerity—till now.
Serenely purest of her sex that live,
But wanting one sweet weakness—to forgive,
Too shock'd at faults her soul can never know,
She deems that all should be like her below:
Foe to all Vice, yet hardly Virtue's friend,
For Virtue pardons those she would amend.

But to the theme:—now laid aside too long,
The baleful burthen of this honest song—
Though all her former functions are no more,
She rules the circle which she served before.
If mothers—none know why—before her quake;
If daughters dread her for the mother's sake;
If early habits—those false links, which bind
At times the loftiest to the meanest mind—
Have given her power too deeply to instil
The angry essence of her deadly will;
If, like a snake, she steal within your walls,
Till the black slime betray her as she crawls;
If, like a viper, to the heart she wind,
And leave the venom there she did not find;
What marvel that this hag of hatred works
Eternal evil latent as she lurks,
To make a Pandemonium where she dwells,
And reign the Hecate of domestic hells?

Skill'd by a touch to deepen scandal's tints
With all the kind mendacity of hints,
While mingling truth with falsehood—sneers with smiles—
A thread of candour with a web of wiles;
A plain blunt show of briefly-spoken seeming,
To hide her bloodless heart's soul-harden'd scheming;
A lip of lies—a face formed to conceal;
And, without feeling, mock at all who feel:
With a vile mask the Gorgon would disown;
A cheek of parchment—and an eye of stone.
Mark, how the channels of her yellow blood
Ooze to her skin, and stagnate there to mud,
Cased like the centipede in saffron mail,
Or darker greenness of the scorpion's scale—
(For drawn from reptiles only may we trace
Congenial colours in that soul or face)—
Look on her features! and behold her mind
As in a mirror of itself defined:
Look on the picture! deem it not o'ercharged—
There is no trait which might not be enlarged;—
Yet true to "Nature's journeymen," who made
This monster when their mistress left off trade,—
This female dog-star of her little sky,
Where all beneath her influence droop or die.

Oh! wretch without a tear—without a thought,
Save joy above the ruin thou hast wrought—
The time shall come, nor long remote, when thou
Shall feel far more than thou inflictest now;
Feel for thy vile self-loving self in vain,
And turn thee howling in unpitied pain.
May the strong curse of crush'd affections light
Back on thy bosom with reflected blight!
And make thee in thy leprosy of mind
As loathsome to thyself as to mankind!
Till all thy self-thoughts curdle into hate,
Black—as thy will for others would create:
Till thy hard heart be calcined into dust,
And thy soul welter in its hideous crust.
Oh, may thy grave be sleepless as the bed,—
The widow'd couch of fire, that thou hast spread!
Then, when thou fain would'st weary Heaven with prayer,
Look on thine earthly victims—and despair!
Down to the dust!—and, as thou rott'st away,
Even worms shall perish on thy poisonous clay.
But for the love I bore, and still must bear,
To her thy malice from all ties would tear—
Thy name—thy human name—to every eye
The climax of all scorn should hang on high,
Exalted o'er thy less abhorred compeers—
And festering in the infamy of years.

His Lordship, then, is determined that nothing shall stand between him and public animadversion.—He will compel that notice which an honorable sense of delicacy would have withheld, if he had been content to offend in silence. The better part of the Press will always be cautious of engaging in the dangerous and disagreeable task of interfering with the vices of private life,—for the principles on which the safety of society rests, will usually be more injured by such intrusion, than improved by any correction that is thus applied to the violation of virtue. The extreme difficulty of settling the proper exceptions to the general rule, and the horror which every respectable author must feel of being confounded with the noxious tribe of sordid slanderers, cannot but occasionally operate to screen enormities, that have no claim to forbearance, from receiving the full measure of that castigation and exposure which is their due, and which the public interests require should be bestowed. But this is an evil that lies on the safest side; and it is most creditable to the tendency of that freedom of inquiry and expression, which, by some timid minds, is regarded with much alarm, that, in the country where

The news media exposed, commented on and condemned Lord Byron.

Ignoring the likely social consequences, Byron wrote and authorised for private printing two poems about the separation: 'Fare Thee Well!' and 'A Sketch from Private Life'. These were swiftly leaked to *The Champion* newspaper, which viewed the personal and vindictive nature of the poems as licence to break with publishing decorum, publicise the material and condemn Byron for the poor treatment of his family and dependents: 'receiving the full measure of that castigation and exposure which is [his] due, and which the public interests require should be bestowed'.[5]

The publication of the poems in *The Champion* caused outrage in polite society, and inspired a number of other unflattering newspaper editorials as well as a scurrilous satirical print by Isaac Robert Cruikshank (1789–1856), narratively titled 'The separation, a sketch from the private life of Lord Iron who panegyrized his wife, but satirized her confidante!!'.[6]

Byron's twenty-first-century biographer, Fiona MacCarthy, cites the initial printing of the poems as 'a prime example of Byron's irresistible urge to make the private public, to justify himself in a reckless flow of words'.[7] The criticism of the news media, combined with the rumours of Byron's infidelities, his relationship with his half-sister Augusta Leigh (1783–1851) and his dalliances with young men (then a hanging offence and deemed more taboo than incest), spurred Byron to flee England in self-imposed exile.

Just as the news media exposed, commented on and condemned Lord Byron for his personal and legal transgressions, so too are more recent celebrity activities amplified in news coverage for moralising or civic purposes. For example, Muhammad Ali's (1942–2016) highly publicised refusal to fight in the Vietnam War broke United States law and (temporarily) ended his boxing career. However, his actions received extended news coverage globally and galvanised support for both the civil rights and anti-war movements in the US.

At the same time that Ali was actively campaigning against the Vietnam War, news coverage of the Rolling Stones was unexpectedly shaking up the social status quo in Britain. The 1967 Redlands drugs bust and subsequent trial gathered popular momentum, garnered numerous headlines and broke through into the national consciousness. The *News of the World* – while on an anti-drugs, sex and rock 'n' roll crusade – tipped police off about a party at guitarist Keith Richards'

'Lord Byron's Poems on His Own Domestic Circumstances', *The Champion*, 14 April 1816, featuring Lord Byron's leaked poems 'Fare Thee Well!' and 'A Sketch from Private Life'.

(born 1943) house where, they believed, debauchery and heavy drug use would be rife. However, the raid was a relative failure: singer Mick Jagger (born 1943) was charged with possessing four amphetamine tablets, while Keith Richards was penalised for permitting his premises to be used for smoking cannabis. Regardless of the minor criminal charges, both Richards and Jagger were sentenced to imprisonment. News coverage of the events was extensive and divisive, with widespread engagement in the story spanning television, radio and tabloid as well as broadsheet newspapers. The case became a lightning rod for debate about the Sixties counterculture, drugs, sex and the new 'permissive' society.

The case became a lightning rod for debate about the Sixties counterculture, drugs, sex and the new 'permissive' society.

On 1 July, the day after Richards and Jagger were sentenced, the editor of *The Times*, William Rees-Mogg (1928–2012), published his now infamous leader 'Who breaks a butterfly on a wheel?' In it he questioned the prosecutions and asked whether 'Mr Jagger received the same treatment as he would have received if he had not been a famous figure, with all the criticism and resentment his celebrity has aroused'.[8] Critically, Rees-Mogg also waded into the counterculture debate, acknowledging that the case had come to symbolise the struggle between the British establishment and 'hedonism'. *The Times* was backing hedonism.

The article elevated discussion about the trial, drug culture and whether the existing legal framework for dealing with drug offences was fit for purpose to a serious national level. Both Richards and Jagger had their sentences quashed or suspended on appeal. The trial is widely held up as a defining moment in twentieth-century cultural history. It marked a turning point in the establishment's attitude to the younger generation and inched counterculture further towards mainstream acceptance.

Celebrity news stories can speak to the broader cultural climate, but on a more day-to-day basis, they can also speak to individuals on a personal level. Regardless of a celebrity's credentials – whether they're famous for being talented, knowing someone else who's talented or just being really, really good-looking – exposure in the media makes them seem accessible and familiar, and can encourage audiences to invest in their lives as they would a friend or acquaintance.

Jade Goody's special appeal was her ordinariness. Catapulted into the spotlight as one of the first British reality TV stars, Goody (1981–2009) was celebrated for being a 'working-class girl done

'At Peace on Mother's Day', *The Sun*, 23 March 2009. *The Sun* commemorates the death of reality TV star Jade Goody.

good'. Her fame and fortune seemed attainable to audiences and they clamoured to know more about who she was, how she'd succeeded and what she planned to do next. The tabloids and celebrity press obliged. However, her relationship with the news media was unstable and ricocheted between being mutually beneficial, overly invasive and, in relation to her racist behaviour in the *Celebrity Big Brother* house, justifiably hostile.

Ultimately, Goody's battle with and death from cervical cancer re-established the goodwill of the public and press. The extent of the authorised news coverage of her illness and the media reaction to her death were extraordinary and inspired a national outpouring of grief of a kind not seen since the death of Princess Diana, 'the People's Princess', in 1997. But unlike Diana's sudden death – involving the paparazzi and implicating celebrity newsmongers – Jade Goody's last moments were not shocking or intriguing: they were commonplace and recognisable. Her illness was newsworthy because of the nature of her celebrity; her relatability acted as a conduit for public empathy and created a focal point for many people's own experiences with cancer and grief. On 23 March 2009, the morning after her death, *The Sun* devoted its front page, the following nine pages and a special sixteen-page pullout to mourning Goody. Gordon Brown (born 1951), then prime minister, issued a statement to say that she was 'a courageous woman both in life and death and the whole country has admired her determination to provide a bright future for her children'.[9]

Of course, not everyone shared in the national mood of mourning, but the celebrity press and its buying public carried the day.

Olaudah Equiano

Profile by Beth Gaskell

Olaudah Equiano (*c.* 1745–1797) was a writer and abolitionist. He was enslaved as a child, bought his freedom and then travelled to England, where he became an important activist and celebrity.

There are question marks over Equiano's early life. By his own account he was born in Nigeria and transported across the Atlantic once enslaved. Other sources point to him being born in South Carolina. Either way, Equiano spent his childhood and early adulthood enslaved, and was bought and sold several times, travelling around the world with his various owners. He bought his freedom in 1766, and then travelled to England, somewhere he believed it was safer for a freedman to live.

After settling in England, Equiano quickly became involved in the abolitionist movement. With their encouragement he wrote his life story. He published his autobiography, *The Interesting Narrative of the Life of Olaudah Equiano*, in 1789, and it shot him to instant celebrity. It made him a bestselling author and the wealthiest

Black man in the English-speaking world at the time. While recent research has questioned the veracity of early sections of the autobiography, both then and now Equiano's writing had a huge impact on the way that people understood the experiences of enslaved people.

Equiano became a prominent spokesman for the Black community in Britain, as well as a campaigner for various abolition movements and groups. An important part of his activism was using the media of his time to help change minds. He frequently published comments and articles in British newspapers, particularly the *Public Advertiser* and the *Morning Chronicle*, around issues facing Black communities around the world, and advocating on behalf on abolition. He became such a well-known figure that his death was reported in both British and US newspapers.

In the years since his death Equiano has been honoured and commemorated in several ways. In 1976 a crater on Mercury was named after him, and in 2019 Google Cloud named a subsea cable connecting Europe to Africa after him, greatly and appositely extending connectivity to African nations.

Joad Raymond

Spectacles of woe: Reporting disasters

What constitutes a disaster, and what makes it newsworthy? At about 9.15 a.m. on Friday 21 October 1966 a waste tip from Merthyr Vale Colliery slipped down a mountainside a few miles south of Merthyr Tydfil in the Taff Valley, and crashed into the mining village of Aberfan.

The slag and slurry overwhelmed about twenty houses and Pantglas Junior School; 144 people died, 116 of them children. Welsh towns were accustomed to the loss of life, even the mass loss of life, through the hazardous practices of the mining industry, but not the loss of children's lives. After the roar of the rubble there was silence. 'In that silence you couldn't hear a bird or a child,' said one resident.[1]

The press rushed to Aberfan. The following day the newspapers, including the Welsh national newspaper the *Western Mail*, offered good coverage. Some of the initial reporting did identify the actual cause of the tragedy – the tip had been placed on a well-known spring – though this insight disappeared amid the obfuscations of the National Coal Board (NCB) and the attorney general, Elwyn Jones (1909–1989). The London newspapers reported lower fatalities (though with more unaccounted for) than the Welsh.[2]

The press reported it as a shocking tragedy, and some, following local voices, accused the NCB of negligence. 'Why were the warnings ignored?' asked the *Sunday Mirror*. Two patterns

THE LARGEST
PRESS BRAKE in WALES
CAPACITY 320
SIDNEY WELDING & ENG
CO.LTD. Tel.Cardiff 77676

WESTERN MAIL

THE NATIONAL NEWSPAPER OF WALES

SATURDAY, OCTOBER 22, 1966.

LONDON EDITION

for COMMERCIAL
PHOTOGRAPHY
WESTERN MAIL & ECHO STUDIOS
CARDIFF 33633

71 KILLED, 60 STILL LOST

The two-million-ton black avalanche which slid half-a-mile down from the coal tip above Aberfan and engulfed a farm, crushed Pant-Glas Junior School and swept away a row of cottages in Moy Road is clearly shown in this aerial picture by a Western Mail photographer. The main rescue operation is centred (far bottom) and other houses in the area showed cracks because of the pressure.

Hopes fade as thousands dig through night

Duke of Edinburgh to visit Aberfan

THE Duke of Edinburgh is flying to Wales today to visit the disaster area. It was announced late last night. Lord Snowdon was flying down yesterday.

SEVENTY-ONE bodies, most of them children's, have been found and about 60 are feared still buried under the massive avalanche of colliery waste which engulfed a school, farmhouse and row of houses at Aberfan.

'71 killed, 65 still lost', *Western Mail*, 22 October 1966. Welsh newspaper *Western Mail* report on the disaster at Aberfan following the collapse of a colliery spoil tip. 116 children and twenty-eight adults died.

characterised the reporting: in presenting it as a tragedy the reporting increasingly implied that it was a tragic accident rather than a criminal act. Secondly, the journalists and photographers who descended on Aberfan wished its citizens to follow a script of grief. Reporting disasters carries ethical responsibilities. Of course to some extent this is merely a matter of 'decency'. But contradictory imperatives are in play that can be particularly acute around disasters. The journalist (and photographer) is expected to show empathy; to present to an anonymous public circumstances that the subjects (or 'victims', to use a very loaded word) might prefer to be private; and to represent to the reader a story that can clearly be understood.

One bereaved father said, twenty years later, 'I remember more than one interviewing me, wanting me to give certain answers.' And another: 'During that period the only thing I didn't like was the press. If you told them something, when the paper came out your words were all the wrong way round.' And a rescue worker: 'I was helping to dig the children out when I heard a photographer tell a kiddie to cry for her dead friends, so that he could get a good picture – that taught me silence.'[3]

'I heard a photographer tell a kiddie to cry for her dead friends, so that he could get a good picture – that taught me silence.'

Aberfan: Government and Disasters

Three hundred years earlier, on 2 September 1666, a fire broke out in Pudding Lane that engulfed hundreds of acres of London (recorded fatalities were suspiciously few). The path of the conflagration was reported in detail – covering all of the front page and one-fifth of the second and final – in the weekly *London Gazette*, published on 10 September (a week after the fact; but remember that it was set and printed by hand, and the printing and bookselling district of London was burned). The *Gazette* polemically praised the caring concern of the king, and the absence of social unrest, while reporting that various foreigners, 'Divers Strangers, Dutch and French', were arrested 'upon suspicion that they contributed mischievously to it'.[4] However, the author concludes that the causes were only indirectly human: 'The whole was an effect of an unhappy chance, or to speak better, the heavy hand of God upon us for our sins, shewing us the terrour of his Judgment in thus raising the fire, and immediately after his miraculous and never enough to be acknowledged Mercy, in putting a stop to it when we were in the last despair.'

So the fire was a providential reprimand for unspecified 'sins'. This was a common and consistent theme in the reporting of disasters from the origins of newswriting through the eighteenth century. When terrible things happened for which there were not clear causes they were attributed to divine judgement, or interpreted as warning messages counselling future amendment or just punishments for transgressions past. When the floor of the French ambassador's house in Blackfriars collapsed

The London Gazette.

Published by Authority.

From Monday, Septemb. 3. to Monday, Septemp. 10. 1666.

Whitehall, Sept. 8.

THe ordinary course of this Paper having been interrupted by a sad and lamentable accident of Fire lately happned in the City of *London*; It hath been thought fit for satisfying the minds of so many of His Majesties good Subjects who must needs be concerned for the Issue of so great an accident to give this short, but true Accompt of it.

On the second instant at one of the clock in the Morning there hapned to break out, a sad deplorable Fire, in *Pudding-lane* neer *New Fishstreet*, which falling out at that hour of the night, and in a quarter of the Town so close built with wooden pitched houses, spread it self so far before day, and with such distraction to the inhabitants and Neighbours, that care was not taken for the timely preventing the further diffusion of it, by pulling-down houses, as ought to have been; so that this lamentable Fire in a short time became too big to be mastred by any Engines or working neer it. It fell out most unhappily too, That a violent Easterly wind fomented it, and kept it burning all that day, and the night following spreading it self up to *Grace-church-street*, and downwards from *Cannon-street* to the Water-side as far as the *Three Cranes in the Vintry.*

The people in all parts about it distracted by the vastness of it, and their particular care to carry away their Goods, many attempts were made to prevent the spreading of it by pulling down Houses, and making great Intervals, but all in vain, the Fire seising upon the Timber and Rubbish and so continuing it self, even through those spaces, and raging in a bright flame all Monday and Tuesday, notwithstanding His Majesties own, and His Royal Highness's indefatigable and personal pains to apply all possible remedies to prevent it, calling upon and helping the people with their Guards; and a great number of Nobility and Gentry unweariedly assisting therein, for which they were requited with a thousand blessings from the poor distressed people. By the favour of God the Wind slackned a little on Tuesday night & the Flames meeting with Brick-buildings at the Temple, by little and little it was observed to lose its force on that side, so that on Wednesday morning we began to hope well, and his Royal Highness never despairing or slackning his personal care, wrought so well that day, assisted in some parts by the Lords of the Council before and behind it, that a stop was put to it at the *Temple-church*, neer *Holborn-bridge*, *Pie-corner*, *Aldersgate*, *cripplegate*, neer the lower end of *Coleman-street*, at the end of *Basing-hall-street*, by the *Postern*, at the upper end of *Bishopsgate-street*, and *Leadenhall-street*, at the *Standard* in *Cornhill*, at the Church in *Fanchurch-street*, neer the lower workers Hell in *Mincing-lane*, at the middle of *Mark-lane*, and at the *Tower-dock.*

On Thursday by the blessing of God it was wholly beat down and extinguished. But so as that Evening it unhappily burst out again afresh at the *Temple*, by the falling of some sparks (as is supposed) upon a Pile of Wooden buildings; but his Royal Highness, who watched there that whole night in Person by the great labours and diligence used, and especially by applying Powder to blow up the Houses about it, before day most happily mastied it.

Divers Strangers, Dutch and French were, during the fire, apprehended, upon suspicion that they contributed mischievously to it, who are all imprisoned and Information's prepared to make a severe inquisition hereupon by my Lord Chief Justice *Keeling*, assisted by some of the Lords of the Privy Council, and some principal Members of the City, notwithstanding which suspicions, the manner of the burning all along in a Train, and so blowen forwards in all its way by strong Winds, makes us conclude the whole was an effect of an unhappy chance, or to speak better, the heavy hand of God upon us for our sins, shewing us the terrour of his Judgment in thus raising the fire, and immediately after his miraculous and never enough to be acknowledged Mercy in putting a stop to it when we were in the last despair, and that all attempts for the quenching it however industriously pursued, seemed insufficient. His Majesty then sat hourly in Council, and ever since hath continued making rounds about the City in all parts of it where the danger and mischief was greatest, till this morning that he hath sent his Grace the Duke of *Albemarle*, whom he hath called for to assist him in this great occasion, to put his happy and successful hand to the finishing this memorable deliverance.

About the Tower the seasonable orders given for plucking down Houses to secure the Magazins of Powder, was more especially successful, that part being up on the Wind, notwithstanding which it came almost to the very Gates of it, so as by this early provision, the several Stores of War lodged in the Tower were entirely saved: And we have further this infinite cause particularly to give God thanks, that the fire did not happen in any of those places where his Majesties Naval Stores are kept, so as tho it hath pleased God to visit us with his own hand, he hath not, by disfurnishing us with the means of carrying on the War, subjected us to our enemies.

It must be observed, that this fire happened in a part of the Town, where tho the Commodities were not very rich, yet they were so bulky that they could not well be removed, so that the Inhabitants of that part where it first began have sustained very great loss, but by the best enquiry we can make, the other parts of the Town, where the Commodities were of greater value, took the Alarum so early, that they saved most of their Goods of value, which possibly may have diminished the loss, tho some think, that if the whole industry of the Inhabitants had been applyed to the stopping of the fire, and not to the saving of their particular *Goods*, the success might have been much better, not only to the publick, but to many of them in their own particulars.

Through this sad Accident it is easie to be imagined how many persons were necessitated to remove themselves and Goods into the open fields, where they were forced to continue some time, which could not but work compassion in the beholders; but his Majesties care was most signal in this occasion, who, besides his personal pains, was frequent in consulting all wayes for relieving those distressed persons, which produced so good effect, aswell by his Majesties Proclamations, and the Orders issued to the Neighbour Justices of the Peace, to encourage the sending in provisions to the Markets, which are publickly known, as by other directions, that when his Majesty, fearing lest other Orders might not yet have been sufficient, had commanded the Victualler of his Navy to send bread into *Moore-fields* for the relief of the poor, which for the more speedy supply he sent in Bisket out of the Sea Stores; it was found that the Markets had

Qqqq   been

in 1623, under the weight of around 300 Catholic worshippers, almost one-third of whom died in the accident, the London Protestant press gloated at the just punishment meted out in these 'fatal vespers'.[5] Just as 'monstrous' births, strange lights in the sky and fish with books in their bellies were interpreted as hidden messages, so disaster, natural and man-made, was at once described as inexplicable chance and as a meaningful sign.[6] It was both apparently random and laden with significance.

We will find this throughout the history of reporting disasters: the grasping for formulae that help not only to communicate but also to explain the event. A tragedy for a people used to losing lives; a judgement by God; a glimpse of a pattern that confers meaning. Horror is presented as both unpredictable and knowable, and the journalist or photographer finds ways of fitting the story to a familiar template. It is in the nature of disasters that they both surprise us and confirm what we already know.

The Lisbon earthquake of 1755, widely felt and reported across Europe, was a local natural disaster that became international news. The tremors began at about 9.30 a.m. on 1 November, All Saints' Day, when many were attending church. Three tremors, destroying many buildings in the city centre, were each followed by a tsunami or tidal wave, drowning many fleeing residents, then a fire that raged for a week. Aftershocks continued through the following year. The magnitude of the earthquake is estimated at between 8.75 and 8.9, and it lasted ten minutes. It was felt not only across the Iberian peninsula but also in France, Italy, Switzerland, Britain and across North Africa, where further tsunamis damaged coastal towns. The tremors travelled faster than the news; news followed to explain what had already been experienced. Thus the newspapers in Hamburg, The Hague and Utrecht reported local tremors (and others at Portsmouth, Rotterdam, Amsterdam, Hamburg and Lübeck) before news of the destruction of Lisbon arrived.[7] Over the following years, while Lisbon was being rebuilt, there were

It is in the nature of disasters that they both surprise us and confirm what we already know.

economic aftershocks in England and the German states, and philosophical aftershocks in France (in Voltaire and Rousseau's debate about optimism).

The earthquake was reported quickly in Seville and Madrid, from where news spread to Barcelona and thence Italy, and to Paris and northern Europe. The first report in Britain came via Spain: the British envoy to the King of Portugal wrote to his counterpart in Madrid, who then wrote, on 10 November, to a London politician. This letter formed the basis of a report in the *London Gazette* on 29 November 1755. The *Caledonian Mercury*, a thrice-weekly paper printed in Edinburgh, had reported news of an earthquake on 27 November, though stating that it had struck Madrid. It proceeded to report that the news of an earthquake in Lisbon was in fact fake news – invented in Paris by the French, seeking to disconcert and disrupt English merchants. This was soon corrected, as British commercial interests in Lisbon were extensive, and British merchants wrote home to their families. Some of these letters were then printed, in Britain and elsewhere. *The Scots Magazine* reported on the ways in which the intertwining of mercantile interests gave domestic significance to a distant event:

> *The dreadful calamity befallen this city, next to the miserable inhabitants, the Brazilians and the English may probably be the greatest sufferers; next to them, the Genovese, and merchants of Leghorn, who supplied this city and the Brazils, with silks, velvets, &c. The French, Dutch, Hamburghers, and indeed most commercial nations, were concerned in the trade here, and must needs be affected by a calamity which extends itself to all Europe.*[8]

Was the fascination with a disaster that happened to others based on self-interest as much as empathy?

Was the fascination with a disaster that happened to others based on self-interest as much as empathy and the recognition of shared humanity?

News came to England indirectly, and also directly to Falmouth. The further away from the epicentre, the more significant the printed news was, as it was less likely to have been widely disseminated by word of mouth. Overseas earthquakes were frequently reported in the British press, even before a series of light earthquakes shook Britain in 1750. The stories from Lisbon were largely descriptive, including eyewitness accounts, though they also

A disaster is a special kind of news; it is self-evidently news, news as spectacle, stirring pity and terror in the audience.

discussed the causes and the death toll, estimates for which ranged from 10,000 to 100,000 (modern estimates suggest 30,000–40,000 fatalities in Lisbon, which was then a city of 275,000 inhabitants). In England, as elsewhere, there were three overlapping kinds of response. First, there were attempts to explain the causes in natural terms, ranging from Aristotelian to the then-contemporary (underground explosions, or the build-up of an electrical charge).[9] Secondly, there were providential explanations, which posited that the disaster was a sign of divine displeasure. By the following year some English authors were proposing that it was a warning to England. Thirdly, there was the precursor of 'fake news': some writers claimed that it was significant that very few Protestants had died, in contrast to Catholics.[10] The same three strategies were found in Iberian news publications, *relaçoes de sucessos* and *relaciones de sucesos*, though their fake news was the claim that survivors were saved by the apparition of the Virgin Mary.[11]

In 2020–1 we experienced another disaster that was at once local, regional and international, one with higher fatalities and more profound aftershocks. The journalism covering COVID-19 (which was initially slow to appear) also combined scientific with providential explanations, and even more 'fake news'. Does it make sense to compare this with earlier reporting, to put the pandemic in the same category as these other disasters? A disaster is a special kind of news; it is self-evidently news, news as spectacle, stirring pity and terror in the audience. While other events and stories are selected by an editor from a wide range of possibilities, according to one or more criteria, the disaster forces itself upon the editor's attention and demands to be addressed, somehow or other.

Various approaches to understanding newsworthiness have been developed by sociologists and historians. One is to examine news publications and identify the characteristics shared by stories (and those characterising overlooked stories). This approach – examining how events become news – resulted in the widely discussed criteria proposed in 1965 by the Norwegians

Johan Galtung and Mari Holmboe Ruge (developed through analysis of foreign news). Their criteria include: frequency (its temporal profile has to fit the medium of publication); scale (big is preferred); unambiguity; meaningfulness (to the readers' own experiences); predictability (and therefore fitting expectations), but also unpredictability; continuity (with previous reporting); and composition (offering a degree of balance to the publication). They add that in Europe there is an additional concern with elite nations, elite people, the extent to which a news event can be seen in individual terms (or personification), and negative consequences.[12]

Disasters are surprises that affirm our expectations.

The approach is open to criticism. It supposes, for example, that an event has an atomistic identity, that it has relatively defined boundaries. It assumes that the event is out there, waiting to be selected, not something that is transformed into news by being shaped in a specific way – given continuity and temporality – and recreated by the editing process. It assumes that events become news because of qualities of the events themselves, not because of commercial structures, or the interests of media owners.[13] News media and institutions transform things that happen into news: i.e. they may claim to publish 'all the news that's fit to print', but it may be truer to say that 'all the news that fits we print'. Emphasising the role of institutions attributes more instrumental power to news media.

However, the disaster, natural or man-made, is precisely the kind of news that matches this event-centred approach. Disasters happen at a particular moment (frequency); they are large-scale; they are unambiguous and negative in their consequences; they can be personified (particular individuals can be singled out for affective force); and, as I have suggested, they are both unpredictable and predictable. They surprise us, but invariably have meaning conferred on them by assimilation to a world view, an understanding of providence or history. They are surprises that affirm our expectations. If news is a spectrum, these kinds of disasters are at one end.

This should make us ask: what is at the other end of this newsworthy spectrum? And are there disasters that do not fit the event-centred model, ones that we normalise?

Consider the phone hacking scandal, an intricate series of events extending from investigations into hacking and police bribery starting in 2005, resulting in revelations in 2011 that the hacking was far more extensive (and socially offensive) than had hitherto been assumed, resulting in the Leveson Inquiry of 2011–12; the imprisonment in 2014 of Andy Coulson (born 1968), journalist and former communications director to prime minister David Cameron, one of twenty-six journalists and others charged with criminal offences; the rejection of the recommendations of the 2012 Leveson Report (notably the recommendation of the creation of an independent body to replace the Press Complaints Commission, by which the press self-regulates); and in 2017–18, the decision by the Conservative government to stop part two of the inquiry. This was news, but also a series of events so much harder to parse than the Great Fire of London or the Lisbon earthquake; easier for some parts of the press and its interested owners to sideline; and something at the far end of the spectrum from the natural or man-made disaster.

Are there disasters that do not fit the event-centred model, ones that we normalise?

And what of climate change, a disaster that happens in slow motion, the evidence for which has been frequently disregarded or made to seem (almost) normal? To understand the shape of news in the twenty-first century, we should reflect on the ways in which disaster is not always a spectacle or spectacular.

Mohamed Amin

Profile by Beth Gaskell

Mohamed 'Mo' Amin (1943–1996) was an award-winning Kenyan photojournalist who specialised in covering African news and events. He gained world renown for his coverage of the Ethiopian famine in 1984.

Amin was born in Kenya, the son of South Asian immigrants, and spent much of his childhood in Tanzania. He developed an early interest in photography and photojournalism, and by his late teens he was already working for international news agencies. He founded his own photography agency, Camerapix, in 1963, and went on to cover many of the key African news stories of the late twentieth century, including the Zanzibar revolution (1964), the exodus of Asians from East Africa (1967–72) and the Biafran War (1967–70).

Amin became well known among his peers as a resourceful and, at times, ruthless journalist. His network of contacts across East Africa, alongside his own local knowledge, provided him with information and access that was often unavailable to other members of the press, the majority of whom were European. His friendly relationship with the Ugandan dictator Idi Amin (c. 1925–2003) – they shared the same name – made him one of the few journalists able to enter Uganda freely, with unique access to the man and the regime.

One story in particular would cement Mohamed Amin's place as one of the twentieth century's most influential journalists: the Ethiopian famine in 1984, which he covered alongside the BBC's Michael Buerk (born 1946). The footage and photographs that Amin took illustrated the sheer scale of the humanitarian disaster, highlighting scarcely imaginable human suffering. Amin and Buerk's reporting jolted the world, and led to international fundraising on a scale never previously seen. As Bob Geldof (born 1951), founder of Live Aid, recalled, 'The pitiless, unrelenting gaze of this camera was different. Somehow this was not objective journalism but confrontation. There was a dare here – "I dare you to turn away, I dare you to do nothing."'

Mohamed Amin continued to work after losing his arm as a result of an explosion during the Ethiopian Civil War in 1991. He died in November 1996, aboard a hijacked flight, which crash-landed off the coast of the Comoros Islands.

Political theatre: The fall of Margaret Thatcher

'She wore,' I wrote, 'very dark green with black collars, and a diamond star on one lapel.' Was this news? On at least one level what this *Times* parliamentary sketch reported was trivial and personal, drawing on an earlier time when I'd worked in her office.

Now (with me writing for *The Times*) Margaret Thatcher had popped into an empty Commons chamber just after the last Parliament she'd ever be part of had wrapped up the remaining Commons business before a general election. And she couldn't resist neatly tidying the papers on the dispatch box, though she had long since ceased to be prime minister. Alone in a deserted press gallery, I watched.

Nothing important happened: I simply described the scene, that was all. But readers of *The Times* thought it mattered, and as their parliamentary sketch writer it was my job simply to write what we judged would gain our readers' attention, keep them reading, and amuse or interest them.

'She seemed,' I wrote, 'quite composed. [Prime minister] John Major was absent. Mrs Thatcher made for the front bench, which was empty. What, one wondered rather nervously, had she in mind?'

The table on which the dispatch box sits – where she had stood so many thousands of times – was littered with papers. Mrs Thatcher walked up and tidied the mess. She put the documents together

> *History has difficulty in reporting not what happened, but how things felt.*

into neat little piles, glanced at her handiwork, and left. I remembered how, when she was Leader of the Opposition, she would climb onto chairs to check for dust on top of the picture frames in the shadow cabinet room. 'It's the way a woman knows that a room's really been cleaned,' she once told us.[1]

I thought the incident amusing but minor, and my newspaper put it on page eighteen, next to an item relating to what once seemed a much bigger story about the (now completely forgotten) 'Iraqi super-gun' affair. In the event, my sketch attracted a good deal of comment. Looking back now to that day in March 1992 when Thatcher thought she was unobserved, noticing the detail I offered of her dress, her every step, her every movement, it's evident that national attention was still intensely focused on the previous prime minister, even though she had left Downing Street in 1990. 'The lady sails proudly away' was the headline my sub-editor gave that sketch.

And so she did. But what filled those sails? What filled the sails of politics at that time? We reach into memory and our hand comes back clutching recorded events, 'hard news', but somehow missing the sense of what impelled them. In Thatcher's case there was a very public perception of tragedy; there was an uneasy feeling that something big had imploded, leaving a hole; there was the fascination she still held for both friends and enemies: the widespread sentiment that somehow she still mattered.

Such prevailing winds are so very hard for historians later to track and report. You cannot photograph the wind. It's unseen, yet it blows people and events around. History has difficulty in reporting not what happened, but *how things felt*. And how things felt at the time often drove what happened. Without a sense of these winds, history's sails flap idly, reporting facts but leaving us stumped for any explanation that feels satisfactory to a generation looking back.

The reasons for and causes of the First World War, for instance, are a case in point. From our vantage point today it's evident to us that conflict was in nobody's interests; and modern readers get an impression only of some invisible force pushing the Europe of 1914 towards the abyss. How then do we assess, record, describe such winds? I believe that what my trade sometimes disparagingly

Frame still from television coverage of Prime Minister Margaret Thatcher in the House of Commons, 22 November 1990.

calls 'colour' journalism – word-pictures of a mood, a scene, the small, revealing, personal things, the straws (if you like) in the wind, the trivia that interested folk *at the time* ... this kind of reporting plays an indispensable part in bringing to life the unseen forces that help shape events. As an increasingly forgetful old lady and finally as a ghost, the late Lady Thatcher has hovered over the Conservative Party for the last thirty years. Her memory is part of the wind that has blown Brexit.

Unless you read the sketches, the whimsies, the gossip and the tremulous accounts of now-negligible things, the sails of history will flap for you. 'Observational' journalism (as, to distinguish it from simple news reporting, we might call it) may therefore have huge explanatory power. It's what we were all looking at then.

But hand in hand with the way observational journalism can give explanatory shape and colour to events, it also has a power to distort: not least because it is what sinks in, to be remembered long after the nuts and bolts are forgotten. Andrew Marr, in his book *My Trade*, notes that many political events are too complex for a good news story. He mentions, from the Thatcher days, the Westland affair – a fiendishly complicated tale of helicopters and defence procurement whose plot some of the best of us have now forgotten: politically big but journalistically tough to explain. Instead we can consider Margaret Thatcher's final days in power,

Many political events are too complex for a good news story.

because of the high drama and the tragic, epic qualities of the story.[2]

The legend helped drive history. But it has also distorted history, precisely because it is so memorable.

That episode has become legendary. Westland has not. And it was in the sheer theatre that her downfall generated that Mrs Thatcher (or an idea of Mrs Thatcher) became, posthumously to her admirers, a martyr, a supposed victim of the pro-European Tories, a mascot for a breed of younger Conservatives who idealised her but had never themselves witnessed her in her pomp and glory days, and a patron saint of Brexit. The legend helped drive history. But it has also distorted history, precisely because it is so memorable. To this I will return in a moment.

Up in the press gallery it was my good fortune to observe at close range the Commons part of the drama that surrounded the fall of Thatcher in 1990. I had a ringside seat. It started with Michael Heseltine's challenge to her leadership, her disappointing first-round result in the leadership election, the sounding out of colleagues to assess her chances after a skirmish that wounds but does not kill her leadership; and the immediate aftershock, as Thatcher consults further, and realises her first-round victory has been insufficiently decisive, and resigns.

Then the colleague who wielded the dagger, Mr Heseltine, fails to win the crown: John Major does. And almost from the start Mr Major is being routinely described as 'grey'. Commentators want colour. Interest never leaves the outgoing prime minister. Her final appearance in the Commons is sensational, and the newspapers find it hypnotic. And all the while, a legend is being born. She helps cement it later in an interview with the BBC. 'It was treachery,' she told them: 'Treachery with a smile on its face.'[3] Such traction did that phrase of hers attract that later there were legal battles about who owned the copyright to the sentence.

Let's look at observational, 'colour' accounts that accompanied the actual news reports, and see their power in shaping that legend: a legend of which the *Daily Express* was quick to offer a first draft: 'What have they done?' bawls the headline ('SPECIAL REPORT: PAGES 2, 3, 4, 5, 7, 8, 9, 10, 12, 17, 21' says the strap below the front page) beside a picture of Mrs T with some of the flowers well-wishers have sent. Within, the paper's chief feature writer gives us colour, illustrated by a picture of a kindly aide offering her a helping arm at the Downing Street door. '"Do you think she cried?" asks woman in the crowd at No. 10.'[4]

The *Daily Express*'s sketch writer, Peter Tory, piles in on the same theme: 'She was splendid. Magnificent. Triumphant ... Could this woman really have been hacked down only hours before? ... Behind her, those men and women who had savagely drawn her blood hunched uncomfortably. Their daggers were still dripping. Their victim brightly blue-suited, trim and composed.'[5] From his seat in the press gallery, the *Daily Mail*'s veteran sketch writer, Colin Welch (under the headline 'What have we done?') tells readers 'I saw the Tories down there looking woebegone and guilty. Most of them must have been thinking "what have we done? We've made the most frightful mistake."'[6]

The Independent is more measured, but describes the 'spirited defence' she made of her record, above a huge picture of her looking composed in pearls and not a hair out of place, checking her appearance in a dressing-table mirror.[7] Even *The Guardian*'s Andrew Rawnsley, then his paper's sketch writer, pays her ('Dying Swan Gives Commons a Command Performance') a sideways compliment. 'The Tories rose, cheering and waving their order papers, many of them the same men and women who had just pulled the lever to send her through the trapdoor of history. "Hypocrites!" yelled Labour MPs, many of whom are genuinely distressed to see her go.'[8]

But it is *The Daily Telegraph* that, in its respectful farewell, signals the next chapter in the developing legend. Their cartoonist Matt unwittingly joins in, his cartoon showing a bartender telling his customer 'There's a 10p fine every time you say "It's the end of an era."'[9]

On the same front page, beside a photograph of a spotlit and radiant-looking Thatcher (in camera focus) against the backdrop of two unnamed male Tories (out of focus and in the shadows behind her), the paper's Philip Johnston notes that

Her speech was an exposition of her beliefs in freedom, justice, the market economy and individual choice ... Free of the need to dissemble or compromise, she ... once again exposed the Tory rift over Europe, repeating with gusto the views on monetary and economic union which had contributed to her downfall.[9]

Here we see the legend moving on from a human story of personal betrayal to a putative theory: that

> *'She was splendid. Magnificent. Triumphant ... Could this woman really have been hacked down only hours before?'*
>
> Peter Tory

Thatcher, Thatcherism and her memory stand for the Eurosceptic cause within the party, and that her defenestration is some kind of a revanchist putsch against the Tory belief in national sovereignty. She has been, in short, martyred for her patriotism, and the canonisation is now under way. Mrs Thatcher was soon clothing herself in this version of her downfall, building upon and reinforcing the legend.

Which suited her very well, moving the story on, as it did, from the question Labour's Denis Healey asked in *The Independent*. 'If she really is this paragon of political and national virtue, why the hell have you ditched her?'[10] For by no means was it all about Europe, or the free market, or individual liberty. Most immediately it was about the poll tax, which – whatever view one took of its theoretical merits – had proved a catastrophic political misjudgement which she was refusing to reverse. There had been riots. More generally her downfall was about a widespread perception among her parliamentary colleagues that she was

'What have they done?', *Daily Express*, 23 November 1990. *The Express* asks the question over pages 2, 3, 4, 5, 7, 8, 9, 10, 12, 17 and 21.

going bonkers and dragging her party towards defeat in the next general election. That, let me assure you, was the general view – now almost buried by the legend.

A simple, gripping story was just too good to subject to critical scrutiny.

So I'm afraid Andrew Marr is right. A simple, gripping and (to many) moving story about a heroic leader brought down in cowardly fashion by lesser beings, nicely reinforced by the picture of a brave woman, composed and defiant in the face of a shadowy gang of treacherous males, was just too good to subject to critical scrutiny.

And, my goodness, did we colour writers assist in projecting it! Even at the time I was becoming aware of the template we were following for the creation of the legend that has become the right's preferred version of history. After her fall, and after Michael Heseltine too had been knocked off the ballot, I wrote this in my parliamentary sketch:

What happened next is now folklore. With the leader wounded but still alive, her own senior tribesmen drew back with one accord, and left her. Suddenly alone, she hesitated, then staggered from the stage. The tribe mourned her departure. Not falsely or without feeling, they wept. Then last night the final twist occurred. The tribe fell upon her assailant, Michael Heseltine, and slew him too. With many shouts of anger. Real anger.

It could have been done as a ballet. It had all the elements of a classical drama. Like Chinese opera or classical Greek tragedy, the rules required that certain human types be represented; certain ambitions be portrayed; certain actions punished. Every convention was obeyed, every actor played out his role ...

It started with an old leader, who was assassinated, as she deserved; then her assassin was assassinated, as he deserved. Then the new leader stepped forward; and here the ballet ended.[11]

Or so we thought. But even today, her ghost, whom we colour writers helped create, dances on.

Malala Yousafzai

Profile by Beth Gaskell

Malala Yousafzai (born 1997) is a Pakistani campaigner for female educational rights who was attacked by the Taliban when she spoke out against them for the right of girls to attend school. She survived the attempted assassination, and went on to become a world-renowned activist and Nobel Peace Prize laureate.

Malala Yousafzai was born into a Pashtun family in the Swat region of northern Pakistan. Her father was the principal of three local schools, including a girls' school, and education played an important part in her life from a young age. When the Taliban began to gain power in the region, her father risked his life to speak out against them, and Malala followed his example.

In 2008, when she was just eleven years old, Malala began writing a diary for BBC Urdu about her experiences as a schoolgirl under Taliban control. While the diary was published under a pseudonym, it soon became common knowledge in the area that Malala was the author. The following year *The New York Times* made a documentary following her life as the Pakistani military and the Taliban fought for control of the Swat Valley. She also gave interviews to a wide range of print and broadcast media, with the aim of publicising the plight of girls in her region, gaining international recognition.

In October 2012, when she was only fifteen, Malala's school bus was attacked by Taliban militants, who targeted her in retaliation for her activism. She was shot in the head, but miraculously survived. After receiving initial treatment in Pakistan, she was evacuated to the UK, both for her safety and for specialist medical care. The murder attempt received worldwide coverage; in trying to silence Malala, the Taliban had inadvertently brought her story to an international audience.

The news media continued to follow Malala's story, through her recovery, her family's relocation to the UK and her schooling. She has used that as a platform to spread her word, campaigning for women and children's rights, particularly focusing on women's education. In 2014, at seventeen, Malala became the youngest ever winner of the Nobel Peace Prize.

Luke McKernan

We win! The news and celebration

At the end of the evocative opening credits to the American television sitcom *Cheers* (1982–93) there is a vintage, colour-tinted photograph of a bar. The drinkers are holding up their glasses; the bartender is holding up a newspaper. The headline, in giant letters, reads 'We Win!'

Cheers, as the title song puts it, is the place 'where everyone knows your name', a communal home from home. With other elements of the front page deliberately blurred, the headline could represent any place, any community, any news story where identity is affirmed through celebration.

'We Win!' is both inclusive and exclusive. It announces something that belongs to all, while narrowing down its message to a particular group. *Cheers* was designed around the idea of being a home to all, while at the same time being emphatically defined by its Boston location and Bostonian habitués. This is what makes the choice of a newspaper so apposite. Newspapers, indeed any form of news publication, aim for inclusivity yet operate exclusively: that is, they are defined by the needs and understanding of their particular audience. That audience may be determined by region, age, class, gender or occupation, though it may always be shifting as tastes or aspirations change. The news will only ever be as fixed as its audience is fixed.

These points are demonstrated by the way news treats the celebratory story. 'We Win!' was originally a headline from New York newspaper the *Brooklyn Eagle* (its non-Bostonian origins are diplomatically blurred in the programme's title sequence), probably a special issue celebrating local baseball team the Brooklyn Dodgers winning the National League pennant in 1941.[1] It is narrowly triumphant. It speaks with the thrill that a news publication senses when it understands its audience completely and can be the purveyor of its joys. This is the news at its happiest.

The celebratory news story documents triumph. It may be a sporting victory, the end of a conflict, a scientific breakthrough, a coronation or the success of a heroic undertaking. The diamond jubilee of Queen Victoria, the ending of the two World Wars, the 1953 coronation, the climbing of Mount Everest and the 1966 World Cup are all notable examples from British history when the news spoke for all in acclaiming a triumph – or assumed that it did. Of course, not everyone among the British audience rejoiced in the reign of Queen Victoria, or thought that the conquest of Everest mattered, or cared much for football, but the presumed universality made such contrariness redundant in news terms. The celebratory news story affirms a community's sense of itself, that which makes it proud, an emotion that the news publication crystallises.

The celebratory news story affirms a community's sense of itself, that which makes it proud.

Three stories from three centuries demonstrate different facets of the celebratory news story, from the particular, to the national, to the global.

THE GREAT PUGILIST OF ENGLAND

The first story comes out of a remarkable image. On 14 February 1863 the *Illustrated Sporting News and Theatrical News Review* published a double-page illustration entitled 'The Great Pugilists of England'.[2] The *Illustrated Sporting News* was one of a number of specialist newspapers serving a growing market for sporting information, as sports such as football, golf, athletics, cricket and boxing grew in popularity.

It made a special feature of illustrations, which were so popular that they were made for sale separately, often ending up on the walls of homes or public houses. But though sport was growing in popularity, many associated it with disorder, gambling or the improper use of leisure time. The *Illustrated Sporting News* not only reported but also championed its subject, identifying strongly with the aspirations of its readership, taking a firm stance against those who would curtail such enjoyments. It was celebratory in all that it published, in support of its audience.

'The Great Pugilists of England' portrays what looks, at first sight, like a collection of prosperous mid-Victorian gentlemen. If one did not know the title or the content, one might think that here was a gathering of local politicians, or merchants of some kind, preening themselves with civic pride. But these were men who fought for a living, at a time when boxing was bare-knuckle, with brutal contests that could last for hours. The police were never too far away, ready to break up what were viewed as riotous assemblies.

On the right-hand side of the illustration is its most remarkable feature: a Black boxer, presented without qualification as an Englishman among Englishmen, someone to be admired. He was Bob Travers (1832–1918), in fact an American, one of a number of African Americans, either born slaves or the freeborn sons of slaves, who managed to cross the Atlantic to try their chances in a land where pugilism had an avid following and they might enjoy a greater degree of freedom. Travers, born in Norfolk, Virginia in 1832, came to Britain as a child. He began boxing in 1854 and had a nine-year career. He was a moderate but tenacious fighter, always a tough proposition for his opponents, but smart enough to get out of the game when he could. He retired to run a London pub, though sadly ended his days in Wandsworth workhouse.[3]

The Illustrated Sporting News *championed its subject, identifying strongly with the aspirations of its readership.*

What is notable about Travers, and some other Black sportsmen of the mid-nineteenth century who were reported on in the pages of the sports-focused papers that sprung up at this time, is how they were taken entirely at their own merits. Of course, in real life they were subjected probably to daily racial prejudice. For those such as Travers who toured the country, appearing before rough audiences, there would have been much abuse to endure. Even friendly accounts in boxing memoirs of the period use language to describe him that we would now find offensive.

But in the pages of the *Illustrated Sporting News and Theatrical and Musical Review* things are different. Travers is one of us. More than that, he is an admired figure, a notable exponent of pugilistic science, an exponent of sporting virtue, despite what censorious authorities might say about the rough world of bare-knuckle fighting. His colour is certainly referred to – he is variously referred to as 'the Black' or 'the Ebony Gentleman' in the characteristically florid style adopted for fight descriptions – but for most of the time he is simply Travers, or Bob. He is our fighter.

'The Great Pugilists of England' champions more than sport; it champions the socially transformative effects of sport, breaking down the barriers that would restrain it. In lauding that which it cherished, the *Illustrated Sporting News* pointed to a new kind of society, based not on race or class, but on personal merit. It defined, and celebrated, a new *us*.[4]

THE LAST LEG

A century and a half later, the London 2012 Olympic and Paralympic Games were an expression of sport's profoundly moral and uplifting quality. Political machinations and drug-taking scandals had done much to tarnish Olympic ideals, but London 2012 – and particularly the Paralympic Games – was seen as a reaffirmation of the better things to which Olympism and Paralympism might make people aspire.

The opening ceremony of the Olympic Games championed an inclusive society forged by historical progress, setting the tone for the summer. The

London 2012 was seen as a reaffirmation of the better things to which Olympism and Paralympism might make people aspire.

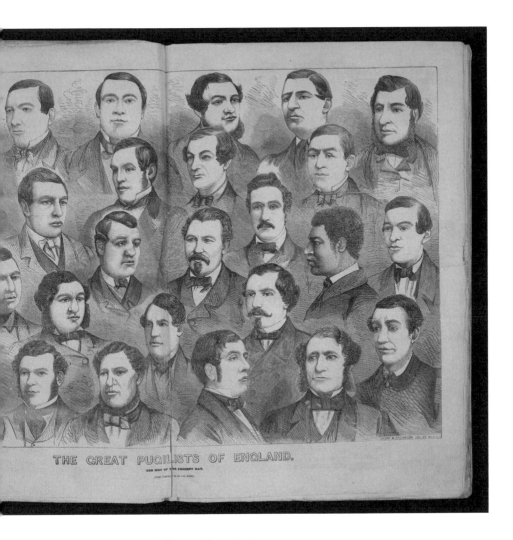

THE GREAT PUGILISTS OF ENGLAND.

THE MEN OF THE PRESENT DAY.

Paralympic Games built on this optimism, as can be seen in the guidelines given to journalists by the British Paralympic Association. This document advised on language, behaviour and perceptions, asking that Paralympic athletes be understood as 'elite athletes first and foremost, rather than seen primarily as people who have overcome great adversity'. The goal was change perceptions, to change the general public's idea of *us*.

Paralympics GB's success in 2012 will be measured not just in gold medals and our final position on the medal table, but also by the effect that the Paralympic Games has on the general

'The Great Pugilists of England', *Illustrated Sporting News and Theatrical and Musical Review*, 14 February 1863. Bob Travers centre row, second from right.

From the start it was clear that this was a different kind of television programme.

public and by the shift in perceptions of disability sport and disability that we can, and must, affect.[5]

This spirit informed every part of host broadcaster Channel 4's coverage, notably so in a television series shown late at night from the first day of competition, *The Last Leg with Adam Hills.*[6]

The programme, produced by Open Mike Productions, was presented by Australian comedian Adam Hills (born 1970), who was born without a right foot, with Alex Brooker (born 1984), who has hand and arm disabilities and a prosthetic right leg, and comedian Josh Widdicombe (born 1983), who has no physical disability. From the start it was clear that this was a different kind of television programme. It discussed the day's sporting events with both humour and unabashed enthusiasm at athletic excellence, establishing a warm, inclusive tone. Inclusive in this case meant not just the Paralympians (several of whom featured as guests) but also apprehensive viewers. In the second episode the programme introduced a Twitter hashtag, #isitok, that encouraged viewers to ask questions about disability, not least on what sort of humour was appropriate. It was a programme built around understanding.

The programme learned as it went along, establishing a form – and quickly building up an appreciative audience for this – that found a harmonious balance between comedy, comment and reportage. Such was its success that the series returned in 2013, the title simplified to *The Last Leg*, with a brief to provide a commentary on the week's news. Unlike other news satire programmes, *The Last Leg* engaged with its political subjects as much as it mocked them. An interview conducted by Brooker with deputy prime minister Nick Clegg (born 1967) on 30 January 2015, complete with a 'bullshit' button for answers Brooker felt were evasive, has been held up as a model example of the breaking down of the barrier between public and politicians.[7]

It continued to cover issues of disability, but the broadening of questions under the #isitok hashtag showed how its remit had been extended. Nevertheless, the programme remained grounded in the good-natured activism that characterised the first series. Astutely attuned to an audience both in the studio and online, as much a news programme as a comedy show, *The Last Leg* exemplifies honest engagement. At the time of writing the series is still running, grounded in the lessons and the triumph of the Olympic and Paralympic Games.

THE MOON

Global celebrations are rare. When are we all one audience? The Olympic and Paralympic Games may aspire to such universality, but ultimately their focus is national, for each of us cheers on different competitors. A better example, at least at face value, is the moon landing.

The landing on the moon by two Apollo 11 astronauts, Neil Armstrong (1930–2012) and Buzz Aldrin (born 1930), on 20 July 1969 had been preceded by a long campaign of news management by NASA (the National Aeronautics and Space Administration). A narrative of heroic endeavour representing the peak of human achievement was fed to the media, which resonated with notions of Manifest Destiny and cherished stories of journeys of discovery that expanded human horizons (circumnavigating the globe, reaching the South Pole, climbing Everest). This helped offset the nakedly political aspect of the space programme – the United States sought to conquer space ahead of the Soviet Union – and the huge costs involved.

The moon landing itself took place at 15.17 Eastern Standard Time, with Neil Armstrong setting foot on the moon at 21.56 EST. 'You guys are getting prime TV time,' spacecraft communicator Charlie Duke told Armstrong and Aldrin when they decided to walk on the moon earlier than planned.[8] The lander was equipped with a light black-and-white Westinghouse 16mm camera operating at ten frames a second, with images and sound signals transmitted via an antenna on the top of the lander.[9] In the UK more than 26 million people saw the landing broadcast by the BBC and ITV (at 21.17), with the moonwalk inconveniently taking place at 03.56.[10]

Global celebrations are rare. When are we all one audience?

Crowds in Sheep Meadow in Central Park, New York, 20 July 1969, watching the moon landing on a giant television screen.

Globally an estimated 650 million people, or around 20 per cent of the world's population, saw the landing live or in later news programmes. Others followed the story on radio, while newspapers – unable to compete on equal terms with live broadcasting – recorded the triumph but could not quite live up to it.

It was an American victory. For the losers in the space race (the Soviet Union), for anti-Americans anywhere, for non-white Americans who felt the event summed up their alienation from mainstream society (memorably expressed in Gil Scott-Heron's song 'Whitey's on the Moon'), and for anyone who felt the estimated $19.4 billion ($116.5 billion in today's money) might have been better spent on the needy, the moon landing was no cause for celebration.[11]

Yet the world celebrated nonetheless. It was an unparalleled human achievement; any human had to share in that. Television created the moment, firstly as the most notable achievement in long-distance communications, secondly as a means of binding the world together. All were interconnected in a common experience through a common technology (at least, all those who had access to a television set). Though the moon landing was seen, listened to and read about in many media produced by myriad publishers in multiple languages, such differences disappeared for a moment in time. The triumph was as much the audience itself as the story that audience was witnessing.

The news loves to celebrate with us. The opportunity confirms its sense of being the voice of a people. However, saying 'we' with confidence has become ever harder given the shifting loyalties of our present news world. The internet, which was seen as something to bring the world together, in doing so has created news communities that lie beyond those of class, region or nation whom the traditional news media reached. Online, we can choose whoever we want to be. Technology has given us the power to be citizens of anything and anywhere, dividing us up in every possible way in the process. The global *we*, if ever it existed, has gone. It is as far away from us as the moon.

The triumph was as much the audience itself as the story that audience was witnessing.

2

WHAT DOES A FREE PRESS MEAN?

Jackie Harrison

INTRODUCTION

It is reasonable to suppose that we live in a world where there are only three fundamental sets of civil and political circumstances in which a free press operates independent from control by any vested interests. These circumstances are where the idea of a free press is tolerated, often disliked, but reluctantly endured; where it is constantly attacked (for whatever reason but usually for being on the 'wrong side'); and where the press is repressed or completely oppressed. The chapters in this section concern themselves with some of the details of these circumstances that surround the issue of a free press by looking at the relationship between the context of a news event and how the reporting of it can be suppressed; the history of the partisan press and its taste for battle and crusade; and the deep value of visual satire (mainly pocket cartoons) and its potency. The chapters ultimately point to the kinds of precariousness that surround a free press, and how it has over time resisted those who would ensure that it only provides news stories that serve particular outlooks and causes.

Suppressing the news

Extinction Rebellion (XR) protesters divided opinion when they used vehicles, bamboo structures and their own bodies to blockade three major printing plants, delaying distribution of many of the UK's leading national newspapers one night in September 2020.

Their action was aimed at highlighting the role of the commercial press in general, and Rupert Murdoch's international media empire in particular, in downplaying or denying the extent of the climate crisis confronting the planet. However, even many XR sympathisers thought it an odd look for environmental campaigners to be disrupting the free flow of news. Rebels are usually the ones protesting *against* suppression. Indeed, at around the same time as those XR activists were gathering outside News UK's Newsprinters sites in Glasgow, Hertfordshire and on Merseyside, the streets of Belarus, Bangkok and Hong Kong were witnessing state forces clamping down on such free assembly and expressions of opinion.

As Dominic Ponsford, editor-in-chief of industry website *Press Gazette*, mused:

Many are left scratching their heads about Extinction Rebellion's willingness to extinguish freedom of expression in order to exercise their right to protest. It is quite a contrast to countries like China and Russia where those protesting against the status quo would dearly love to have the sort of free press we enjoy in the UK.[1]

However, whereas limiting the circulation of information is an everyday occupation of authoritarian states, for XR the targeting of printing presses was more of a one-off stunt. It annoyed many people, but it also got activists invited onto news broadcasts, where they seized the opportunity to argue that much of the 'free press' had for years chosen to ignore or question the extent of the climate emergency. It seemed that their case required the peg of a provocative action before it would be reported as news.

Context is important whenever the issue of a 'free press' is discussed. The concept is generally taken to mean that news organisations are free to report without being subject to prior restraint, censorship or regulatory systems that entail the official licensing of journalists. The trouble with the state having authority to grant licences to practise journalism is that such power also entails *refusing* or threatening to revoke such licences, with all the fear and timidity that is apt to engender. A free press is therefore held by many to be a bulwark of democracy and an informed citizenry. More critical commentators dismiss such talk as self-serving mythology, arguing that freedom of the press exists only for those rich enough to own a media empire, with billionaire proprietors treating the concept more as a property right than a human right.

Yet 'knowledge is power', according to a well-worn saying, commonly attributed to the philosopher and scientist Francis Bacon (1561–1626). The extent to which knowledge on its own can really be empowering in a social or political sense might be debated, but what is beyond question is that a tendency for the powerful to fear the free circulation of news and views among the wider population goes back a very long way. The first recorded case of the suppression of 'free speech' in England was literally of *speech* rather than writing, when an ecclesiastical court in twelfth-century Oxford ordered people to be branded and flogged for uttering heretical thoughts.[2] Printing went on to increase the speed at which unofficial information could circulate among the population – along with plenty of misinformation and imminent predictions of the end of days, of course – and from the fifteenth to the seventeenth centuries the court of Star Chamber maintained strict control of what could and could not be published, with gruesome

> *Context is important whenever the issue of a 'free press' is discussed.*

Once in post, he enforced the draconian Licensing Act 1662 with gusto, formalising a system of news censorship.

punishments awaiting those who disobeyed its edicts.

This system of censorship began to break down during the period of political, religious and intellectual ferment that culminated in the execution of King Charles I in 1649. Numerous newsbooks and pamphlets were printed around this time, many combining comment with the reporting of something that we might recognise as news, prompting *The Times*'s editor Henry Wickham Steed (1871–1956) to conclude: 'Regular English journalism began with the Civil War and the political strife that led up to it.'[3] Moves by Parliament to reimpose controls on printing prompted the republican poet John Milton (1608–1674) to write and publish *Areopagitica: A Speech for the Liberty of Unlicensed Printing* (1644), in which he argued that denying people access to printed material 'kills reason itself'.[4]

A rival pamphleteer took a rather different view. Roger L'Estrange (1616–1704), an absolutist Royalist, celebrated the defeat of the Commonwealth and the restoration of the monarchy by calling for a return to the strict censorship of pre-revolutionary days. It has been observed that L'Estrange was 'a rather unusual newspaper man in that he believed that in a well-ordered world newspapers should not exist at all'.[5] 'I do declare myself,' wrote L'Estrange in the *Intelligencer*, one of several news-sheets he edited, that:

supposing the Press in order, the people in their right wits, and news or no news to be the question, a Public Mercury shall never have my vote, because I think it makes the multitude too familiar with the actions and counsels of their superiors … and gives them not only an itch but a kind of colourable right and licence to be meddling with the Government.[6]

With such an attitude towards the dangers of giving 'the multitude' too much access to information, it is little surprise that L'Estrange's *Considerations and Proposals in Order to the Regulation of the Press* (1663) led to his becoming official licenser of the press. Once in post, he enforced the draconian Licensing Act 1662 with gusto, formalising a system of news censorship that has even drawn comparisons with that later established by Joseph Goebbels in Nazi Germany.[7] According to Anna Beer:

The extremism of men like L'Estrange was embarrassing to more moderate members of the Royal

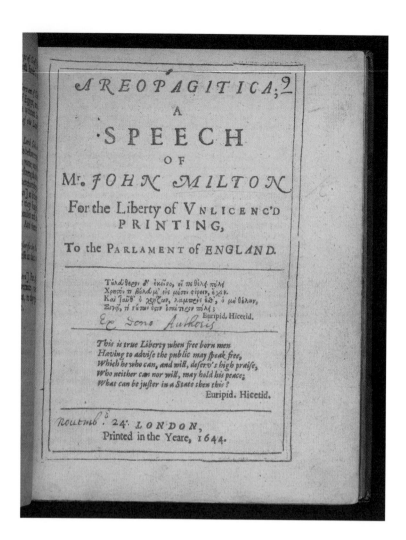

Printed border content:

AREOPAGITICA;

A

·SPEECH

OF

Mr. *JOHN MILTON*

For the Liberty of Vɴʟɪᴄᴇɴᴄ'ᴅ
PRINTING,

To the Pᴀʀʟᴀᴍᴇɴᴛ of Eɴɢʟᴀɴᴅ.

Τὸν δ᾽ ἐκεῖνο, οἵ τι θέλᾳ πόλᾳ
Χρηστὸν τι βέλμ᾽ εἰς μέσον φέρειν, ἔχᾳ ν.
Καὶ ταῦθ᾽ ὁ χρήζων, λαμπρός ἐσθ᾽, ὁ μὴ θέλων,
Σιγᾷ, τί τούτων ἐστιν ἰσάίτερον πόλᾳ ;

Euripid, Hicetid.

This is true Liberty when free born men
Having to advise the public may speak free,
Which he who can, and will, deserv's high praise,
Who neither can nor will, may hold his peace;
What can be juster in a State then this ?

Euripid. Hicetid.

LONDON,
Printed in the Yeare, 1644.

Areopagitica: A speech of Mr. John Milton for the liberty of unlicensed printing to the Parliament of England (London, 1644). A presentation copy of the first edition from Milton to bookseller George Thomason.

court and government, including the King himself, but it was L'Estrange who demanded and got tougher laws and penalties to stamp out the publishing underground. Appointed in 1663 as Surveyor of the Press, he was granted formidable powers to search for unlicensed books, illegal presses and all those involved in the production of illicit material. Dawn raids, rewards for informers and imprisonment without trial characterised his rule. The punishments for authors and printers could be severe. On 20 February 1664, the printer John Twyn was executed.[8]

L'Estrange may have gone down in history as the 'bloodhound of the press', but he was not against *all* printing, just that which circulated nonconformist arguments among the people.[9] Indeed, despite the regime of censorship he had been instrumental in establishing, he continued as a writer, editor and publisher himself, justifying his own polemical output in the following terms: 'Tis the Press that has made 'um mad, and the Press must set 'um right again.'[10] Even L'Estrange knew that suppression alone could not win hearts and minds.

Pre-publication censorship may have ended but the extent of the freedoms enjoyed by the 'free press' remains contested.

It was a heavy weapon while it lasted, though, and it hampered would-be commercial publishers as well as political radicals and anybody else who desired to have their say in print. The Licensing Act was renewed several times before eventually being allowed to lapse in 1695, a year referenced in much press commentary on the Leveson Report into press ethics in 2012.[11] According to this rhetoric, the glorious year of 1695 marked the end of pre-publication censorship in what was to become the UK, and ever since we have enjoyed more than three centuries of untrammelled press freedom.

It is not quite as simple as that, argues Stanley Harrison in *Poor Men's Guardians*, his account of the struggles of the radical press. Pre-publication censorship and outright suppression of certain publications may have ended in formal terms more than 325 years ago – apart from the occasional exception, such as the banning of the communist *Daily Worker* in 1941 – but the extent of the freedoms enjoyed by the 'free press' remains contested:

In truth, the ending of pre-censorship marked not an end but a beginning. All the main battles – against legislation to make newspapers prohibitively dear, countless prosecutions for sedition, criminal libel and blasphemy, involving sentences of imprisonment and transportation totalling hundreds of years – still lay ahead.[12]

The early years after the lapsing of the Licensing Act certainly saw the 'truly astonishing' growth of a national and local newspaper industry, with an estimated total of 70,000 copies bought every week in 1712.[13] Yet it was also in 1712 that the authorities imposed the first of the newspaper stamp duties to which Harrison (above) alludes, which had the effect of limiting the circulation of news among poorer sections of the community. Such measures were directed only at a mischief-making 'pauper press', Parliament was assured by Lord Ellenborough (1790–1871),

Stamp duties on paper, advertising and newspapers were condemned by democrats as 'taxes on knowledge'.

who added that depriving 'the lowest classes of society of all political information' was a good thing, on the grounds that he could see 'no possible good to be derived to the country from having statesmen at the loom and politicians at the spinning jenny'.[14] His lordship was speaking just four months after the Peterloo massacre.

Stamp duties on paper, advertising and newspapers themselves were condemned by democrats as 'taxes on knowledge' and were defied and resisted by 'the great unstamped', demonstrating a recurring theme that press freedom in practice is not granted to the people from on high in a certain year, but remains an arena of contestation. In the eighteenth and nineteenth centuries, countless people risked prosecution to write, print and distribute cheap but unlawful 'unstamped' newspapers to a wider working-class readership; titles included *The Poor Man's Guardian* itself, published from 1831 to 1835, which made its point by using as its masthead the perennial motto, 'knowledge is power'. Some of the radical press wore their unstamped status as a badge of honour, while others adopted more oblique forms of defiance, claiming not to be newspapers at all on the grounds that they were not printed on paper; Henry Berthold's calico *Political Handkerchief* (1831) was one cheeky example, and the *Political Touchwood* (1832) was printed on thin plywood.

Taxes on knowledge began to be reduced from the mid-1830s and were abolished in 1861, partly because of continued defiance by the working-class press but also because of the potential for cheap newspapers to be targeted at a mass market by commercial publishers, or 'men of good moral character, of respectability and of capital', as one put it.[15] Since then, the power of the market has been the main regulator of the UK press, with circulation wars, takeovers, (over-)mighty proprietors and the influence of advertisers all tending to have the effect of reducing media plurality and suppressing – or marginalising, at least – alternative voices.

The arrival of broadcasting in the twentieth century met with significantly tighter forms of state regulation of news, in part because technology made restricting output via licensing a feasible option, and in part because of fears about the potential dangers of allowing the voice of an electronic 'guest' to speak directly to people in their own homes. Hence the system of licensing and regulation under which TV and radio operate to this day, sometimes

The newspaper was an attempt to avoid paying Stamp Tax by claiming that as it was printed on calico it did not qualify as a paper.

Berthold's Political Handkerchief, 8 September 1831.

augmented by even stricter prohibitions such as when the government of Margaret Thatcher (1925–2013) outlawed broadcast interviews with members of various groups in Northern Ireland. The UK broadcast ban, which operated from 1988 to 1994, was aimed at denying 'the oxygen of publicity' to organisations such as Sinn Fein during the Troubles. The National Union of Journalists, among others, opposed the ban on the grounds that it also deprived citizens of the right to information. Within just a few years of the restrictions being lifted, some of those political activists who had once been silenced – or whose words had been re-voiced by actors – became regulars on TV and radio news as members of the power-sharing Northern Ireland Executive. One-time *persona non grata* Martin McGuinness (1950–2017) even ended up taking tea with the queen.

In comparison with broadcast journalism, newspapers and online media in the UK face far fewer formal restrictions on what they can and cannot report, and on how they may go about doing so. This contrast was frequently highlighted during the Leveson Inquiry. While many newspaper editors stressed the importance of resisting the 'shackles' of state regulation, some of their broadcast counterparts pointed out that TV and radio journalists also produce hard-hitting investigations that challenge authority, but only when it is undeniably in the public interest to do so. Not that the press is a complete free-for-all, as the authors of the journalist's Bible, *McNae's Essential Law for Journalists*, point out: 'Although the UK has a free press in comparison to the censorship which stifles liberty in many other nations, the description must be qualified because of the many and growing restrictions on what can be published', which range from the Official Secrets Act 1989 to the Defamation Act 2013.[16] But since 2008 – in England and Wales, at least – these restrictions have no longer included the blasphemy law that was used to prosecute a UK newspaper as recently as the 1970s.

When Gay News *ceased publication it was less to do with legal suppression and more to do with financial pressures.*

Two years after launching as a fortnightly publication in 1972, *Gay News* had fended off one obscenity charge – the 'offending' image was a cover photograph of two men kissing – but it would prove less successful in defending itself against a private prosecution for blasphemous libel. That case, brought by the morality campaigner Mary Whitehouse (1910–2001), was prompted by the paper publishing a poem by James Kirkup (1918–2009), which imagined a Roman soldier's sexual fantasies following the crucifixion of Jesus Christ. Publishing the poem in 1976 earned editor Denis Lemon (1945–1994) a suspended prison sentence, and the paper itself was fined £1,000. The case dragged on for years afterwards, with unsuccessful attempts at overturning the verdict on appeal and via the European Commission for Human Rights, but when *Gay News* ceased publication in 1983 it was less to do with this legal suppression for blasphemy and more to do with the financial pressures of seeking to survive as an independent voice in a marketplace.

As an indication of how some things *do* change, it is worth recalling that when the writer David Widgery (1947–1992) was preparing a piece on the demise of *Gay News*, he visited the British Library's former newspaper archive at Colindale to consult some back issues, only to be told: 'Oh no, you won't find *that* here. It's a cupboard number you see.' As Widgery noted at the time: 'Homosexuality out of the closet? After fourteen brave years of gay liberation, it hasn't even got out of the British Library's dirty books cupboard.'[17] Well, it has now. And Kirkup's poem was itself liberated twenty-five years after the original court case, when the human rights campaigner Peter Tatchell (born 1952), among others, presaged the end of the blasphemy law by reading the poem aloud and handing out printed copies on the steps of St Martin-in-the-Fields, Trafalgar Square.[18] It was an event that echoed the outspokenness of heretics and democrats of centuries past, but this time no action was taken against the brazen blasphemers. Fittingly, the title of the poem was 'The Love That Dares to Speak Its Name'.

Gay News may have been a commercial publication, but it was also more than that, because it reflected and served a wider social and cultural movement and community. Its legal problems were similar to those of other sections of the so-called 'underground' press, such as the high-profile prosecutions of people associated with the magazine *Oz* and the newspaper *IT*. However, it could be said that the trials and tribulations of such media pale into insignificance when considered alongside attempts to suppress a genuinely underground press.

Consider, for example, the case of *GUNS* – the *Guernsey Underground News Service* – and its deadly serious instruction to readers to 'burn after reading'. *GUNS* was a (more or less) daily news-sheet, typed up on the ultra-thin paper used for packing tomatoes and distributed in clandestine conditions from 1942 to 1944, while the Channel Island of Guernsey was under Nazi occupation during the Second World War. *GUNS* was a perilous project, with those caught just reading it likely to be sent to prison. Five islanders accused of actually distributing *GUNS* were deported to concentration camps in Germany, suffering a regime of 'beatings, starvation, and other mistreatment' under which two died and the other three were liberated only days from their likely deaths.[19] And what was the vital news these 'brave Guernseymen who served as resisters' risked their lives to communicate to their fellow citizens, and of which the occupying forces were so fearful?[20] *GUNS* and the similar news-sheet *GASP* (*Guernsey Active Secret Press*) mostly comprised items simply transcribed from BBC news broadcasts that volunteers picked up on the crystal radios that were produced and listened to furtively after the Nazis confiscated wireless sets from every home on Guernsey.

The fact that islanders would risk imprisonment and death to type up the contents of a regular BBC

The trials and tribulations of such media pale into insignificance alongside attempts to suppress a genuinely underground press.

radio bulletin, then pass it around for others to read in secret, surely says something about the strength of people's itch for news, particularly at times of crisis, threat and oppression. It also suggests that, whenever there is suppression of news, there is also likely to be resistance, however terrifying the potential consequences. Perhaps most of all, it brings home the fact that, when it comes to understanding the continuing contestation around concepts such as freedom of the press, context is everything.

Guernsey Underground News Sheet, 4 August 1943. The secretly-produced *GUNS* was a single sheet, printed on tomato-packing paper, comprising transcripts of BBC news broadcasts.

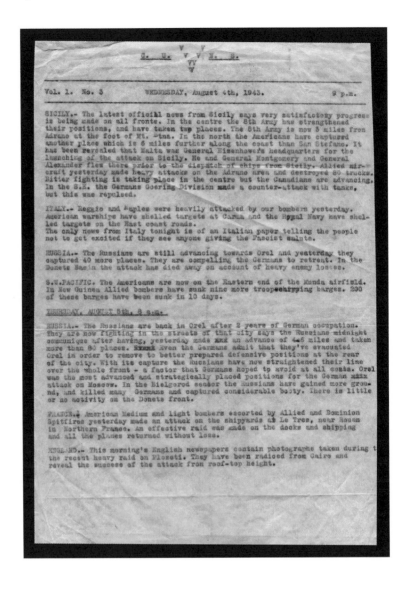

The Voice

Profile by Beth Gaskell

The Voice is an award-winning newspaper aimed at a Black audience. It was founded in 1982 and has been a launchpad and a platform for a number of illustrious Black journalists and broadcasters to investigate and write about a wide range of issues that affect Afro-Caribbean people living in the UK.

The Voice was founded by Val McCalla (centre, 1943–2002), who, while working on a local East End newspaper, saw a gap in the market. The pioneering team working with McCalla included editor Peter 'Flip' Fraser (left, 1951–2014) and deputy editor Sharon Ali (right), while broadcaster Alex Pascall (born 1936) was McCalla's business partner, helping the fledgling newspaper get off the ground.

It was the first news publication for a Black British audience interested in Black British life, as opposed to earlier titles such as the *West Indian Gazette*, which had given a first-generation immigrant readership news of the Caribbean. It was launched as a weekly publication in August 1982, to coincide with the Notting Hill Carnival, but was also a response to the Brixton riots which had taken place the previous summer. It was hoped that *The Voice* could speak to and for the Black community, who felt that they had been marginalised both by the UK authorities and by the British press.

The Voice's subject matter is wide-ranging and diverse, including local, national and international news and politics; sport; entertainment; crime; education; and issues surrounding race and ethnicity. Key issues that it has covered include the aftermath of the Brixton riots, violence and policing around the Notting Hill Carnival, investigation of and dialogue about Stephen Lawrence's murder and the police response, and the Windrush scandal. The publication also focuses on Afro-Caribbean food, business, music and film, and civil rights around the world.

Over the years many journalists have been part of *The Voice* team, but some important members have included Trevor Phillips, Rageh Omaar, Martin Bashir, Brenda Emmanus, Gemma Weekes, brothers Diran and Dotun Obedayo and Vanessa Walters. The publication and its journalists have won numerous awards, including the BBI Media and Entertainment Award in 2008, and 'Best Magazine' from the Urban Music Awards in 2009 and 2010. The newspaper became a monthly publication in September 2019.

Adrian Bingham

The partisan press

The British press was born amid the heat and fury of conflict, and has never lost the taste for battle. The first significant blossoming of printed news in Britain came during the early stages of the Civil War in the 1640s, as the mechanisms of state censorship collapsed and the opposing sides produced newsbooks and news-sheets to win over and mobilise opinion.

P re-publication censorship was reimposed under the regimes of Oliver Cromwell (Lord Protector 1653–8) and Charles II (r. 1660–85), but it did not last beyond 1695, and fierce rhetorical clashes in print resumed. Over subsequent centuries, the state would bring in various measures to control and restrict the press, from duties and taxes that kept newspapers expensive to legal obligations against defamation, obscenity and the release of 'official secrets', but these did not prevent the culture of British journalism remaining deeply partisan or stop journalists vehemently criticising those in power.[1]

As the press industrialised and mass-market newspapers emerged in the late nineteenth and early twentieth centuries, the tendency for publications to align themselves with political causes and to campaign on behalf of their readership did not diminish. In Fleet Street there was little of the reverence for 'objectivity' in reporting that developed in the United States; and when the

BBC was established in 1922 with a mandate for 'impartiality' and 'balance' in its broadcasting, it only reinforced the belief of many print journalists that newspapers and magazines should provide something more distinctive and full-blooded. The British press has continued to display its partisan colours prominently, and at moments of high political drama, such as during the turmoil created by the vote to leave the European Union in a referendum in 2016, the bitter language of the Civil War period did not seem far away.

Press partisanship has been exercised in many different ways, and with a variety of justifications. It is possible to identify three broad types of partisan behaviour. The first draws on the long-held ideal, first articulated by the politician and writer Edmund Burke (1729–1797), of the press as a 'fourth estate', scrutinising and critiquing the actions of the other three estates (monarchy/aristocracy, clergy and MPs assembled in the House of Commons).[2] In this model, the press represents and defends the interests of the public against those wielding power, by investigating and exposing incompetence, inefficiency, lassitude or corruption. Such an approach lends itself to a populist or anti-establishment rhetoric, arguing that individuals or institutions are incapable of serving the real interests of the nation, perhaps because they lack the fortitude, common sense or honesty of ordinary citizens.

The second approach adopts more of an 'insider' perspective, and aligns itself to the conventional political system by exercising support for one or other of the main political parties. For all its claims of independence, the press has been intimately tied to party politics for centuries. Many publications have been financed by donations from politicians and party associations; proprietors and editors have traded access and information for supportive articles and headlines; at election times, above all, newspapers and magazines have been expected to campaign vigorously for their favoured party. In Britain's first-past-the-post electoral system, traditionally dominated by two main parties, that has often resulted in a sharp polarisation of press output.

The final type of press partisanship seeks to provide a platform for marginalised or under-represented voices. If the 'fourth estate' rhetoric invokes the broad public, and party campaigning

Press partisanship has been exercised in many different ways, and with a variety of justifications.

aligns itself with the main national and local political structures, these publications – often poorly financed and with relatively low circulations – advocate for those who feel excluded from the political mainstream or who wish to challenge conventional wisdoms. This alternative journalism spans the political spectrum, from publications for radical, socialist or communist organisations, feminist campaigns and BAME (Black, Asian and minority ethnic) populations to titles supporting radical right movements, anti-immigration groups or fundamentalist religious sects. Such journalism might have a limited reach in the first instance, but it not only offers an important rallying point for campaigners; it can also be an important testing space for ideas that gradually percolate into the mainstream. This chapter will explore in turn each of these types of partisan voice to provide an overview of the cacophony that is British journalism.

'FOURTH ESTATE' CRUSADING

Press crusades against the mistakes, misdeeds and iniquities of elites and authorities have a long history. In its short run between 1762 and 1763, John Wilkes's (1725–1797) *North Briton* vehemently attacked George III's government. The first issue defiantly declared that: 'The Liberty of the Press is the birthright of a BRITON, and is justly esteemed the finest bulwark of the liberties of this country. It has been the terror of all bad ministers.'[3] Ministers were indeed sufficiently terrorised to call, after the particularly vituperative issue 45, for Wilkes and the *North Briton*'s writers and publishers to be arrested on a general warrant. The defendants were eventually released in what became a long-run *cause célèbre* about the rights and freedoms of the press, one result of which, in 1771, was the winning of the right of newspapers to print the proceedings of the Houses of Parliament. Another editor who found himself facing legal penalties for his controversial journalism was W.T. Stead (1849–1912). His 'Maiden

'The Liberty of the Press is the birthright of a BRITON, and is justly esteemed the finest bulwark of the liberties of this country. It has been the terror of all bad ministers.'

North Briton

Tribute of Modern Babylon' series, published in *The Pall Mall Gazette* in July 1885, sought to expose the prevalence of child prostitution in the nation's capital. Stead proved his point by showing how easy it was to buy thirteen-year-old Eliza Armstrong for £5, and ended up serving three months in Holloway Prison. But his revelations had a significant impact, notably helping to secure the passage of the Criminal Law Amendment Act, which raised the age of consent from thirteen to sixteen and increased police powers over brothels.[4]

The most striking example of fourth estate crusading in the twentieth century is perhaps the Northcliffe press's assault on Liberal prime minister Herbert Asquith's (1852–1928) government during the First World War. Lord Northcliffe (1865–1922) was the most powerful 'press baron' of the period, having founded the *Daily Mail* (1896) and the *Daily Mirror* (1903); he subsequently acquired *The Observer* (1905) and *The Times* (1908). Northcliffe had repeatedly warned about the emerging threat from Germany in the years before 1914, and when war broke out he was determined to ensure that it was prosecuted urgently and efficiently. He feared, as did many other editors and journalists, that the strict censorship regime imposed by the government and the military authorities would hide failures in the management of the war effort; he believed, too, that while there was a political truce in Parliament, it was the responsibility of the press to keep up the pressure on Britain's leaders.

On 30 August 1914 *The Times* caused a furore by printing a special Sunday edition with a front-page report – the so-called 'Amiens Dispatch' – detailing the 'Heavy Losses of British Troops' and 'Broken British Regiments' retreating from German advances.[5] Unexpectedly passed by the Press Bureau – which soon disassociated itself from the decision – and roundly criticised in the House

Northcliffe had repeatedly warned about the emerging threat from Germany in the years before 1914.

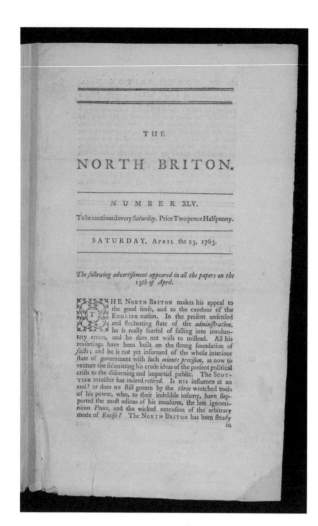

The North Briton
no. 45, 23 April 1763.
The notorious issue
no. 45 of John Wilkes's
The North Briton criticised
King George III, which led
to a warrant for his arrest.

of Commons for its negativity, the report was markedly different
from the bland coverage that had filled most newspapers in the
preceding days, and illustrated the serious predicament the nation
was in. The report and the controversy it generated contributed to
a rise in the level of recruitment in the following days.[6]

As the war continued, Northcliffe became increasingly
convinced that several men in leading positions were not up to
their job – including Asquith, Lord Kitchener (1850–1916), the
secretary of state for war, and Winston Churchill (1874–1965), the
first lord of the Admiralty. The episode that crystallised his concern
was the 'shells crisis' of May 1915. On 15 May, *The Times* published
a telegram from its respected military correspondent, Lieutenant-
Colonel Charles à Court Repington (1858–1925), arguing that the

Allies had failed to capitalise on an initial breakthrough at Neuve Chapelle due to a lack of munitions. Northcliffe decided to go on the offensive. After some critical editorials, the *Daily Mail* on 21 May published an incendiary piece personally written by Northcliffe and headlined 'The Tragedy of the Shells: Lord Kitchener's Grave Error'. Northcliffe pinned the blame for the shells scandal directly onto Kitchener: 'The admitted fact is that Lord Kitchener ordered the wrong kind of shell,' he declared. 'The kind of shell our poor soldiers have had has caused the death of thousands of them.'[7]

Members of the London Stock Exchange burned copies of both The Times *and the* Daily Mail.

Such a direct, and grave, public attack on a widely esteemed figure at time of national crisis was shocking, and generated fury among many of Northcliffe's critics. Members of the London Stock Exchange burned copies of both *The Times* and the *Daily Mail*, and thousands of readers stopped buying the papers. Northcliffe, however, was soon vindicated. By the end of the month, the Liberal government had fallen, to be replaced by a coalition administration. Asquith remained as prime minister, and Kitchener stayed in post, but David Lloyd George (1863–1945), whom Northcliffe admired, was appointed as minister of munitions to address the supply problems. These changes were not enough to stem the criticism from the *Mail*, which continued to call for conscription (eventually introduced in 1916), more equipment for frontline troops and more decisive leadership at the top. In the final months of 1916, the *Mail* stepped up its campaign, attacking the 'limpets' that were clinging onto power and arguing that 'Government by some 23 men who can never make up their minds has become a danger to the Empire'.[8]

Behind the scenes, Northcliffe and Lord Beaverbrook (1879–1964), the new owner of the *Daily Express,* assisted the manoeuvres of those conspiring to replace Asquith as prime minister. Asquith eventually stepped down in December 1916 and was replaced by the more dynamic and decisive Lloyd George. To his critics, Lloyd George was now beholden to the press barons, an accusation that was redoubled when he offered them positions in his administration. In 1917 Northcliffe was appointed head of the war mission to the United States, before becoming head of propaganda in enemy countries. Lord Rothermere (1868–1940), Northcliffe's brother and since 1914 the proprietor of the *Daily*

Used at the right moment, the press crusade retained considerable power.

Mirror, became air minister, while Beaverbrook was appointed minister of information. Lloyd George's cynical use of patronage would have damaging long-term effects on his reputation, but it helped keep his press critics onside for the duration of the war – and eventual victory in November 1918 seemed to vindicate the press's support of Lloyd George.

These dramatic events did much to reinforce the idea of the press having a powerful hold over British political life, and the reverberations of Asquith's resignation were felt for several decades. Such momentous interventions were rare, but press crusading continued in various forms. In the 1960s, press investigations into security scandals involving figures such as John Vassall (1924–1996), John Profumo (1915–2006) and Kim Philby (1912–1988) aimed to expose the incompetence, nepotism and sexual hypocrisy of the British establishment. More recently, *The Daily Telegraph*'s revelations about MPs' expenses in 2009 generated a wave of outrage against the political classes. Used at the right moment, the press crusade retained considerable power.

PARTY POLITICAL CAMPAIGNING

For all their claims of 'fourth estate' independence, however, the reality is that most newspapers are fairly closely and consistently aligned to political parties and positions. If individuals are described as, say, a '*Guardian* reader' or a '*Mail* reader', we can immediately conjure up an image of their political worldview, and this idea of newspaper choice as a marker of political affiliation has a long tradition. In the second half of the nineteenth century, provincial newspapers – many subsidised by politicians or political associations – played a key role in consolidating the emerging Conservative and Liberal party identities.[9] In the early twentieth century, the new national popular dailies, such as the *Daily Mail*, the *Daily Express* and the *Daily Mirror*, were powerful exponents of Conservative and imperialistic thinking, and helped the Tory Party maintain and extend support as the electorate expanded.

The fledgling Labour Party was acutely conscious of the disadvantage that it faced in the battle of ideas and there were various attempts to establish supportive titles that could counter what they regarded as the 'dope' peddled by the 'millionaires'

In the early 1920s, the right-wing popular dailies were unsparing in their attempts to associate Labour with 'Bolshevism'.

press'. *The Daily Citizen*, set up with official Labour Party backing in 1912, failed within three years, but the *Daily Herald*, originally launched in 1911 as a publicity vehicle for striking print workers, proved more long-lasting, and had a period of real circulation success in the 1930s.[10] When the *Daily Mirror*, after a tabloid relaunch in the mid-1930s, gradually developed a left-of-centre political outlook, the playing field started to become more even between the two leading parties, but it was only at the end of the century, under the leadership of Tony Blair (born 1953), that the Labour Party managed to attract the support of a majority of the national press; that, too, proved only temporary.

During general elections, national newspapers have all but given up any pretence of balance in favour of joining the political combat. At times, their interventions have been both dramatic and ruthless. In the early 1920s, the right-wing popular dailies were unsparing in their attempts to associate Labour with 'Bolshevism'. The most notorious example of this 'Red Peril' scare came four days before polling day in the 1924 election when the *Daily Mail* published the notorious 'Zinoviev letter' under the headline 'Civil War Plot by Socialists' Masters'. This forged letter, purporting to be from Comintern chief Grigory Zinoviev (1883–1936), offered financial backing for revolutionary activity to the Communist Party of Great Britain.[11] The fact that Ramsay MacDonald's (1866–1937) Labour government had not taken any action to counter this unwelcome foreign intervention indicated, in the *Mail*'s eyes, that Labour was beholden to the Communists. The dramatic revelation of 'a great Bolshevik plot to paralyse the British Army and Navy and to plunge the country into civil war', the culmination of weeks of inflammatory rhetoric, seems to have successfully fanned public anxieties about the left. The heated political atmosphere led to the highest voter turnout of the inter-war period, and although Labour's overall tally increased, the anti-socialist propaganda seems to have driven some former Liberal voters into the arms of the Conservative Party. The result was a crushing majority for Stanley Baldwin's (1867–1947) Conservatives.

Papers on the left could be equally vicious. Winston Churchill was so infuriated by the *Daily Mirror*'s election day issue in 1951 that he sued for libel. The front page featured a sketched hand holding a gun above photographs of Clement Attlee and Churchill: the provocative headline, 'Whose Finger?', hammered home the message that Churchill was a warmonger who could not be trusted to maintain peace as Cold War tensions intensified. Churchill eventually settled for compensation and an apology for another, earlier, *Mirror* story.[12] Ultimately, though, the long-term dominance of the right-wing press has meant that Labour and the left have suffered disproportionately. During the 1980s – by which time the Labour-supporting *Daily Herald* had been bought by Rupert Murdoch and restyled into the right-wing *The Sun* – the stark polarisation of views and the press attacks on the so-called 'loony left' recalled the 'Red Peril' scare of the 1920s. *The Sun* and the *Mail*, in particular, with their combination of brash conservative populism, capitalist cheerleading, glitzy consumerism and self-confident moralising, articulated prime minister Margaret Thatcher's (1925–2013) views more faithfully and completely than any other media channel.

'Civil War Plot by Socialists' Masters', *The Daily Mail*, 25 October 1924. *Daily Mail* front page revealing the supposed existence of the 'Zinoviev letter'.

It was after Thatcher was replaced by John Major (born 1943) as Conservative leader that the influence

Press partisanship shapes political culture by newspapers framing issues in particular ways.

of the press's election campaigning came under the closest scrutiny. In the fiercely contested 1992 general election campaign, the right-wing tabloids put all their weapons at the disposal of the Conservative cause. The Labour leader, Neil Kinnock (born 1942), was subjected to merciless criticism, and his party's tax plans were cynically distorted ('£1000 a Year Cost of Labour'). *The Sun*'s polling day front page pictured the Welshman's head in a lightbulb alongside the headline 'If Kinnock wins today will the last person to leave Britain please turn out the lights.' When a Conservative victory was declared in what had been seen as a tight race, Murdoch's daily famously declared that 'It's the *Sun* Wot Won It'.[13]

Do such press campaigns sway voters? Scholars have debated the question endlessly, and have not reached a consensus. It is likely that newspapers do mobilise voters and consolidate their views during election campaigns, but for all the focus on these key headlines and front pages, the evidence suggests that the greater influence is longer-term and cumulative. Press partisanship shapes political culture by newspapers framing issues in particular ways and repeatedly placing them high on the public agenda. Years of tabloid headlines about Brussels' meddling and the problems associated with Eastern European immigration are likely to have swayed voters in the 2016 referendum on European Union membership more than the headlines in the days immediately before the vote. Even if well-crafted headlines ('If Kinnock wins …') grab the attention, the cumulative weight of partisan reporting and commentary is ultimately more decisive.

ALTERNATIVE JOURNALISM

The most visible political impact of the partisan press has usually come through 'fourth estate' crusading or party campaigning, but the influence of smaller and more marginal publications should not be underestimated. There is a long history of editors and journalists trying to provide a platform for voices that were not well represented in the existing political structures or which challenged conventional thinking. In the first half of the nineteenth century, radical newspapers sought to reach a working-class audience by avoiding

'It's the Sun Wot Won It', *The Sun*, 11 April 1992. *The Sun* newspaper boasts that it was influential in the Conservative Party winning the 1992 general election.

the taxes that kept them expensive: some 560 'unstamped' papers of this kind were established in the politically turbulent period of 1831 to 1836, including Henry Hetherington's (1792–1849) *Poor Man's Guardian*, with its defiant slogan 'knowledge is power'.[14] The Chartist movement, which campaigned in the late 1830s and 1840s for manhood suffrage and annual elections, developed a valuable mouthpiece and information source in the form of the *Northern Star*, which sold around 50,000 copies a week at its peak.

In the second half of the nineteenth century, the women's movement fostered a similarly rich print culture. It has been estimated that female proprietors published more than 150 political periodicals aimed at women readers between the late 1850s and the 1930s; the most successful was *Votes for Women*, selling around 50,000 copies a week in the first decade of the twentieth century.[15] These titles helped to sustain the intellectual vitality and the political networks of a campaign that faced considerable opposition in Parliament and the mainstream press. In the second half of the twentieth century, newspapers and periodicals offered a platform for Black and minority ethnic groups to resist the stereotypes that were so frequently used in

By 1986 more than seventy newspapers and magazines were being published specifically for ethnic minority readerships.

the national press. An early example was the *West Indian Gazette*, founded by Claudia Jones in 1958.[16] By 1986 more than seventy newspapers and magazines were being published specifically for ethnic minority readerships, including *The Voice*, *Caribbean Times*, *New Life* and the *Asian Times*.[17] All of these publications provided important spaces to incubate ideas, articulate identity and support campaigns. Many had influence over the longer term, as mainstream media picked up new ways of thinking and sometimes personnel from these titles.

In the late twentieth and early twenty-first centuries, as news media channels proliferated on television and radio and then online, national newspapers and mainstream news programmes have faced declining audiences and have struggled to retain their previous authority. The generalising language of the mass newspaper seems increasingly dated in a more pluralistic, individualistic and mobile society, and has been undermined by the personalisation, niche marketing and social networking enabled by the new media. The range of opinions in the public sphere has increased, and alternative journalism has broken free of the economic and cultural restrictions it faced in previous decades. News and commentary can travel across borders and be exchanged between individuals in ways that were not previously possible. Fourth estate crusading and party political journalism will not lose their influence, but will find it harder to get heard among the increasing babble of conflicting voices shouting to be heard. If partisanship may take different forms, though, we can safely predict that the appetite for debate will not diminish.

William Hone

Profile by Beth Gaskell

William Hone (1780–1842) was a journalist and publisher who rose to prominence when he successfully defended himself against charges of blasphemous libel brought by the British government. At a time of considerable political oppression, he became a figurehead for press freedom and the fight against censorship.

Hone rose from humble beginnings. His father was a lawyer's clerk, and he received only a rudimentary education. At the age of twenty he set up his first bookshop. This and several other early ventures failed, but his experiences taught him much about hard work and poverty, and he became aligned with reform movements campaigning to extend democracy to all men, to improve workers' rights and protections and for freedom of the press.

Hone began writing for newspapers and periodicals to make ends meet. He quickly developed skills as an investigative journalist, and his writing became a tool in his fight for social justice and political reform. His investigation into the conditions at Bethlem Hospital ('Bedlam') caused public outrage and resulted in the resignation of the hospital's governor.

He wrote a series of articles in *The Examiner* and *The Traveller*, a newspaper he was editing and publishing, in an unsuccessful attempt to save a servant, Eliza Fenning, who had been accused of murdering her employer. Fanning was executed, but Hone uncovered the corruption surrounding the case, once again causing a scandal.

Hone's journalism frequently brought him to the attention of the authorities. This was particularly true after he launched his *Reformists' Register*, a weekly news pamphlet, in 1817, which frequently criticised the government. He also produced a number of satirical squibs and parodies, illustrated by George Cruikshank (1792–1878), which landed him in court, facing charges of blasphemy, although his prosecution was politically motivated. He successfully defended himself at all three of his trials (held on three successive days), ridiculing the legal process he was facing, in court and then in print.

Legal problems and a generous nature meant Hone and his family often struggled for money. He frequently relied on help from friends and subscriptions. By 1842, with the fight against press censorship largely won, his fame had diminished, and he died in relative obscurity.

James Whitworth

Low and Lancaster: Visual satire in the Second World War

In June 1940 SS General Walter Schellenberg was working on a book that would be put to deadly use in the planned German invasion of mainland Britain.

Sonderfahndungsliste GB – the title can be translated literally as the Special Search List for Great Britain, but it is now widely known as the 'Black Book' – was in essence a list of almost 3000 people who would be rounded up and, in most cases, handed over to the Gestapo. On what was essentially a death list, populated by critics of the Third Reich and those who it was felt would oppose a German occupation, was the name of cartoonist David Low (1891–1963).

By the time the Second World War had begun Low was an established presence in Lord Beaverbrook's (1879–1964) *Evening Standard* and a long-established thorn in the side of the appeasement movement. When he was proven right in his fear of the real intentions of Hitler's Germany, Low's cartoons moved from prophetic warning to finely developed satire of the Nazis. 'The Angels of Peace Descend on Belgium', published on 10 June 1940, is in many ways typical of both his style and the satiric approach of the majority of Fleet Street's news cartoonists of the time. Low uses caricature, a long-established tool of the political cartoonist, but rejects gross exaggeration in favour of a more realistic depiction of facial features, in this case Heinrich Himmler (1900–1945), the chief of German police and leader of the Gestapo.

It was unlikely that those who had opposed and lampooned the likes of Hitler and Himmler would escape serious punishment.

The cartoon depicts Himmler, along with two fellow Gestapo officers, as angels descending on a recently defeated Belgium with a Death List, truncheon and whip. The caption is, of course, ironic and helps give the illustration a feeling of both pathos and intense malice. The reader is left in little doubt as to what will be the result of the Nazi 'peace'.

As well as Low's use of caricature, it is revealing to look at the portrayal of the Belgium town. It makes the most of Low's development of a less detailed style, something that he and other cartoonists such as the *Daily Express*'s Sidney Strube (1891–1956) had been developing over the previous decade. While realistic enough for us to identify that it is a city or town, it is also generic enough for it not to resemble a specific location. It could be anywhere: it could be Britain. Low is not only passing a satiric comment on the Nazis' concept of peace; the cartoon also acts as a warning. This may be Belgium now, it appears to suggest, but soon it could be your home. Low, like most people in Britain at the time, was under little illusion as to the precariousness of the situation facing the country. The threat was real – within a month of the cartoon's publication Hitler had ordered preparations for the invasion – and Low would have known that ridiculing and satirising Nazi Germany, while a key role of a free press, was also extremely dangerous. When the German invasion came, it was unlikely that those who had opposed and lampooned the likes of Hitler and Himmler would escape serious punishment.

Just eight days after publishing the 'Angels of Peace' cartoon, Low produced what must rank as one of his – and for that matter one of *the* – most powerful British cartoons of the entire war. Initially published in the *Evening Standard* on 18 June 1940, the cartoon was drawn in the aftermath of Dunkirk and the surrender of France. A British soldier stands resolute on a cliff edge, shaking his fist at the waves of enemy bombers that are crossing the rough sea. The caption reads: 'Very well, Alone'. It is an acceptance that Europe has succumbed to the Nazi war machine and therefore Britain stands 'alone'; but it is also defiant and inspirational. In his autobiography, Low recalled how he 'tingled when I drew it' and that the 'anguish which infused the great occasions imposed

HIMMLER, HAVING "DONE" THE NETHERLANDS, IS NOW AT WORK ON BELGIUM.

GESTAPO "DEATH" LIST

THE ANGELS OF PEACE DESCEND ON BELGIUM

(Copyright in All Countries.)

David Low, 'Angels of Peace Descend on Belgium', *Evening Standard*, 10 June 1940. Low depicts Heinrich Himmler and two Gestapo colleagues hovering over Belgium, bearing a death list ready for use.

a pregnant simplicity on their interpretation'.[1] This last phrase is particularly telling as it foregrounds the development of a less cluttered drawing style. Building on the work of late Victorian cartoonist Phil May (1864–1903), Low's work can be seen to be of the 'it's not what you draw, but what you don't draw' attitude to satiric illustration. In this example, the soldier is almost all outline with little shading; Low is letting the paper do the work. There are a number of reasons for this. One was the influence of Japanese art on his work, but more importantly he seems to have realised that an extra dimension could be added to visual satire by removing extraneous detail to create a more simplistic, yet powerful, commentary on the deadly threat to the country's freedom.

Britain has a long history of visual satire – from the days of copper engravings to the penmanship of the twentieth century. The fathers of the genre, William Hogarth (1697–1764), James Gillray (1756–1815) and George Cruikshank (1792–1878), while not newspaper cartoonists as such (their work was originally sold as prints), can be seen to have influenced generations of news cartoonists including the likes of *The Times*'s Morten Morland (born 1979), who updated Hogarth's 'Gin Lane' during David Cameron's premiership, and *The Guardian*'s Steve Bell (born 1951), who reworked Gillray's caricature of Pitt the Younger and

Napoleon with Donald Trump and then British foreign secretary Jeremy Hunt feasting on Theresa May as a dead duck. Ben Jennings (born 1990) brought Gillray's print even further up to date, with the COVID-19 virus replacing Gillray's pudding. Despite the popularity of the likes of Hogarth, Gillray and Cruikshank, it would take an advance in printing technology, along with the ambitions of an Edwardian insurance clerk, to bring visual satire to what many argue is its true home: the daily pages of a British newspaper.

William Haselden (1872–1953), an underwriter at Lloyd's, approached Alfred Harmsworth, later Lord Northcliffe (1865–1922), with examples of his topical sketches, and duly became the first full-time daily newspaper cartoonist at Northcliffe's *Daily Illustrated Mirror*, producing political satire until his retirement in 1940. During the First World War his characters Big and Little Willie mocked Kaiser Wilhelm and his son, foreshadowing Low's work

James Gillray, 'The Plumb-pudding in danger, or, State Epicures taking un Petit Souper' (1805). Gillray shows British prime minister William Pitt and Emperor Napoleon of France carving up the globe.

twenty years later, and in doing so helped create a template for using the press as a platform for freedom of expression through the prism of visual lampooning of both domestic and foreign targets.

By the time Haselden retired, Low was arguably the premier political cartoonist in Britain and therefore the responsibility lay with him to lead the satiric assault on Germany. Yet Low was not alone in his attacks on the Third Reich. The aforementioned Strube worked in a similar way, as did the *Daily Mail*'s Leslie Illingworth (1902–1979) and the *Daily Mirror*'s Philip Zec (1909-1983). However, it was at the *Daily Express* that a form of visual satire was establishing a new front from which to engage with contemporary politics, society and of course the war. This was the pocket cartoon, a form pioneered by Osbert Lancaster (1908–1986) at the end of a decade in which he had steadily built a reputation with his architectural drawings and the publication of a number of books, including *Pillar to Post* (1938) and *Home Sweet Homes* (1939).

Steve Bell, 'The dead Duck in danger', *The Guardian*, 4 June 2019. Bell's homage to Gillray shows Theresa May being carved up by Donald Trump and Jeremy Hunt.

Lancaster's new form of topical cartoon debuted in the Daily Express *on 3 January 1939.*

Named after the pocket battleship, portrait in orientation and only a single column wide, Lancaster's new form of topical cartoon debuted in the *Daily Express* on 3 January 1939. The decision initially to place his pocket cartoons within the 'Hickey' gossip column is most instructive and

'There will be no Great War in Europe in 1939'

Daily Express

informative about how the newspaper initially viewed its latest innovation. Tom Driberg's column covered not just politics, but social issues as well. This demonstrates one of the key differences between the long-established news cartoon drawn by the likes of Strube, Low and Illingworth and Lancaster's fresh creation. The pocket cartoon would tackle politics, of course, but it would also move away from the Westminster-centric editorial cartoon to focus on topical stories that involved ordinary people, such as the building of air raid shelters and the rationing of food.

While pocket cartoons did not focus exclusively on politics, it would be a mistake to assume that they dealt with less weighty subjects, as demonstrated in Lancaster's earliest cartoons. During the 1930s the *Daily Express*, of which Lord Beaverbrook was proprietor, had advocated appeasement towards Germany – although it is important to note that, unlike Lord Rothermere's (1898–1940) friendship with Hitler, Beaverbrook's motivation was not based on a sympathy with the German leader, but rather had its roots in his desire for isolationism, which fuelled his imperial obsessions and the Empire Free Trade Crusade (a political party founded to help fulfil the press baron's plan to create a free trade bloc for the British Empire). This in turn can be linked to the *Express*'s desire to be 'relentlessly cheerful and optimistic ... at a time when economic and political storm clouds were gathering over Europe'.[2] Just six months before Low's Belgium cartoon, the *Daily Express* was still firmly in a state of denial about the coming war. On 2 January 1939, the day before Lancaster's first cartoon, the paper's leader page featured an editorial headlined 'This is why you can sleep soundly in 1939' and which was followed with the unequivocal statement 'There will be no Great War in Europe in 1939.' This had been the newspaper's position for most of the decade, and Beaverbrook did not encourage divergence from this editorial line in the *Express*.

Four days later, the editorial cartoon used President Roosevelt's radio speech as its topic. Strube drew an arm emerging from a giant radio and a fist banging on a table, around which sit nine men. The cartoon employs the long-established editorial cartoon trope of labelling the people with names such as Hate, Aggression and Lawlessness. The arm is labelled 'Roosevelt's Speech'. It is certainly not a poor cartoon, nor is it atypical for its time; yet the image of the thumping fist is perhaps unintentionally revealing, as it encapsulates the didactic nature of the editorial cartoon as a genre. When we compare it with the pocket cartoon from the same day, the difference in style is of course clear, but it is the marked difference in content that is most revealing. Lancaster's cartoon is simply drawn – a church is represented by just an outline – but it is the content that holds the greatest impact. Two men dressed in black stand over a hole in the ground. The caption reads 'No perhaps they won't be much use now as air raid shelters in the next war, but they'll come in very handy as cemeteries in the next peace.'[3] It is an extraordinary cartoon in the sense that it completely contradicts the paper's editorial stance by implying that war is coming. Just four days into his role as pocket cartoonist, Osbert Lancaster can be seen to be both creating and defining the parameters of what the new form can achieve.

Lancaster demonstrated both aspects of editorial freedom: freedom of the press and freedom to contradict the editorial line.

The importance of this should not be understated, as Lancaster was working in an environment in which striking a note contrary to the proprietor's position and which countered what the cartoonist called 'the unhealthy optimism which still remained the corner-stone of editorial policy' was extremely difficult.[4] The *Daily Express* 'stoutly maintained day after day that there would be no war in Europe' and any 'unkind and possibly aggravating jokes about the Fuhrer and his minions, was rigorously taboo'. The cartoonist negotiated this situation by approaching the topic, as in the above example, in a way that subtly undermined the editorial line.[5] In doing so, Lancaster demonstrated both aspects of editorial freedom: freedom of the press in general, but also the freedom to contradict the editorial line. This was to become a recurring theme with Lancaster's early cartoons, which continued to anticipate war, such as when a town planner says 'if it comes to war these houses may be bombed before we've had time to knock them down and build flats'; and with the depiction of a tank adorned with the slogan 'Stop Me and Buy One', to which the tank driver says 'Don't blame me! It's all a clever idea of the camouflage department.'[6]

The increasing use of humour was part of a wider general trend in the depoliticisation of the popular press, which began to foreground human-interest stories, competitions and photographs. Lancaster's use of humour was a new way to engage with social and political themes that was as subtle as it was effective.

As the first weeks of the war progressed, editorial cartoonists continued to use metaphor-based tropes such as the Nazi fist crashing down, whereas Lancaster's work employed what can be seen to become one of the pocket cartoon's defining tropes: the foregrounding of a direct style of humour which did not require the reader to decode metaphor or symbolism. Even at the time of greatest danger in the first years of the war, Lancaster made great use of the concerns about German parachutists dropping in disguise into England, such as the cartoon published in the week before the first Christmas of the war in which he drew two German paratroopers dressed as Father Christmas. One says to the other 'I suppose, Heinrich, that the credulous English do still believe in Santa Claus?'[7] Of course, other cartoonists had ridiculed Germans – Low had been particularly good at this in the run-up to the war, as in his cartoon showing Stalin as a ventriloquist's dummy on Hitler's lap – but there is a subtle yet important change here that would characterise Lancaster's work for the next forty years. His cartoons laugh at their subject, as do editorial cartoons, but in addition to this they break new ground by subtly allowing the readers to laugh at themselves. There was a genuine fear at this time of fifth columnists infiltrating British society, but Lancaster inverts this fear via the visual construct of taking disguise to an extreme degree. He also uses a type of humour that has its roots in vaudevillian tropes of cross-dressing, adding a sense of the ridiculous to the image.

Central to this was the new form of topical humour which was intrinsic to the way in which newspapers such as the *Daily Express* and *Daily Mirror* sought to develop and present a new relationship with their readers. They sold an idea of togetherness by working to create strong brands that would engender reader loyalty, and in doing so became the ultimate

The increasing use of humour was part of a wider general trend in the depoliticisation of the popular press.

"I suppose, Heinrich, that the credulous English do still believe in Santa Claus?"

Osbert Lancaster, 'I suppose, Heinrich, that the credulous English do still believe in Santa Claus?', *Daily Express*, 19 December 1939. Lancaster invites readers to laugh at their fears, in this case German paratroopers landing in Britain.

expression of the popular in the British mass-market press.

It is perhaps little surprise that, following the outbreak of the Second World War, both the *Evening Standard* and the *Daily Express* immediately changed their editorial position, backing Britain's involvement and becoming pro-Churchill. Both Low and Lancaster continued to use visual satire to engage with contemporary news stories. On Low's part this was often through cartoons that were intended to motivate, inspire and boost morale, such as his drawing showing Churchill rolling up his sleeves and leading the War Cabinet into the war effort, with the caption 'All behind you, Winston.'[8] Lancaster took a different route, using humour to undermine the horror of the Nazi war machine, such as his depiction of two senior German officers with one saying 'Sometimes, Ulrich, I get so depressed that thinking about the next war doesn't cheer me up.'[9] Lancaster's work, with its blending of humour and satiric attack, made his readers laugh as they faced adversity. Like Low, he became a prominent national figure. The novelist Anthony Powell (1905–2000) commended Lancaster's impact on home front morale, writing that he 'kept people going by his own high spirits and wit'.[10]

David Low and Osbert Lancaster, both leaders in their own cartooning genres, made a contribution to the war effort and the morale of the nation through visual satire that we should not underestimate. Hitler certainly did not. When Low learned that his name had been on the Nazi death list he remarked, 'That is all right, I had them on my list too.'[11]

3

WHAT ARE THE ETHICS BEHIND THE NEWS?

Jackie Harrison

INTRODUCTION

'Ethics', here, refers primarily to occupational standards of behaviour typically reflected in the professional codes of ethics adopted by public and private news organisations. These codes act as the basis for justifying what stories should be covered and what is professionally permissible when it comes to obtaining information deemed relevant to a particular story. They do this by pointing to some set of ideals about the purpose of news journalism, such as serving the public's right to know, acting in the public interest, informing public reasoning and deliberation and holding power to account. These codes of ethics underwrite the particular ethical significance or principle attached to reporting an event, and in so doing they provide a justification for why a particular story should be covered and how it has to be covered in terms of both the methods and resources used. As the following chapters show, these justifications can be used in news reporting to inspire expressions of civil idealism, or be deployed as the basis for defying political power, or be used as an excuse for the worst excesses and illegal practices. Ultimately, news journalism does not always come with a guarantee of ethical decency.

In the public interest

Where the press is free and every man able to read, all is safe.[1] As many of the stories in this volume show, the media could not have grown and prospered over five centuries without a willing, attentive and paying audience.

To sustain profitable consumption, what the media traditionally offered needed to be of some interest to the consuming public. This should not be confused with a discussion about news-making in the public interest, which requires a good deal more than merely being interesting to the public.

There is no single definition of the public interest. It depends on the publication and often the interpretation of the government of the day. However, the principal public broadcaster in Britain, the BBC, helpfully outlines to its journalists what in practice public interest has come to mean:

It includes freedom of expression; providing information that assists people to better comprehend or make decisions on matters of public importance; preventing people being misled by the statements or actions of individuals or organisations. The public interest is also served in exposing or detecting crime or significantly anti-social behaviour and by exposing corruption, injustice, significant incompetence or negligence.[2]

The journalist's test is to distinguish between the public actions of the individual person or organisation and individual

The facts and truth need even more robust defence if the news is to serve the public interest.

attitudes or morality. As we shall explore later on in this chapter, however, sometimes social mores play a part in defining what is asserted to be in the public interest.

In the emerging digital ecosystem of news, often characterised as heralding an era of 'information disorder', it is widely agreed that the facts and truth need even more robust defence if the news is to serve the public interest. However, it still needs to be recognised that since there is no single universally accepted definition of the public interest, nor what is increasingly regarded as public-interest journalism, it is often easier to define what is *not* in the public interest, as in the phone hacking scandal that presaged the demise of the *News of the World*. Lord Brian Leveson (born 1949), who chaired an inquiry into the culture, practices and ethics of the press (2012), sparked by the wholesale abuse of people's private telephone conversations and email traffic, put it this way: 'There has been a willingness to deploy covert surveillance, blagging and deception in circumstances where it is extremely difficult to see any public interest justification.'[3]

In its broadest sense, journalism underscored by a conception of the public interest as facilitating the activities of the 'well-informed citizen' relies upon a set of normative practices, within regulated institutions that apply common ethical principles to news-making. In the digital age, fragmentation and an explosion of voices in the public spaces of the internet have re-emphasised the desirability of codes of ethics that underpin good journalistic practice in the public interest. What Lord Leveson acknowledged time and again in his inquiry was that journalism that defended the public interest was a cornerstone of good journalistic practice: 'I repeat my view that the majority of editors, journalists and others who work for both the national and regional press do good work in the public interest.'[4]

The spirit of public interest evokes journalism that brings to public attention something that 'someone, somewhere, wants concealed'.[5] The defence of the public interest is something that newspapers and broadcasters have often used to justify publication, but equally they have occasionally interpreted it in a proprietorial fashion, choosing not to publish material that their editors believe not to be in the public interest. Looking at examples from news history, it is clear that the UK media does not necessarily speak with one voice on this issue of the public interest.

The Manchester Guardian (it became The Guardian in 1959) from its inception had the character of an oppositional publication, with a clarion call to make facts sacred. It made the claim that it was not the newspaper of the establishment and published on issues that spoke to the public interest and not the London elites. At the height of the Second Anglo-Boer War (1899–1902) the British military leader Herbert Kitchener (1850–1916) used a scorched-earth strategy to isolate the Boer guerrilla fighters and displace their wives and children, interning the women and children in tented camps beyond Afrikaner strongholds. Conditions in the camps were appalling, with high mortality rates among the children.

Emily Hobhouse (1860–1926) came from a religious family with traditions of pacifism. She travelled to South Africa to help with relief efforts of those in the camps. Her narrative reports for The Manchester Guardian in 1901 made the case for more humane management and British government intervention in the camps to improve the misery of these Afrikaner victims. The Manchester Guardian reported that the conditions, in what were widely characterised as 'concentration camps' (on account of their tented layout and overcrowding), were a matter of public interest. Challenging the British government approach in time of war was unpopular, but helped carve out a distinction between the national interest and the public interest. Despite real public support for this imperial war, there was a sense that it was neither humanitarian nor honouring imperial ideals to stand by while women and children died of disease and starvation in camps set up and run by the British colonial authorities.

Challenging the British government approach in time of war was unpopular, but helped carve out a distinction between national and public interest.

The sympathetic portrayal of the victims in the camps meant Hobhouse faced a hostile reception on her return to Britain, openly criticised by the government and many in the media more loyal to the government position. However, *The Manchester Guardian*'s stance raised the profile of the story and succeeded in getting more financial assistance for the victims. The government also ordered a commission under Millicent Fawcett (1847–1929, widely known later on as a suffragette) to investigate the claims, and this corroborated the appalling conditions. To this day Hobhouse remains a folk hero in many parts of South Africa.

The actions of the royal family have consistently remained a newsmaking realm where privacy and the public interest are regularly contested.

Publishing information that is not readily available sometimes means transgressing the laws on privacy that are designed to avoid unnecessary breaches of trust. For example, BBC editorial guidelines make it clear that private behaviour, information and correspondence and conversation should not be brought into the public domain unless there is a public interest that outweighs this expectation of privacy.[6] The next example from British news history exemplifies how for much of the twentieth century, newspapers and then broadcasters found deciding between public interest and privacy difficult to justify. As a deferential attitude has long governed relations between the press and the monarchy, the actions of the royal family have consistently remained a news-making realm where privacy and the public interest are regularly contested.

An early illustration of this tension between private behavior and public interest in relation to the monarchy was the abdication crisis of 1936. The diaries of the journalist and publicist Sydney Walton (1882–1964) capture the tensions produced by Buckingham Palace wanting to keep 'schtum' on Edward VIII's liaison with Wallis Simpson, in an attempt to protect the monarch from scrutiny and unwanted speculation about his conduct. The issue for Walton was the perennial question of what exactly was in the public interest and what was not. Walton's concern was exacerbated by the fact that that while the British press may have deferred to the Palace, foreign publications certainly did not. The resulting rumour mill, aided by these foreign missives, in

'The King Abdicates: Will Broadcast To-Night', *Daily Herald*, 11 December 1936. A factual headline that somewhat belies the extent of the emerging constitutional crisis.

fact began to put a strain on the reputation of the monarchy. As the Walton diaries illustrate, subjects' learning of the king's liaison from unofficial sources fuelled a crisis of legitimacy over the monarch's determination to wed the American divorcee.

The Bishop of Bradford, Alfred Blunt (1879–1957), brought the constitutional crisis to a head when the regional press finally broke ranks by reporting on a rather innocuous speech to parishioners.[7] In it the bishop questioned the king's loyalty to his faith as head of the Church of England.[8] This prompted the national press to speculate on a matter now seen to be of grave public interest. Once the relationship was out in the open, reports of conflicts between the Cabinet and the king about Mrs Simpson meant the abdication die was cast. Although not all newspapers, as the Walton diaries show, were hostile to the king, the prevailing view was that the public interest consisted of a desire to preserve a constitutional monarchy and that the king's behaviour undermined what was expected of a constitutional monarch. Thus the king came under huge pressure to abdicate. The abdication occurred just ten days after Blunt's speech. Deference to the Crown continued in the press until the late 1950s, but there remains a fraught and tetchy relationship between Buckingham Palace and the media on where the balance between individual privacy and the public interest lies.

The prevailing view was that the king's behaviour undermined what was expected of a constitutional monarch.

In the 1970s greater media competition led to broadcast journalism in particular tackling more difficult (even sensational) subjects and a greater willingness by broadcasters to challenge and criticise government. Relations between government and the media often erupted into outright hostility to the point where they found themselves arguing over what the government felt be in the national interest and the media felt to be in the public interest. A pivotal moment, which was to cement the idea that public interest broadcasting was a key part of the duty of broadcasters, was Thames Television's broadcast of the 'Death on the Rock' documentary (ITV, tx. 28 April 1988). 'Death on the Rock' consisted of an account of the shooting of three Provisional Irish Republican Army (IRA) operatives on an active operation in Gibraltar, which contradicted the government account of the incident. Members of the SAS (Special Air Service) killed Danny McCann, Sean Savage and Mairéad Farrell in an operation that the documentary suggested might have been outside the rule of law. The three IRA operatives had all been involved in previous acts of terror and were being actively tracked by security services and Spanish police. Prime minister Margaret Thatcher (1925–2013) was incensed at the programme, which called into question the legitimacy of the actions of the British state. The documentary makers asked rhetorically if this was an example of a 'shoot to kill' policy with IRA suspects. In trying to prevent the programme being broadcast, both national interest and due process (the public inquest was still due to be held) were invoked. But the broadcaster and the regulator defended the issue as a matter of huge public interest. British constitutional arrangements and the rights of citizens depend on the rule of law and, they argued, this meant government actions, in this case the rules of engagement with terror suspects, should be scrutinised to establish if there was evidence they had operated outside the law. It confirmed that the tussle between state and broadcasters for primacy in determining that public interest would remain active. Some argue that in fact government anger led to Thames Television losing its ITV franchise and to the Broadcasting Act (1990) that changed the way the industry was structured and regulated.

It is worth considering at this point how editorial processes in most legacy news organisations oblige journalists to consider the public interest when engaged in news-making. As an investigative TV journalist, it is often necessary to delve into the private spaces of the subject of a story if there is believed to be a substantial risk to the public of fraud, harm through terrorism or just plain wrongdoing. In late 1999 I began an investigation into the poor management of some of Britain's mosques for the Channel 4 *Dispatches* programme. We needed permission to gather evidence of things I had personally witnessed and others had alleged in a number of mosques around the country. For an investigative journalist, the mechanics of being allowed to investigate the truth of serious allegations of misconduct, which necessitates venturing into the private affairs of individuals or organisations, are onerous but, in my view, need a public-interest justification. When I was approached with serious allegations against Abu Hamza al-Masri (born 1958), an imam at Finsbury Park mosque, for example, it was clear they would not be easy to substantiate without a proportionate level of intrusion.[9] Primarily this

> *The mechanics of being allowed to investigate the truth of serious allegations of misconduct need a public-interest justification.*

Transparency of public information can both protect the public interest and hold those who act (or should act) in the public interest to account.

was because many of the allegations related to activities in a place of worship that was difficult to access by non-members. We also needed to investigate allegations of contact with minors by a religious teacher who was now on the sex offenders register.

These serious allegations could not be published without gathering information that breached the rules on the privacy of the individuals and organisations involved. No broadcaster steps lightly into this territory, and the process of seeking permissions and justifying your actions to senior executives and the broadcaster's legal advisers are demanding and intense. It took us several months of written submissions to justify and secure permission. There is a very real sense in which secretly filming individuals and gaining access to buildings to film surreptitiously requires the highest level of proof that the exercise will deliver evidence. It is not in anyone's interest to be caught out in what in the industry journalists often call a 'fishing expedition'. In the end the documentary, 'Trouble at the Mosque' (Channel 4, tx. 14 February 2002) was successful, because it revealed a range of issues that we believed could be justifiably said to be in the public interest to expose. Not everyone agreed: there were those who argued we made a minority community look bad in the eyes of the broader community. This is the kind of balancing act that is important to consider but, I would argue, impossible to avoid if journalism is to be valued as a tool of oversight and reform where circumstances are harmful to citizens.

Journalists are now assisted in these investigative endeavours, after the Labour government passed the Freedom of Information Act (2000). This has provided citizens (journalists included) with access to information held by public authorities. It does this in two ways. Public authorities are obliged to publish certain information about their activities; and members of the public are entitled to request information from public authorities. At its heart is the idea that transparency of public information can both protect the public interest and hold those who act (or should act) in the public interest to account. There are thousands of examples of journalists using this law to extract information from public bodies reluctant to make it available. In the wake of the Lakanal House fire of 3 July 2009, which killed six residents in a tower block inferno, I worked with BBC colleagues to establish whether the risks of the spread of fire in tower blocks were known to the authorities and what precautions were being taken to mitigate these risks.[10] We quickly established that Fire Risk Assessments (FRAs) were the crucial, legally required document for landlords to document each tower block. Initial approaches to local authorities for information were rebuffed. So we used a series of freedom of information requests to all London public authorities to see if their blocks were missing FRAs. Shockingly, many tower blocks had none, including the block where the fire happened. Fire safety in public housing was pushed up the political agenda and a number of reforms were recommended in the 2013 inquest into the fire. Unfortunately, many of these official recommendations were ignored and led directly to the fire tragedy at Grenfell Tower in 2017 where seventy-two people lost their lives in a West London tower block.

The Freedom of Information Act reinforced the Public Interest Disclosure Act (1998), also known as the 'whistleblower's charter', which provides officials in public organisations with a public-interest defence if they choose to leak information to the press which they believe shows harm could come of a public decision kept from the public. It does not prevent prosecution, nor in fact the suppression of information if the state deems that the national interest trumps the public interest. But even here there are increasingly problems for a government wishing to suppress publication, if it can be argued that information should rightfully be presented to the public.

Edward Snowden (born 1983) is an American whistleblower who copied and leaked highly classified information from the National Security Agency in 2013 when he was a Central Intelligence Agency employee and subcontractor. It was one of the most significant leaks of intelligence secrets in history. Snowden has defended his leaks as an effort 'to inform the public as to that which is done in their name and that which is done against them'.[11] He said the leak raised legitimate concerns about mass surveillance and the breaches of information security in the interest of national security: a clash

It does not prevent prosecution, nor in fact the suppression of information if the state deems that the national interest trumps the public interest.

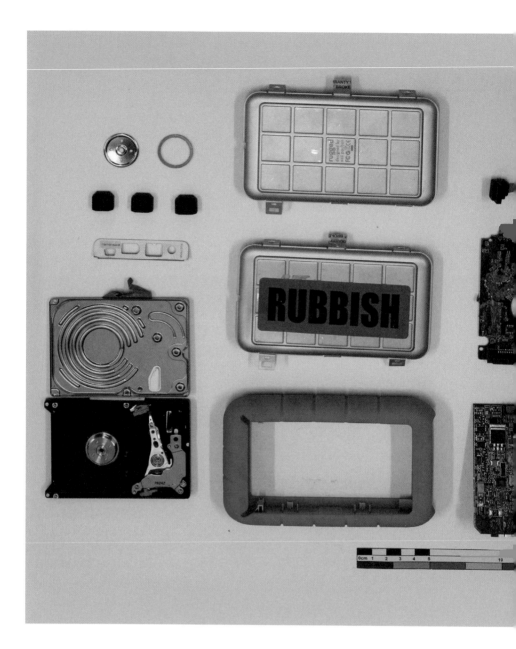

Destroyed objects from
H Compaq 8200 elite
convertible mini tower,
one of the *Guardian*
computers used to store
Edward Snowden's data.

between national and public interest. The collection
of smashed-up hard drives and computer hardware
from *The Guardian* offices now held in the Guardian
News & Media Archive shows what measures the
British state took to defend that national interest,
even when the newspaper believed the story it had
was squarely in the public interest. A substantial

issue for *The Guardian* was that many other newspapers did not share this view. Editor Alan Rusbridger (born 1953) found himself under intense scrutiny, with the threat of prosecution and being openly questioned in Parliament about his patriotism. Was publication treasonous?[12]

The Guardian argued that the Snowden documents raised a number of issues of public interest. Just because security and intelligence were important and sensitive did not mean, in its view, that they should be outlawed from informed discussion. It was supported in this view by American judges who had had to address a similar question after publication of material from the same source in *The Washington Post* and *The New York Times*. These judges had come out on the side of the journalist's freedom to publish in the public interest, even if this inconvenienced government.

The British government took a very different and dimmer view, and made that clear in a series of increasingly intense confrontations with Rusbridger. *The Guardian* was reluctant to test its own reasoning, and the government's will, in an expensive court battle. This led to a rather Kafkaesque resolution where the government demanded that the machines in London that had the important data on them be destroyed under supervision, knowing full well this would not prevent further publication of the story because the data was held on computers in other countries. *The Guardian* was never prosecuted for publication, but it did lose some computers. Perhaps what this reveals is the difficulty with which the public-interest argument in one jurisdiction can be suppressed when the internet makes it possible for people to read the same material

What this reveals is the difficulty with which the public interest argument in one jurisdiction can be suppressed when the internet makes it possible for people to read the same material published elsewhere on the planet.

We as a society are dependent on news-makers applying these codes to serve us well.

published elsewhere on the planet: a rather pyrrhic victory, it might seem, for the government, although a clear warning to publishers of the risks they run if their notion of the public interest conflicts with a government determined to uphold its view of the national interest.

I would argue that progressively through the twentieth and twenty-first centuries, journalism has grown in confidence, and the advent of broadcasting and latterly the digital ecosystem has reasserted the centrality of that public interest to the purposes and defence of journalism. Codes of ethics such as the BBC editorial guidelines enshrine public interest at the heart of the journalistic enterprise. Public interest is freedom of expression itself.

In the digital age, when anyone can publish, one of the defining features of journalism will necessarily be that which is published with the normative principles and processes this chapter has dealt with in mind. More recent laws have reinforced the ability of news-makers to hold power to account, and the digital age, with its propensity for flows of misinformation (not in the public interest), has led to a renewed interest in attempts to codify how journalism is defined and who can be defined as a journalist. As more actors make the claim to be journalists, it is increasingly important that they can be held accountable, demonstrating they abide by a set of practices or codes that are buttressed by ethical conduct in a way that involves the reliable handling of information.[13] While it is now more readily recognised that what is in the public interest does not always align with what the public is actually interested in, we as a society are dependent on news-makers applying these codes to serve us well.

The Bristol Cable

Profile by Beth Gaskell

Adam Cantwell-Corn (right, b. 1990) and Alon Aviram (left, b. 1990) are co-founders of *The Bristol Cable*, a co-operatively owned independent media company that has won international recognition for its investigative journalism.

In 2014, when they were not long out of university, Cantwell-Corn and Aviram established *The Bristol Cable* alongside their friend Alec Saelens, having initially thought to apply their business ideas to creating a baking co-operative. *The Bristol Cable* produces a free quarterly hard-copy news publication alongside a news website, both focused on local news. The company is funded via membership, with all members having a say in the strategic aims of the publications. The aim of *The Bristol Cable* is to challenge the hold that large media conglomerates have on local news outlets, and to revitalise the local newspaper industry.

The Bristol Cable's main focus is investigative journalism: uncovering stories that affect the people of Bristol and holding local authorities to account. It has covered stories as wide-ranging as covert police surveillance of mobile phones, immigration stops and racial profiling, problems with local housing development and prices and the experiences of refugees living in Bristol. Because of this broad scope, the *Cable* does not think of itself as a 'hyperlocal' operation. Nevertheless, it is a notable example of the independent, community-focused news publishers that have sprung up in the UK, changing perceptions of who can produce the news and for whom.

As well as being co-founders of the *Cable*, both Cantwell-Corn and Aviram work as journalists for the publication. Their most high-profile story was the 'Ice-Cream Slavery Case', a five-year investigation in which they, along with colleagues Matt Woodman and Will Franklin, exposed a local businessman for exploiting vulnerable workers, ending with a prosecution under modern-day slavery laws. The stylishly presented story won the *Cable* the 2019 Local Journalism prize at the *Press Gazette* British Journalism Awards, and saw them shortlisted for the 2020 Orwell Prize for Exposing Social Evils.

Crossing the line

Investigative journalism is particularly vulnerable ethically to the temptations of 'crossing the line'. When an investigation is pursued over months or years, the pressure to 'get' the story can be irresistible, especially if the ethos of the paper endorses it and financially rewards it, or when the public interest seems overriding, even when the leaked material is illegally obtained.

xamples include W.T. Stead's (1849–1912) 'Maiden Tribute of Modern Babylon' report on child prostitution, published in *The Pall Mall Gazette* (*PMG*) in July 1885, for which he and several of his accomplices were prosecuted and jailed, but which ultimately led to a change in the law covering the age of consent; Mazher Mahmood's (born 1963) celebrity stings as the 'Fake Sheikh' for News International between 1991 and 2014, whose final sting led to his conviction for conspiracy to pervert the course of justice; the exposure of phone hacking in 2010–13 at the *News of the World* (hereafter *NOTW*), which led to the closure of the newspaper; and Edward Snowden's (born 1983) leak of global surveillance by America's National Security Agency (NSA) in 2013, curated and published by a global consortium of newspapers.[1]

Although Stead and Snowden were primarily driven by ethical and ideological motives, and the *NOTW* journalists by commercial and professional competition, both groups share an indefatigable commitment to the investigative process, and a determination to reveal and print their findings. Freedom of speech and public interest are precious but complicated rights, and press regulation and control vary in different legal jurisdictions. Always nuanced, they are subject to historical change, multifaceted, messy and above all porous, having to be defined characteristically by litigation, by the state and by individuals. All the journalists named here were finally charged as individuals, and any regulation of the press was self-imposed.[2]

The objects illustrated in this chapter articulate the borders of journalism, the existence of restrictions and a legal framework of reporting and punishment for 'crossing the line'; the changing forms *of media* that circulate the stories – the newspaper, the internet and the rest (film, broadcasting and video); and the changing technology and hardware of newsgathering and media history that underpin these stories – the printing press, the telegraph, telephone, the computer, the internet and the mobile phones that enabled hacking.[3]

That the three journalists discussed in detail below are all male reflects the unmistakable dominance of men in print journalism to date, and especially in political and economic news and investigative journalism. Likewise, the character of the investigations and stings in the cases of Stead and the *NOTW* – focusing pruriently on sex trafficking, prostitution, adultery and women's bodies – echoes the highly gendered discourse of the popular press. However, my account of the investigative newsgathering and dissemination by Stead and Snowden does include women as key agents: Josephine Butler (1828–1906) in 1885, an activist campaigner on women's rights, and Laura Poitras (born 1964) in 2013-4, a film director and documentary maker.

In journalism stories are not usually traced through the name of their author, but from a keyword drawn from their title, and the name and date of the relevant paper. Bylines are increasingly collective, listing multiple authors and collective responsibility. Nevertheless, 'crossing the line' usually but not always refers to the culpability of named individuals under the law. The stories in this chapter reflect tensions in investigative journalism between individual and collective responsibility, and the newspaper as a corporate entity and the medium of dissemination and storage.

The stories reflect tensions in investigative journalism between individual and collective responsibility.

THE
PALL MALL GAZETTE
An Evening Newspaper and Review.

No. 6337.—Vol. XLII.   *TUESDAY, JULY 7, 1885.*   *Price One Penny.*

A GOOD START.

THE new Cabinet made a good beginning yesterday. The ministerial manifestoes of Lord SALISBURY and Lord CARNARVON were admirable alike in tone and in substance ; and, although we cannot profess to rejoice at the latest and final vote against liberty of conscience recorded in the House of Commons in the case of Mr. BRADLAUGH, Ministers may well feel exhilarated at carrying a majority of 44 into the lobby in the first important division that has taken place since they accepted office. If for the rest of the session they can keep up to yesterday's level they will do more to convince the country of their statesmanship than by all the speeches which they have made during the last five years.

Take, for instance, the way in which the new Lord Lieutenant discussed the affairs of Ireland from his place in the House of Lords. Nothing could be more statesmanlike and lofty than the tone in which Lord CARNARVON addressed himself to the consideration of the great problem of the reconciliation of Ireland. No Radical in the House of Commons could have been more frank and courageous in his recognition of the necessity for a change in the abandonment of the miserable habit of constant recourse to exceptional and special legislation, by which, as by a series of temporary stopgaps, peace and order have been maintained in Ireland for the last forty years. It is a great thing to have the official chiefs of the Conservative party committed to a declaration in favour of some wholesome and better solution, based upon that feeling of trust, "which is after all the only foundation upon which we can hope "to build up amity and concord between the two nations." There is a better ring about Lord CARNARVON'S little speech than we have heard in any of the speeches dedicated to Irish affairs for some years. If the new Administration fails in Ireland, it will not be for lack of a noble ideal ; and, with Lord CARNARVON, we cannot and will not believe that the combination of good feeling to England and good government to Ireland is a hopeless task. The new Government intends to rely upon the firm and effectual administration of the ordinary law for the maintenance of order, while they proposes to amend the Labourers Act and pass a Land Purchase Bill as a means of establishing better, more wholesome, and kindlier relations between the rulers and the ruled. Nothing could possibly be better than the spirit which breathed throughout Lord CARNARVON'S speech, and if only the new Viceroy is not fatally hampered by his sinister alliance with the Irish Chancellor we may venture to hope for better things in Ireland.

Lord SALISBURY'S declaration of the foreign policy of the new Administration was dignified and effective. Of course it is easy to deal in sounding generalities, and the test of an Administration is not in its formulæ, nor even in its ideas, but in its ability to act upon the one and to realize the other. Still, so far as mere programme can go, Lord SALISBURY did his work very well. His speech was devoted solely to the Afghan and Egyptian questions, and on both he spoke with a very certain sound, and in a much more reasonable fashion than might have been imagined considering some of his own utterances when in opposition. On the question of the Afghan frontier he somewhat unnecessarily committed himself to a declaration which might compel him to go to war with Russia as to the precise point where the Pass of Zulfikar begins, or concerning the definition of the positions which command the entrance to that place. But that, we may take it, is governed by the significant remark that "he was bound to say that the promise given to the Ameer was only consequent upon another promise given by Russia." From which it follows that the definition as to what we are to give to the Ameer is bound by the interpretation which Russia attaches to the particular phrase, "the Pass of Zulfikar." On the general principles of Afghan policy Lord SALISBURY spoke wisely and well :—

Although we shall cultivate the confidence and friendship of the Ameer of Afghanistan, it is not to the friendship of the Ameer of Afghanistan that we must trust for the protection of our interests. It is to preparations skilfully devised and vigorously and rapidly carried out for the defence of our frontier at all points where it is weak, and to bulwarks which shall not only defend the frontier when it is attacked, but which shall stretch out far enough to prevent the tide of war rolling to its foot.

There is a danger of course that the last phrase may be held to apply to Candahar, but we prefer to believe that it refers solely to Quetta, and perhaps to Pishin and Sibi. On that point we need more explicit assurances ; but giving the new Cabinet the benefit of that doubt, there is no exception to be taken to the policy of defending India on the frontier of India, and not on the frontier of Afghanistan.

In the references to Egypt and the Soudan there was not much that is new, but its strain was good, straightforward, and manly. The only hint which it contained of any new departure was the allusion to the possibility of obtaining assistance from Turkey in resisting the advance of the Mahdi. Such at least we take to be the meaning of the following allusion :—"The most momentous issue we " have to decide is how we shall apply the forces of Egypt, assisted, no " doubt, in some measure by ourselves—and assisted, it may be, in " other ways—so as to keep this tide of fanatic and san- " guinary barbarism at a distance." Lord SALISBURY definitely put his foot down upon the suggestion that we should sacrifice TEWFIK. The Khedive " throughout the whole of the " calamitous history has shown himself loyal and stedfast " to England. To him, therefore, we are bound by every con- " sideration of honour." The Khedive, therefore, will be maintained, and Sir H. DRUMMOND WOLFF, we suppose, will not go to Cairo. Concerning his general Egyptian policy Lord SALISBURY'S words were weighty and to the point. He said :—

It is impossible that we can restore Egypt to the condition in which she was before our troops landed unless we make up our minds to a somewhat lengthy process. There is really no alternative before us but steadily buckling to with a view of amending all the evils, or a considerable number of the evils, which exist, by a cautious and circumspect policy. There is no alternative between that and taking a course which, it seems to me, would cover England with shame, that of abandoning Egypt to her fate—anarchy and chaos.

A policy of "steadily buckling to" is better than a policy of scuttle, and we cordially wish Lord SALISBURY all success in the difficult task to which he has set his hand. He may not achieve success, but if he and his colleagues continue the same broad and generous spirit which they displayed in their manifestoes last night there is little fear but that they will face the General Election with much better prospects than six weeks ago appeared possible.

THE MAIDEN TRIBUTE OF MODERN BABYLON.—II.

THE REPORT OF OUR SECRET COMMISSION.

I DESCRIBED yesterday a scene which took place last Derby day, in a well known house, within a quarter of a mile of Oxford-circus. It is by no means one of the worst instances of the crimes that are constantly perpetrated in London, or even in that very house. The victims of these rapes, for such they are to all intents and purposes, are almost always very young children between thirteen and fifteen. The reason for that is very simple. The law at present almost specially marks out such children as the fair game of dissolute men. The moment a child is thirteen she is a woman in the eye of the law, with absolute right to dispose of her person to any one who by force or fraud can bully or cajole her into parting with her virtue. It is the one thing in the whole world which, if once lost, can never be recovered, it is the most precious thing a woman ever has, but while the law forbids her absolutely to dispose of any other valuables until she is sixteen, it insists upon investing her with unfettered freedom to sell her person at thirteen. The law, indeed, seems specially framed in order to enable dissolute men to outrage these legal women of thirteen with impunity. For to quote again from "Stephen's Digest," a rape in fact is not a rape in law if consent is obtained by fraud from a woman or a girl who was totally ignorant of the nature of the act to which she assented. Now it is a fact which I have repeatedly verified that girls of thirteen, fourteen, and even fifteen, who profess themselves perfectly willing to be seduced, are absolutely and totally ignorant of the nature of the act to which they assent. I do not mean merely its remoter consequences and the extent to which their consent will prejudice the whole of their future life, but even the mere physical nature of the act to which they are legally competent to consent is unknown to them. Perhaps one of the most touching instances of this and the most conclusive was the exclamation of relief that burst from a Birmingham girl of

That the indictments (in 1885 and 2016) of the two journalists W.T. Stead and Mazher Mahmood are separated by 130 years prompts expectations of differences; so does their difference of rank as respectively editor and staff reporter, with different degrees of agency and responsibility. Both, however, went to prison, enabled by their shared tendency to conflate the distinct roles of reporter and editor: Stead was a London-based editor from the north of England who cultivated his status as an outsider, leaving him free to behave like a hands-on reporter, going into the field with alacrity, where he accrued liability in an unfamiliar world. His collaborators, unlike Mahmood's, included people from outside the sphere of the newspaper, the voluntary sector, among them prominent evangelical activists such as Josephine Butler and institutions such as the Salvation Army. His combination of authority and gullibility left him badly exposed: not only was he jailed, but several of his agents in the community were sent to prison, including a reformed brothel-keeper in Butler's employ.

Snowden opted for the press and journalists rather than the internet on the basis of print's stability and durability.

Mahmood, on the other hand, was larger than life, worldly and adept, deriving confidence and airs from his characteristic disguise as a royal sheikh. Although a reporter, he was 'chief investigator' of the *NOTW*, with his own department at the paper's offices which, in the interests of anonymity, he seldom visited. With a generous bankroll from the paper and the ear of the editor, he was feted and favoured; he accrued prizes from the industry for his reporting, and deftly eluded the law which he brought to bear on his victims/subjects.[4] He exuded authority as he produced a succession of what appeared to be spectacular stings of politicians, footballers and celebrities that sold newspapers in prodigious quantities.

The third figure discussed in this chapter, Edward Snowden, was not a journalist but a whistleblower, the source of a leak from his employer in the International Surveillance (IS) community. In 2012–13, late in the day of print journalism, Snowden opted for the press and journalists *rather than the internet* to circulate his momentous content, on the basis of print's stability and durability, and the expertise of journalists as writers and curators of sensitive material. 'I'm not a writer,' Snowden explained, as he described his decision primarily as the act of a citizen concerned to preserve American democracy and its constitution.[5] Like all the journalists

'The Maiden Tribute of Babylon', *Pall Mall Gazette*, 6 July 1885. First instalment of 'The Maiden Tribute of Modern Babylon' reports on child prostitution.

considered here, Snowden augmented his story with
commentary in other media forms: with two films
(*citizenfour*, 2014 and *Snowden*, 2016) and in a book,
Permanent Record (2019).

Snowden and Stead both used the press to
challenge the state, invoking the notion of the press
taken from Edmund Burke (1727–1797) and circulated
by Thomas Carlyle (1795–1881) in 1837 and 1840,
'the fourth estate'.[6] Stead and Snowden locate their
investigative base strategically at the table with
the other three 'estates', based on the principle of
'public interest' that 'Democracy Dies in Darkness',
as *The Washington Post* avers. Stead, in a delirious moment of
self-justification after his successful campaign to alter the law of
the age of consent, called a subsequent article 'Government by
Journalism'.[7] Although it has been increasingly displaced by the
inroads of entertainment, advertising and profit that followed
from the 'new journalism' (in the 1870s) and its successor mass
journalism (from the mid-1890s), the function of the press that
Stead and Snowden advocated remains.[8] In that tradition, neither
Stead nor Snowden profited financially from their scoops, and
both took responsibility for their stories by name once they were
safely published. Neither initially named names in their copy,

Undercover journalist
Mazher Mahmood,
known as the 'Fake
Sheikh', leaving
the Old Bailey after
being found guilty
of tampering with
evidence in collapsed
drug trial of singer
Tulisa Contostavlos,
October 2016.

News is a never-ending serial, and crime is a more sensational category of news with lashings of scandal and sensationalism.

preferring to target institutions such as Parliament or the NSA, and in Stead's case to change names in his narrative accounts that draw on techniques of fiction and melodrama.

The contrast between their campaigns and those of the heavily illustrated *NOTW* – the elaborate 'stings' of celebrities created by Mahmood – is stark. Mahmood dramatised the subterfuge of his undercover investigations by displacing the customary photograph on his byline block with a blank silhouette, while signing his name to gain professional recognition. Key aspects of his methods were revealed and denounced during his long career at the *NOTW*: his resort to elaborate disguise – as the 'Fake Sheikh' – and his subterfuge amounted to illegal acts of entrapment. That Mahmood and the *NOTW* thrived on the exposure of famous names, and that bankrolling of newsgathering through phone hacking by other *NOTW* journalists was routine, became clear: entertainment (involving titillation and sensation) and commerce crowded more sober news out of the paper's dynamic and competitive pages.

Even the small number of stories discussed here appeared across diverse types of newspapers, not only in the popular press, such as family Sundays like the *NOTW* and *The Sun on Sunday*, but in a clubland evening daily (*PMG*), in daily newspapers of record (*The Guardian, The Washington Post* and *The New York Times*) and in a weekly news magazine (*Der Spiegel*).[9] This is not surprising, as this kind of journalism builds on a basic element of newspaper copy – the frisson of *all* that is 'new' in its broadest sense, which keeps readers returning to papers and screens for more. News is a never-ending serial, and crime is a more sensational category of news, whether it occurs in the formal divorce court reports of the nineteenth-century press, or in banner headlines on the front page. Crime is also a foundational element of the newspaper, and a slot into which our investigative stories fit, with their lashings of scandal and sensationalism.

These stories are often doubly crime stories, being *about* alleged crime such as sex trafficking, and understood as involving high risk in reporting them, or under suspicion of illegal newsgathering or publication. For news readers, the ensuing trials extend the original stories, and renew the pleasure of reading dramatic disclosures and scandal about familiar material in a new legal framework. As for the papers, they also enjoy the opportunity to recycle their investment in the original investigation with newsworthy addenda in plentiful copy which continues to sell papers; even when court cases are lost, cumulative sales help make up costs. In fact, there is a consanguinity between all the stories referred to here and the diverse newspapers that published them, except in the Stead/*PMG* case.

Stead's 'Maiden Tribute of Modern Babylon' is the simplest form of investigative journalism among these examples.[10] But it is an anomaly. Appearing in an upmarket but cheap evening daily, it conformed to genres familiar to readers of the paper – campaign, undercover and investigative journalism – but its unmistakable and shocking sordidness proved a mismatch for many readers, and probably for its proprietor.[11] While investigating the story was the editor's initiative, he was responding to a nudge from a cluster of causes he advocated as an activist Congregationalist Christian: in the words of the time, to 'combat the devil', to protect young girls from 'white slavery' and to pressure Parliament to pass flagging legislation to raise the age of consent from thirteen to sixteen. As with the other examples in this chapter, Stead's goals were already in the sights of like-minded people of the period, including voluntary groups such as the Gospel Purity Association (1885) and the London Committee for Suppressing the Traffic of British Girls for Purposes of Continental Prostitution (1879). Stead himself had published a leader on the subject just before he left the *Northern Echo* to join the *PMG* in 1881.[12]

As the Stead and *NOTW* stories imply, all the titles examined here were responsive to the zeitgeist of their historical moment. Evangelical Christianity and its palpable influence on campaign journalism were common in Stead's day, as were the rudiments of the new journalism Stead developed. If Stead's story was primarily editor-led, the ethos of the *NOTW* and its reporters is outstanding for its embodiment of a particular form of highly competitive, popular tabloid journalism sanctioned by the title and its journalists alike.[13] Snowden was addressing an industry born of the technology, the

The ethos of the NOTW *and its reporters is a particular form of highly competitive, popular tabloid journalism.*

politics and the military-industrial complex of the day. The character of newspapers changes radically over time, and these titles (except the new-born *The Sun on Sunday*) have long histories, during which they were substantially different. A common thread in these examples, irrespective of historical period, is the exposure of the abrogation of legal protocols such as the law and the Constitution by many of those appointed to uphold them, such as the police and members of the US Congress.[14]

'The Maiden Tribute' was predicated on its link to power – the coincidence of investigation and the parliamentary bill.

For Stead the timing of 'The Maiden Tribute' was predicated on its link to power – the coincidence of his investigation and the parliamentary bill. The articles' topicality made the sales of the *PMG* rocket beyond its ability to supply copies, and the revival and passing of the far-reaching Criminal Law Amendment Act (1885) validated the brouhaha they provoked from Stead's proprietor and readers.[15] Similarly, Nick Davies (born 1953), the journalist who developed the phone hacking story, insisted that it only had legs – since hacking of mobile phones by journalists had quickly become commonplace – once power was involved, i.e. because the former *NOTW* editor was now working for the prime minister. Even then, it took a revelation of the crucial role of phone hacking in the police investigation of the missing child Milly Dowler (1988–2002) finally to make hacking itself the story.[16]

The power to affect lives of well-known victims, by imprisonment, shame and humiliation through 'exposure', was a factor in Mahmood's stings (in which he took great pleasure, as his covert filming shows), and in the sensational invasion of celebrities' private lives through illegal phone hacking. Professionally, the need to secure a 'scoop' by being the first to publish exclusive information can fuel journalists who decide to 'cross the line'. For Snowden, the urgency of the countdown stemmed from both the controlled conditions of a scoop and the race to publish and lodge the files safely before his employers discovered the theft.

One of the compelling features of the publication of 'The Maiden Tribute' in the *PMG* was its legacy. As a short, one-off campaign, it might have ended with the passage of the bill that raised the age of consent. Although its author went to prison three months later, his deployment of the campaign as a base for further coverage was prodigious and ingenious. It took the forms of his publication of every type of

Some investigative journalism may have durable effects, for its paper, its authors, in legislation and in later campaigns.

subsequent coverage in the pages of the *PMG* that he could muster: correspondence, snippets from other titles and individuals, and detailed daily accounts of the ensuing trial reprinted from other papers, with headlines such as 'The Government Prosecution of Mr Stead' from the *Methodist Times*.[17] Along with advertisements for a pamphlet of reprints of the original story, these reports swelled the evening daily in an effort to continue the huge spurt in sales that the issue provoked for a week in July.[18]

Stead (unrepentant) also made the most of his imprisonment in the following November, writing and publishing two assertive articles on 'Government by Journalism' and 'The Future of Journalism' (1886) in which an ethical journalism predicated on education and campaigns was envisaged. New spin-offs proliferated. Publicity for the accomplishments of Stead himself, as a force and a personality, was also arranged. A timely penny pamphlet, *The Life of Mr W.T. Stead*, appeared in 1886, by an anonymous third person, but clearly embedding long autobiographical 'descriptions' of his childhood and career supplied by Stead, whose self-portrait comprised an instructive hagiography of a model life.[19] On 1 October 1885, the *PMG* reported the announcement by the *Methodist Times* of a Stead Defence Fund, with two MPs as officers, along with the editor of the *Contemporary Review*, which published Stead's two pieces on journalism soon afterward.[20] On the following day, the paper referred to a meeting of the new National Vigilance Association, created in August in response to 'The Maiden Tribute'. What is evident from this nineteenth-century campaign is that the influence of some investigative journalism, imbued with the added investment of risky newsgathering, does not end with its publication, but may have far-reaching and durable effects, for its paper, its authors, in legislation and in later campaigns.

That the sustained trajectory of success resulting from the *NOTW*'s bankrolling of phone hacking was brought to a sudden halt by the title's demise did not prevent waves of repercussions, for individuals and for the press, including the birth of one title predicated on the destruction of another, and the disclosure of alarming overlaps between the press and government, and the press and police. The closure of the paper put 200 jobs at risk, and involved the sacrifice of the best-selling Sunday title in the UK. Despite this attempt to protect the proprietor, his family and News International, the proprietors and editors were interrogated by a parliamentary committee, a government inquiry conducted

'Thank You & Goodbye', *The News of the World*, 10 July 2011. The final issue of the newspaper, which closed following the phone hacking scandal.

by Lord Leveson (born 1949) and by police, from which charges resulted against *NOTW* employees and managers, some of whom were jailed. The paper's former editor lost his post as head of communications in the prime minister's office, and was imprisoned, and its proprietor withdrew his bid for control of the satellite media organisation BSkyB.

Nevertheless, *The Sun on Sunday* was launched swiftly on the back of an extant daily, to occupy the presses and to recoup sales of the *NOTW* readership for NI Group Ltd, and it was this offshoot of the *NOTW* closure that finally implicated Mahmood, who made the transfer to the new paper. Three years later a drug case against the singer Tulisa Contostavlos (born 1988) resulting from a celebrity sting in *The Sun on Sunday* collapsed in July 2014, due to suspicion that Mahmood lied in a pre-trial hearing. It prompted the judge to question Mahmood's role here and retrospectively in other (*NOTW*) sting cases.[21] A *Panorama* programme on the BBC followed on 12 November 2014. The Crown Prosecution Service investigated, and in 2016 Mahmood and his driver were charged; he was found guilty of tampering with the evidence, and jailed for fifteen months.[22]

One repercussion that failed to materialise was any radical improvement of the regulatory mechanism of the press, with attempts by the government and Max Mosley (1940–2021) having foundered, defeated by perceptions of the dangers of government control and fears of financial liability among proprietors.[23]

Snowden's case, as in Stead's, had a significant impact on the law: seven years later, in September 2020, the NSA programme of surveillance was judged unlawful. But well before that, Snowden's data release energised citizen awareness of the necessity to remain vigilant about the operation of government agencies within constitutional boundaries. It built on the activities and organisation of grassroots anti-surveillance watchers who preceded Snowden, and it encouraged scrutiny of the working of democracy in the US government and internationally.[24]

Journalists and stories that 'cross the line' represent one extreme of the journalist's pursuit of evidence and accountability.

Journalists and stories that 'cross the line' represent one extreme of the journalist's pursuit of evidence and accountability, a standard that underlies all journalism. It is implicit in our dismissal of 'fake' news. As in these instances, 'crossing the line' may be inadvertent (Stead) or meticulously planned (Mahmood and Snowden). It can originate in ideology in the name of public interest (Stead's evangelical 'crusade' and Snowden's citizen democracy) or commercial and professional competition (Mahmood, and the other *NOTW* phone hackers); it can be individual and/or corporate. For those involved, the repercussions are similarly diverse. In the absence of agreed press standards or adequate regulations, and given the complexity of defining the public interest, the charges here are notably diverse, as are the length and nature of sentences. They reflect the history of law, but also the dynamic assessments of the gravity of breaking the law among journalists. Stead returned to his job, and donned his prison uniform annually to celebrate his endeavour; Snowden has survived at the expense of exile from his country. The numerous casualties of the *NOTW* case include not only the victims of the stings and phone hackings, but also the newspaper itself, which was forced to close. Crossing the line can inch forward progress, but it can also wreak destruction.

Grateful thanks to Dr Andrew Hobbs, University of Central Lancashire, for obscure information.

Carole Cadwalladr

Profile by Beth Gaskell

Carole Cadwalladr (born 1969) is an investigative journalist and author who rose to international prominence in 2018, after she uncovered the Facebook–Cambridge Analytica data scandal.

She began her career writing for *The Daily Telegraph*, before moving to *The Observer* and *The Guardian* in 2005, where she is currently a regular features writer. While her writing has covered a wide range of subjects, including travel, food, the property market, film and television reviews, celebrity gossip and politics, she has become best known for her writings on technology and its interactions with modern life, politics and the democratic process.

From 2016 she reported extensively on what she believes to be a 'right-wing fake news ecosystem', paying particular attention to the Brexit campaign, the relationship between the UKIP (and then Brexit Party) leader Nigel Farage

and Donald Trump, and Russian intervention in the 2016 American presidential election. In 2018 Cadwalladr became a household name after playing a role in uncovering the notorious Facebook–Cambridge Analytica data scandal. The scandal involved personal data from Facebook accounts being collected and sold by Cambridge Analytica, largely for political advertising around the American election and Brexit campaigns.

An investigative journalist in a digital age, Cadwalladr has won a number of awards: the Orwell Prize for Political Journalism (2018), a Reporters Without Borders 'L'esprit de RSF' (2018) and Hay Festival's Medal for Journalism (2019). She was also a finalist for the Pulitzer Prize for National Reporting in 2019. However, her work has also drawn criticism, particularly from the Conservative press, and in 2019 she was sued for libel by Arron Banks, the financial backer of the Leave.UK campaign group in an ongoing case (at the time of writing).

Seeing is believing

There has always been a sense that when you view an image in a newspaper or on TV, it is a truthful reflection of what has happened before the eyes of the person capturing the image.

The American philosopher Susan Sontag (1933–2004) wrote, 'A photograph passes for incontrovertible proof that a given thing happened.'[1] Unlike words, which can be crafted after the event, even by an eyewitness, the image is taken to mimic a perceived reality (a mimetic object), and this is perhaps why we give so much weight to the idiomatic phrase 'seeing is believing' to guide our commonsense interpretations of what we are told is the truth.

Of course, representing the truth is not quite that simple. The process of selecting a subject to photograph, presenting it as representing the essence of a story and distributing it through news outlets somewhat transforms the idea beyond what Sontag suggests 'seems to have a more innocent, and therefore more accurate relation to visible reality than do other mimetic objects'.[2] Journalism is about storytelling and creating narratives. Moving the audience with an image is bound up in photojournalistic craft, convention and often conscious or unconscious bias. Taking a cue from the advertising world, it is often said that in journalism 'one picture is worth a thousand words'. For this chapter the question may be: what words does the picture conjure up? What makes an image an authentic representation of reality? To answer these questions we need to understand how an original image is presented, and what might shape both its value and the meaning we take from it. This chapter takes a range of images across time used in the media and provides context for how we might interpret them. Each image represents a particular theme: vulnerability, authenticity, iconic standing, privacy and truth, which, when combined, reveal the range, scope and significance of the image as something that is used to represent an objective reality being reported on by the journalist.

The news-consuming public has entered into a kind of visual contract with the producers of the image or item of news: they assume that it has been gathered, edited and published responsibly. The idea is that the audience can trust that these events happened as they have been told. It is then for the audience to make or add meaning to what the image (or moving images) tells them about the world beyond their own experience.

In traditional news organisations all journalists are guided, although not always strictly bound, by a code of ethics. This is also true for photojournalists. Sometimes these codes are written down. In America the National Press Photographers Association (NPPA) has regularly revised this code since its inception in 1946. In the UK the British Press Photographers Association is guided by the principles that apply to all journalists. The academic Daniel Cornu has talked about the moral framework guiding photojournalists being rooted in three core principles: truth, verification of sources and preserving human dignity.[3] While these may not be a sufficient set of conditions to underpin all acts of creating an image used to represent a perceived reality, they are certainly necessary to support the veracity of that image and not breach the trust the audience has place in the news-maker.

> *The news-consuming public assume that it has been gathered, edited and published responsibly.*

VULNERABILITY: ALAN KURDI, *THE INDEPENDENT*, 5 SEPTEMBER 2018

Every once in a while, a single image becomes emblematic of a global story. The photograph taken by Nilüfer Demir (born 1986) of a prone toddler lying on the shore of the Aegean Sea was one such image. The three-year-old Syrian child, Alan Kurdi (2012–2015), had drowned during the flight of his family from war-torn Syria. The photograph of him quickly came to represent both the vulnerability

of the refugees making the perilous journey across
the Mediterranean Sea to seek refuge in Europe, on
unseaworthy vessels, and the futility of the conflict
that had spawned this epic migration.

This image had a similarly immediate and potent
impact on the viewing public as Kevin Carter's
(1960–1994) image of a starving Sudanese child
stalked by a predatory vulture. That photograph,
taken in 1993, also painted a dramatic scene of
vulnerability. Carter had been advised not to touch
the famine victims because of disease and, although
he scared the creature away and the child survived,

'Somebody's child',
The Independent, 5
September 2018. Front
cover showing the
body of a Syrian child
refugee, later identified
as Alan Kurdi.

when *The New York Times* published it there was sympathy for the victim and a backlash against the photographer. Some judged him for not coming to the child's aid, and this was identified as an example of what Sontag called elsewhere 'war porn'. Denounced as exploitative, sensational and voyeuristic – as putting the ethics of news photography under attack – it fostered an active and ongoing debate about intervention and the individual responsibility of the practitioner on the ground. Carter won a Pulitzer for the photograph, but the afterstory is a sad one. He later took his own life, writing, 'I am haunted by the vivid memories of killings and corpses and anger and pain.'[4]

Carter won a Pulitzer for the photograph, but later took his own life, writing, 'I am haunted by the vivid memories of killings and corpses and anger and pain.'

Both images can be viewed as potent documentary evidence which draws on the vulnerability of the subject to motivate empathy and even activism. By placing an emphasis on identifying and capturing these types of images of excessive vulnerability, news editors are often accused of playing to the depraved gallery and the need to meet the demands of the circulation-hungry newspapers or news channels. This may be a useful critique to guide ethical practices, but it still leaves journalists with the problem of how to confront and reflect serious moral challenges, particularly when children are the victims of society's failures.

AUTHENTICITY: 'HORROR IN OUR TIME', GAUMONT BRITISH NEWS, 30 APRIL 1945

The question of whether such graphic images should be used is not new, but questions about image verification have become more urgently debated as a consequence of user-generated content, which has the power to introduce unverified or manipulated imagery into the public domain. The journalistic quest for authenticity and the editorial need for verification come into sharp focus in historical newsreel footage from the German concentration camps at Buchenwald and Bergen-Belsen.

In between 15 April 1945, when British troops entered the compound of the concentration camp, and 21 May 1945, when they burned Belsen to the ground, moving and still images of real potency and importance to the historical record were captured.

At the time many editors argued these were potentially too graphic and disturbing to be seen by adults, and certainly by those under the age of sixteen. In those five weeks, members of the British Army Film and Photographic Unit (AFPU) were so shocked and appalled by what they found that, while they knew it was important to capture the evidence of the barbarity, cruelty and death that they discovered, they foresaw a danger their footage would not be believed because it was beyond comprehension. They tried hard to ensure that they put figures of authority on camera, to 'prove' the authenticity of their material. Even so, there were those who, seeing the first images brought back to the newsrooms in London, wondered out loud about the credibility of the footage and how it could be verified or authenticated.[5]

In a meeting of the five main newsreel editors almost as soon as the AFPU material started being viewed for distribution, the collective view emerged that the footage 'was not entirely convincing and that, to show such pictures unless they were convincing, might have a boomerang effect since the public might query their authenticity'.[6] This challenge was set against a backdrop of information censorship where the public had been spared images of horror and death throughout the war. This in turn had been

There was a sense that this was important testimony and broadcasting it would help to ensure that the horrors could not be denied and refuted at a later date.

conditioned by the idea that if you showed material that was too bad it might be seen as propaganda to beef up the war effort, and could have the consequence of blighting trust in government and morale both at the same time.

The cameramen believed it was their duty as witnesses within Bergen-Belsen to tell the truth and get their images to be seen by the widest possible audience. In order to achieve that, they tried to convey the humanity of their subjects. The shocking treatment of children played a central role here, and provided an evidential quality to their work so that people believed the circumstances were real.

Back home, the newsreel operators were challenged by the idea that it would be inappropriate to show the harrowing footage in cinemas as part of a light entertainment programme. Of course, before the advent of mass television there was no other means of distributing the moving images. Such objections meant there was a strong possibility that the significance of these crimes might be overlooked or underestimated in the context of winning the war.

Politicians and news providers worked to establish a process of verifying the footage, arranging for reputable people such as a committee of MPs to visit the camps and view the evidence for themselves while on camera. This persuaded the producers of the newsreels that it was possible to share these truths of horror in the camps with the public. There was a sense that this was important testimony and broadcasting it would help to ensure that the horrors could not be denied and refuted at a later date.

All these years later, it is important to remember that our memory of the camps is largely shaped by the Bergen-Belsen footage, so devastatingly presented in Gaumont's first 'Horror in our Time' newsreel, and that the material was gathered over just a short five-week period. Afterwards, within thirty-six days of liberation, the camp at Bergen-Belsen was fully evacuated and burned to the ground to save the lives of survivors vulnerable to a typhus epidemic. Only the marked mass graves remained at the memorial site, but the pictorial evidence of the murder, disease and starvation unleashed on civilians remained for posterity. Many years later, when I interviewed Leslie Hardman (1913–2008), the Jewish British Army chaplain who entered Bergen-Belsen with the troops, and one of the survivors of the camp, Gena Turgel (1923–2018), they were eternally grateful for the work of those AFPU operatives whose work helps maintain the memories of those millions who suffered at the hands of the Nazi system of death camps. In an age of Holocaust deniers, imagine if those images had not been filmed and distributed.

It is worth noting that a full-length documentary film involving Sidney Bernstein (1899–1993), who went on to set up Granada TV, and the British Hollywood director Alfred Hitchcock (1899–1980) was suppressed in 1945, precisely because it was deemed too lurid and – later – counter-productive as the Cold War gathered momentum. *Memory of the Camps* was finally restored by the Imperial War Museum in 1985 and aired on US TV. It was only finally shown in Britain as part of a Channel 4 documentary, *Night Will Fall*, in 2015, seventy years after its initial production.

ICONIC IMAGES? BLOODY SUNDAY, NORTHERN IRELAND, *DAILY MIRROR*, 31 JANUARY 1972

Inevitably, conflict has been a primary subject of journalism and a notable venue for capturing iconic photography. The French philosopher Pierre Bourdieu (1930–2002) argued that the ability of an individual image to have a lasting impact depends on its overarching context, in what social and political spheres the image is recognised or exerts influence and above all their significance in informing public discourse and the collective memory of an event.[7] The iconic power of the image is rooted in its enduring symbolism. This involves the relationships that cut across each other in the fields of cultural production (producing the image), politics (discussing the image) and journalism (a public forum for image and discussion).

The Italian photojournalist Fulvio Grimaldi (born 1934) captured a series of images as British paratroopers

The iconic power of the image is rooted in its enduring symbolism.

opened fire on civilians at the very start of the Troubles in Northern Ireland on 30 January 1972. The image shown here was taken through a hail of bullets and depicts the bravery of the priest who would later become Bishop of Derry, Edward Daly (1933–2016). It was the first time Grimaldi had seen civilians being shot at close range and he knew that he had to keep taking images because he was witnessing an historic act and one where tremendous courage was needed by those he was photographing. He believed it was his duty to show the truth of the situation. This single black-and-white image of the tragedy has become the iconic image of Bloody Sunday.

The image from Derry remains one that captures the pain and anguish of conflict, with bystanders

'Ulster's Bloody Sunday', *Daily Mirror*, 31 January 1972, with Fulvio Grimaldi's photograph of Father Edward Daly giving the last rites to teenager Jackie Duddy.

*How much it
evokes in the
audience and what
kind of response it
triggers is where
the image in news
derives its power.*

cradling the fatally wounded teenager, seventeen-year-old Jackie Duddy, who had just been given the last rites by Daly. So powerful was the legacy of this image of the Troubles that it remains one of the most forceful reminders of a conflict which generated thousands of equally powerful images until the Good Friday Agreement was signed in 1998.

Grimaldi's photograph is perhaps less well known than Joe Rosenthal's (1911–2006) shot of the raising of the stars and stripes at Iwo Jima by American GIs on 23 February 1945, but no less iconic. Rosenthal's image became pervasive: it was replicated in newspapers and on postage stamps, distributed to schools and even used as the source for a war memorial to allow it to trigger emotions in people many years after the image was taken.

The Iwo Jima image reflected the glorification of victory after the titanic struggle against imperial Japan. But in Bourdieu's conception, because it was promoted and functioned across multiple spheres of social activity and power, it became established as a national ideological symbol. There is no doubt that these images, particularly the one of Jackie Duddy, evoke a moral response because they are presented in the context of a journalistic narrative. How much it evokes in the audience and what kind of response it triggers is where the image in news derives its power.

PRIVACY: 'DI SPY SENSATION', *SUNDAY MIRROR*, 7 NOVEMBER 1993

Photojournalists are expected to abide by ethical guidelines. One sacrosanct principle is that no photograph can be said to be in the public interest if it is gained by breaching the privacy of the subject. Both the NPPA code and the journalists' code of ethics in the UK make it clear that photographs taken secretly or with a long lens of someone in a private domain should not be available for publication. It is assumed in this code that subjects are entitled to privacy. There are often caveats to this. If the images are of an illegal activity or one where harm is being caused and the image forms part of an evidential package, secret filming is allowed, subject to editorial approval. One area where this has been sorely tested in recent times is in the insatiable appetite of the tabloid newspapers in the UK for images of celebrities and the royal family.

There was a time, in a more deferential age, when the newspapers were bound by a less formal code which prevented photographers from publishing images of the royal family that were not acceptable to the royals. This approach fractured progressively from the 1960s onwards, especially as those newspapers came under increased pressure through declining circulations. As a result they often opted for more sensational or lurid imagery to boost their readerships at the expense of their competitors. Pictures could command high sums of money and this arguably led other photographers – not professionals, but private citizens – to take even greater risks to secure an image. So, while a story might be argued to be an invasion of privacy, if the source of the story was an image not gathered by a journalist (i.e. it was user-generated content), it might be plausible to mount a public-interest defence argument to publish the material. The public interest is an important principle that can guide journalists through an ethical minefield when reporting difficult stories. In the investigations I undertook into terrorism, for example, 'public interest' was a way to remind myself of when I might consider crossing boundaries that ordinarily should not be breached.

The 'Di Spy Sensation' picture caused outrage when it was published in 1993. The image had been gathered by a camera hidden behind a wall of the gym being attended by Princess Diana in Isleworth, West London. She was shown in a leotard with her legs wide apart. The image demonstrated a blatant disregard for privacy and decency, and undermined the Press Complaints Commission (PCC) code of conduct and ethics, which underpin the usual rules deployed by photographers. Bryce Taylor, who was a director of the LA Fitness Club where the picture was taken, wanted as much money as possible for this gross invasion of privacy and betrayal of trust. Most editors refused to touch the images, but Taylor was ultimately offered £100,000 for publication in the *Sunday Mirror*. The images were purchased by the chief executive David Montgomery (born 1948), who had stepped in to try to stem the collapse of the Mirror Group empire after the death of its proprietor Robert Maxwell (1923–1991).

The media industry, and the tabloids in particular, were under extreme pressure at the time

'Public interest' was a way to remind myself of when I might consider crossing boundaries that ordinarily should not be breached.

If photojournalism neglects trust, truth and human dignity, the value of its contribution to journalism is negligible to non-existent.

to clean up their act under the threat of statutory regulation. The fact that the industry's self-regulator, the PCC, appeared toothless did nothing to stem the tidal wave of opprobrium that hit the *Sunday Mirror* in the days following publication. After the dual threats of legal action from the princess herself and government intervention, the *Sunday Mirror* apologised, stating that it regretted the upset it had caused and acknowledging that sometimes newspapers misjudged their publishing decisions.

This was, of course, not the last of the great media scandals of the late twentieth century, all of which culminated in the Leveson Inquiry (see pages 146–7). The way in which parts of the press practised their craft was placed under an intense spotlight, leading to reform of the codes of practice and press regulation. The power of the image to reflect reality was used entirely inappropriately in the 'Di Spy Sensation' case, according to the code, which reflected legitimate limitations on what it is that the press should show. The incident was also a reminder that if photojournalism neglects the core principles of trust, truth and human dignity, the value of its contribution to journalism is negligible to non-existent.

TRUTH: ROBERTA COWELL, *PICTURE POST*, 13 MARCH 1954

The philosopher Onora O'Neill (born 1941) argued in her 2002 BBC Reith Lectures that 'Press freedom is good because and insofar as it helps the public to explore and test opinions and to judge for themselves whom and what to believe and trust.'[8] This is most commonly thought of as the way in which public discourse on politics is mediated, but over the centuries – and particularly the last seventy years – the press has often been an invaluable means for exploring and even breaking through the boundaries of the sexual norms and mores of the time. Since the 1950s debates on LGBT issues have waxed and waned in our public sphere, often informed by journalistic outputs.

One early example of the power of pictures to assist in challenging the private values of the reader was the *Picture Post*'s revelations of how Roberta Cowell (1918–2011) had transitioned from male to female. In the context of more open current debates on fluid gender identity and sexuality it is difficult to recall the bigoted public attitudes of that time to anything other than cisgender, heterosexual relationships.

POST

4ᴰ ROBERTA COWELL'S OWN STORY —Exclusive

HULTON'S
NATIONAL
WEEKLY

13 MARCH 1954 VOL 62 • NO 11

Roberta Cowell, *Picture Post*, 13 March 1954. Front cover of the picture magazine with account by Roberta Cowell of how she had transitioned from male to female.

Cowell's story disrupted the narratives of the time, which tended to conflate trans identity and homosexuality. Prior to her transition, Cowell had had significant success in traditionally male domains, which made this a counterintuitive tale to contemporary readers. A Spitfire pilot, prisoner of war and husband with two daughters, Cowell challenged the prevailing assumptions about what it was to be male or female.

Perhaps what is more interesting is the fact that although her story presaged a revolution

Policeman pictured during civil disturbances in Toxteth, Liverpool, July 1981.

in our understanding of what it means to be trans, at the time the priority for Cowell was an ethical choice to try to ensure her story was not misrepresented in the media. She sought control of the way her image would be represented by ensuring she trusted the context in which it was presented by the *Picture Post* in 'a straightforward, but sober and decent way'.[9]

CHALLENGING WHAT WE SEE

Each of these images helps us explore the power that photojournalism has added to the mission of news-making. They remind us not only of the mission of journalism to tell the truth, but also the challenges faced by editorial mediators who have to make decisions about how to deliver images in a context that is truthful, ethical and dignified. It also reminds us of the evidential quality of some images that help us remember, long after the event, that things did actually happen that way and afford new generations the opportunity to learn from them.

What we do *not* see in the image sometimes remains as important as what we do see. This is why providing adequate context for any text or commentary accompanying an image or moving image matters. In a world where our newsrooms still lack diversity of people and ideas, sometimes the images chosen are less than optimal because different people observe and understand reality in different ways. For example, I recall the inner city riots in the UK in 1981. They are often still referred to, erroneously in my view, as race riots. The images we were often presented with at the time were of running street battles between young people of many backgrounds and the police. Race riots would suggest that the police were keeping apart communities. Riots triggered by racism in encounters between police and public are something different. Such ill-informed judgements and misrepresentation in newsrooms would be more regularly challenged if there were greater awareness and diversity of views in our newsrooms.

Lastly, it is probably inevitable, as public media literacy increases and viewers become more challenging of what is portrayed through images in the media, that news-makers can expect to be held more accountable for their decisions. The digital transformations of the media ecosystem, particularly the ability to manipulate images, have given rise to a greater degree of scepticism among the consumers of news. Now that manipulation of images is a given (although not necessarily to distort the context), there is a climate in which each controversial news image can be seen as suspect. With the introduction of memes into the public sphere, for example, which often present mimetic additions to photographs, we may observe a loss of capacity of a single photograph to prove enduring or iconic. It is possible, for example, that the mimetic distortions of the Alan Kurdi image – remembering Sontag's observation about 'war porn' – have already worked against the ethical underpinning of that caring act of photojournalism.

How we capture, process and distribute images in the media, as part of the journalistic mission, will continue to be controversial on the biggest and most challenging news stories. It will be difficult to avoid all of the criticisms levelled at journalism and photojournalists, but it is worth concluding this discussion with the scripted words of the 1945 Bergen-Belsen film *Memory of the Camps*, which remained unshown for decades because of sensitivities around its content. The simple words uphold the core values that an ethically guided eyewitness image-taker and a trusting consumer could probably agree upon: 'Unless the world learns the lesson these pictures teach, night will fall. But by God's grace, we who live will learn.'[10]

'Unless the world learns the lesson these pictures teach, night will fall. But by God's grace, we who live will learn.'

Memory of the Camps, 1945

4

CAN THE NEWS EVER BE OBJECTIVE?

Jackie Harrison

INTRODUCTION

As far as the news goes, the pursuit of truthful facts, explanations and understandings of events requires that reporting consists of accurate statements about those events and that they are reported on sincerely and after significant investigative effort. But why is it necessary to affirm this? Partly due to the charge against the news that it is an essential part of a *Lügenpresse* (lying press) – a term that goes back to the middle of the nineteenth century and is still used to attack the press today. Not only does the pursuit of truthfulness in news journalism have to contend with the sheer complexity of events and diminishing resources in many news organisations, but it also has to cope with the desires of people to withhold information, mislead and distort. And this is so because truthful accounts are feared for what they reveal. Part of the armoury of this fear is denying that news journalists can be objective, accompanied by accusations of cultural or political bias, or that they systematically fake their reports. News journalism is constantly being challenged by 'alternative facts and realities', and yet at its best news journalism seeks a public warrant of trust, and that requires a firm attachment to being truthful.

Linda Kaye

Staying alert: The news, COVID-19 and public information campaigns

On 14 May 2020 newspapers racked in shops across England displayed a curious uniformity. Front page headlines, columns of print and photos had been replaced by a rainbow straddling the words 'Stay Alert!'

Closer inspection would reveal a phrase above the spectrum of colours: 'We can help control the virus if we all', and these instructions below the directive: 'Keep our distance, wash our hands, think of others and play our part.' The news of the day was literally wrapped in the latest iteration of the government's campaign against COVID-19. It is indicative of a relationship that stretches back through decades of national public information campaigns spearheaded by slogans such as 'AIDS: Don't Die of Ignorance', 'Dig for Victory' and 'Coughs and Sneezes Spread Diseases', which still trigger our collective memory. Of course, providing the public with information belies the aim, which is to influence personal attitudes and behaviour, with the style and tone of the campaign reflecting whether a 'nudge' or a 'shove' is required.[1] Does the news simply carry the government message or is it a little more nuanced than that? This chapter aims to unwrap a variety of roles enacted by the news – public information distributor, promoter, educator, critic and framer – through examining past public information campaigns and seeing how the government's COVID-19 campaign played out from March to June 2020.

DISTRIBUTOR

On 2 March 2020 the government agreed a COVID-19 advertising deal worth £119m with Manning Gottlieb OMD, managed through OmniGov, its specialist media-buying unit.[2] Two days later, a national public health campaign was launched, urging the public to 'Wash Your Hands More Often for 20 Seconds', accompanied by the slogan 'Protect Yourself & Others'. This was the first of a three-phase campaign, each corresponding to a government response to the virus together with the related public action required.

Phase 1: 'Contain' – Wash Your Hands (launched 4 March)
Phase 2: 'Delay' – Isolate (19 March)
Phase 3: 'Suppress' – Stay Home (25 March)

The first television advert, supported by print, radio and social media activity, was produced in response to the 'Delay' phase by the MullenLowe Group UK for the Department of Health and

Social Security. It featured Professor Chris Whitty (born 1966), the UK government's chief medical adviser, telling people, in a direct address to camera, to isolate at home if they had COVID-19 symptoms, such as persistent cough or fever.

Placing adverts in newspapers, wrapped or otherwise, provides a clear channel of dissemination for government information, but it is the coverage of the campaign that raises public awareness and helps the message to stick. Pre-coverage is a vital part of this, utilising the cross-media channels of the news to provide a wider reach, moving from print to embedding the film advert in online publications, to YouTube channels and social media accounts such as Twitter. Hugh Pym (born 1959), BBC News Health Editor, was one of the first journalists to mention the advert in his profile of Whitty on 17 March 2020, noting that 'He is even fronting a new government TV advertising campaign to reiterate the message about people keeping themselves and their families safe.'[3] The following day newspapers and broadcasters such as *The Daily Telegraph* and Sky News embedded the advert on their YouTube channel and website respectively, ensuring the advice and modified slogan 'Protect Yourself, Others and the NHS' had already been trailed.[4]

News has provided a distribution channel for public information films for over a century, with cinema newsreels providing the conduit before television. These short reels consisting of around six to eight news stories were a staple element within the cinema programme from 1910. *Dr Wise on Influenza* (1919), made for the recently formed Ministry of Health,

English newspapers published on or around 14 May 2020 with government-funded 'Stay Alert' COVID-19 cover wraps.

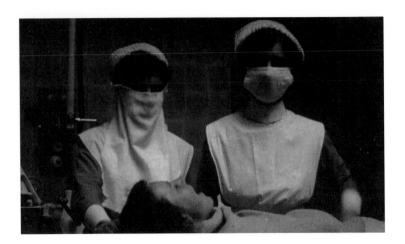

Dr Wise on Influenza (UK 1919). Frame still from Ministry of Health film, shown in UK cinemas during the 'Spanish' Flu pandemic.

was released during the second wave of the 'Spanish' Flu pandemic and shown alongside the newsreel.[5] It is resonant, both in terms of style and content, of the Chris Whitty film. Both are fronted by medical men lending authority to a remarkably consistent government public health message:

> *The ... epidemic can only be controlled if every person will take immediate precaution against infecting others by isolating themselves at home* (Dr Wise, 1919)

> *... even if your symptoms are mild you should all stay at home* (Professor Chris Whitty, 2020)

Although the aftershocks of the influenza pandemic continued to reverberate every winter, with newsreels reporting preventative measures such as disinfecting London buses (20 January 1927) and the benefits of mass gargling (14 February 1929), public health campaigns were left to local health authorities.[6] It was only with the Second World War that the more familiar national multimedia public health campaigns emerged. The Autumn Health Campaign of 1941, conducted by the Ministry of Health through the Ministry of Information, was prompted by the debilitative effect of influenza on the armed forces and, crucially, on manufacturing output. The aim was to reduce the spread of

Both are fronted by medical men lending authority to a remarkably consistent government public health message.

These newsreel stories did more than just repeat slogans; they provided the rationale behind them.

diseases caused by droplet infection, particularly influenza and colds but also diphtheria and measles. The slogan 'Coughs and Sneezes Spread Diseases' was used across a range of newspaper adverts, posters and leaflets, encouraging people to use a handkerchief and stay at home when ill. Audiences in newsreel theatres as well as cinemas watched the popular comedian Cyril Fletcher (1913–2005) deliver his light-hearted ode in *The Careless Sneezer* (1942) as part of the biweekly newsreel programme, a distribution arrangement agreed between the newsreel companies and the government.[7] This provided an additional outlet to newspapers in a campaign that formed part of a barrage of instruction and guidance designed to spur people to take individual responsibility for the 'war effort' while bringing the country together.

PROMOTER

The role of the newsreels on this wartime footing encompassed more than distribution: they actively promoted the sense of mutual responsibility engendered by 'Dig for Victory' and 'Make Do and Mend' by producing stories that echoed campaign slogans, such as student farmers setting off at the weekend to 'Lend a Hand' (27 October 1941). Earlier in the year a Ministry of Health initiative to persuade the public to wear masks resulted in the public information film *A-tish-oo* (1941). It featured a practical demonstration of how to make a mask at home and a glamorous transparent visor that could easily hold its own today. In the *Pathé Gazette* story 'Germ Masks for Crowds' (2 February 1941), three women in the street are shown using their headscarves as masks as the commentator states 'The Ministry of Health wants *us all* to wear germ masks to prevent germs and flu from spreading particularly in the shelters' (emphasis mine). These newsreel stories did more than just repeat slogans; they provided the rationale behind them, and by showing people doing what was asked of them, they encouraged adherence to the measures.[8]

The wartime propaganda propagated by the newsreels quickly threaded its way through official pandemic communications in 2020, most notably in the queen's televised address to the nation on 5 April 2020 as the prime minister Boris Johnson (born 1964) was hospitalised with COVID-19. Drawing on her own experiences during the Second World War, the queen closed with the words 'We'll meet again,' invoking the popular wartime song sung by Dame Vera Lynn (1917–2020) to provide the nation with reassurance. In his letter to the nation in March, the prime minister appealed to the 'great British spirit' in 'a moment of national emergency', a phrase he used in his televised announcement of a national lockdown on 23 March 2020.[9] That morning MullenLowe were briefed for the third phase, 'Suppress', filming Chris Whitty in the evening and recording the actor Mark Strong delivering the refined slogan 'Stay Home, Protect the NHS, Save Lives' on the morning of 24 March 2020.[10] This slogan – which became so redolent of lockdown – was honed successively over the three phases. Although the tricolon was reminiscent of the government's love of the punchy three-word slogan, most recently with 'Get Brexit Done' during the 2019 general election campaign, it was by no means an oven-ready one.

The rationale behind these measures was to ensure the National Health Service was not overwhelmed, and stories emerging on social media that supported this were soon picked up by national news outlets. The most prominent was an idea proposed by Annemarie Plas (@AnnemariePlas) on Twitter to #clapforourcarers, or make any noise at 8 p.m. on Thursday 26 March 2020 to show support

'Stay Home, Protect the NHS, Save Lives'. British government COVID-19 message, issued at the time of national lockdown on 23 March 2020.

The news played an important part in explaining COVID-19, the changing guidance and the reasons behind it.

for the NHS. The message went viral and that evening, public buildings throughout the country shone blue for the NHS, accompanied by millions of 'locked-down' people leaning out of windows clapping and banging saucepans. The NHS clap became a Thursday evening ritual for several weeks and a recurring news story, consolidating a sense of communal support and purpose.[11] Posters made by children supporting the NHS started appearing in people's windows and increasingly featured a rainbow, which came to symbolise the campaign.

The rainbow was utilised for the 'Stay at Home' wrappers that first appeared around newspapers on 17 April 2020, together with the following request: 'When you're out, don't hang about. Clap our carers 8pm every Thursday.' The 'All In, All Together' campaign, part of a three-month advertising partnership between the government and newspaper industry, was designed to 'keep people safe and the nation united'.[12]

EDUCATOR

National consensus can also be cemented through the public education that forms the backbone of health campaigns, providing important context and justification for the guidance given. A notable example of this was AIDS Week, an integral part of the 'AIDS: Don't Die of Ignorance' campaign in February 1987. In a similar 'wartime role', the BBC and ITV worked with the government to provide nineteen hours of programme content following the delivery of leaflets to every UK household.[13] Programmes broadcast on Friday 27 February included *First AIDS*, shown on ITV at 7.30 p.m., where pop stars and medical experts came together for 'a programme unlike any other', and *AIDS – The Facts*, 'A short programme of facts and figures to answer some of the most frequently asked questions and to dispel some myths about AIDS', later that evening, at 9.30, on BBC1 and ITV.[14]

With time at a premium, public education was far more responsive for the COVID-19 campaign. The news played an important part in explaining COVID-19, the changing guidance and the reasons behind it with health editors, such as Sarah Boseley of *The Guardian*, playing a leading role. Boseley recorded short 'video explainers' which could be embedded in related articles and published on the paper's YouTube channel. One example, from 20 March 2020, discusses the symptoms of the

COVID-19 virus, the treatments available, and how people can protect themselves and others from infection.[15] This effectively provided a detailed follow-up to the guidance given by Chris Whitty in the public information film launched five days earlier. News magazine programmes such as the popular weekday evening *The One Show* on BBC One set aside airtime to answer viewers' questions on topics such as social distancing and daily exercise.

The process of reiterating and clarifying guidance played out from 16 March 2020 in the government's daily televised briefings. These live programmes were initially led by Boris Johnson, flanked by Professor Chris Whitty and Sir Patrick Vallance (born 1960), the government's chief scientific adviser, but soon settled into an attendance pattern of cabinet minister, senior medical officer and representative of the theme for that day, such as Sarah Albon, chief executive of the Health and Safety Executive. After briefing the nation on the latest COVID-19 developments and actions taken, questions would be taken from the press and, later, members of the public. The daily briefings were instant news, blogged in real time by newspapers such as *The Guardian* and providing headlines for the evening news. One clear example of clarification given was on 24 March 2020, the day after the announcement of lockdown, by Dr Jenny Harries, deputy chief medical officer for England, as she explained that couples living apart would either have to remain apart or move in together under lockdown rules.[16]

The daily briefings were instant news, blogged in real time by newspapers providing headlines for the evening news.

CRITIC

A request for clarification implies criticism of the way a message has been communicated. While this was muted for the 'Stay at Home' campaign, it was vocal for its successor 'Stay Alert', which marked the easing of the lockdown in England at the beginning of May 2020. 'Stay Alert, Control the Virus, Save Lives' riffed on the original campaign slogan, retaining both the rhetorical force of the tricolon and the visual potency of the hazard chevrons, although the colours were dialled down from red and yellow to yellow and green. The public first caught a glimpse of it on the evening of Saturday 9 May. *The Sunday Telegraph* headline 'Stay Alert: PM's New Message to the Nation' was tweeted, together with a picture of the front page and close-up of the slogan, by Edward Malnick, the paper's political editor.[17]

Set adrift in the ocean of social media, the slogan became a meme within minutes, transmitting its own distress signal of misunderstanding with each transformation. Pre-coverage of the campaign, officially launched on 13 May, was rapidly overwritten by online articles, seeded through Twitter, questioning its ambiguity and a concern that 'Stay at Home' had been dropped, together with 'Protect The NHS'. By midday on 10 May Downing Street had issued a 137-word explanation of the new slogan.[18] 'Stay Alert' meant five actions, including staying at home as much as possible and limiting contact with other people. 'Control the Virus' meant keeping the number of infections down.

The slogan became a meme within minutes, transmitting its own distress signal of misunderstanding with each transformation.

The prime minister's televised broadcast that Sunday evening did little to allay confusion, since Boris Johnson could not refer to the detailed policy behind the guidance. This could only be published the following afternoon after Parliament had first sight of it. By this time YouGov had conducted a poll that showed only 30 per cent of those questioned knew what the new slogan was asking them to do, compared to 91 per cent for 'Stay at Home'. As the government argued its message was nuanced and would make sense over time, Emily Maitlis (born 1970) was excoriating in her opening remarks for *Newsnight* on BBC Two that Monday evening: 'The government has struggled to find a new slogan for this next stage. How about this one? "Muddled messaging costs lives."' Had the government stuck with its original concept of 'ALERT' as an acronym for the five actions, then the message might have gained some traction, both in terms of meaning and in realising the broader aim of shifting responsibility to the individual. However, this idea had not been finalised as adverse coverage of the slogan grew over the weekend and it was dropped by the launch. The critical coverage reflected public confusion and frustration at an important juncture as well as the necessity for clarity in government communications.[19]

This was not the first time the barometer of public opinion had swung to critical in response to a new campaign. The 'Protect and Survive' campaign (1980), publicising a Civil Defence booklet detailing action to be taken in the event of a nuclear strike, and *Monolith* (1987), the 'tombstone' advert supporting the 'AIDS: Don't Die of Ignorance' campaign, attracted controversy for the manner in which they dealt with the subject, the former attracting a degree of ridicule, the latter anxiety at the deliberate shock tactics used.[20] However, while this commentary was clearly in response to publication and broadcast, the criticism of the rail safety film *The Finishing Line* (1977) was published before the film was completed, framing public reaction months before it was shown.

FRAMER

The Finishing Line was a twenty-one-minute film designed to deter children from playing on or vandalising the railway. Directed and co-written by John Krish (1923–2006) for British Transport Films, the film depicts a fantasy sports day where children, risking injury or death, compete for points by crossing busy railway lines, throwing stones at trains or walking into a tunnel. *Nationwide*, the BBC's popular TV forerunner to *The One Show*, devoted its entire programme on Friday 2 September 1977 to railway vandalism. It screened the film in its entirety to a studio audience of parents and children before a discussion with an invited panel including representatives from British Rail. Following the broadcast, the BBC was flooded with distressed calls and later, letters appeared in the *Radio Times* and newspapers objecting to the 'shocking' film.[21]

However, many of these first-time viewers had already formed an idea that the film was horrific from press coverage published during the summer of 1976 as the film was shot on a railway track between Hertford and Stevenage. What started as a small story, 'Safety First', about local children acting as casualties in an anti-vandalism film in the *Welwyn Times and Hatfield Advertiser* on 23 July 1976 quickly spun into 'Shock Film to Fight Vandalism' in the *Hertfordshire Mercury* on 30 July 1976. By 5 August 1976 the child psychiatrist Dr Kenneth Soddy was claiming, in the *Daily Express*, that 'British Rail's Film Frightener' would give 'anxious children the willies'.[22] While the film was designed to shock its audience, specifically eight- to eleven-year-olds, into staying away from

Following the broadcast, the BBC was flooded with distressed calls objecting to the 'shocking' film.

The fear of the NHS being overwhelmed was founded on extensive reports and disturbing images of Italy's health service.

railway tracks, the speculative and sensational framing of *The Finishing Line* ensured the safety campaign was on the defensive before it had started, justifying the film to teachers and parents that had not seen it.

It was shocking rather than sensational news coverage that provided a crucial frame of reference for the COVID-19 campaign. 'Protect the NHS' was identified as the prime motivator to encourage people to 'Stay at Home' and therefore 'Save Lives', but the fear of the NHS being overwhelmed was founded on extensive reports and disturbing images of Italy's health service experiencing just such a scenario in the weeks preceding the launch.

Each role played by the news – public information distributor, promoter, educator, critic and framer – is rarely exclusive. As coverage of the campaign intersects with news of the day, the resonance of the message is subtly altered. The 'Stay Alert' message promoted and distributed by newspapers on 14 May 2020 was quickly submerged by critical news coverage rooted in confusion and frustration. The retention of the rainbow, a residual impression of the now redundant message 'Protect the NHS', stands as a visual counter to the burgeoning public disengagement reported by the media. The role of news in a public information campaign is therefore one of multiple parts, a layered performance constantly adapting and alert to the changing circumstances.

Bradford Community Broadcasting

Profile by Beth Gaskell

Bradford Community Broadcasting (BCB Radio 106.6FM) is an award-winning, volunteer-led community radio station based in Bradford, West Yorkshire. It was launched in 1994 on local cable, gaining an FM licence in 2001. Its goal is to provide an accessible community radio station for the people of Bradford that serves and celebrates the city's diverse, multicultural population. It broadcasts speech and music programmes, working with community organisations and individuals to ensure issues of local concern are covered. It also provides support for community groups that wish to produce their own programmes.

BCB has an average audience of 31,000, but its impact has been far wider. It is recognised as being a model of its kind, responsive to, and indeed run by, the people it seeks to serve. As with most community radio stations across the UK (as of 2021 there are around 300), the station is run by local volunteers and operates on a minimal budget. In normal times the volunteers have numbered around 200, led by a small staff team. Several of these are involved in gathering or presenting news programmes for the different communities of Bradford,

but in a broader sense everything the station does is 'news'. Programmes are made on BAME issues, mental health, the LGBTQ+ community, science, music of all kinds, and topics as varied as gardening and gaming, in a number of languages, for the elderly and the young (in 2020 the youngest presenter was seven). To listen to it is to feel the beating heart of a community.

Since 2020, however, the times have not been normal. The number of volunteers was halved, as the station learned to operate under lockdown, owing to the COVID-19 pandemic. With studios closed, presenters had to broadcast from home under hastily improvised conditions, only increasing the sense of a station at one with its audience. BCB's inventive response to the crisis has been much praised. It boosted its local programming slots, interviewed councillors, carers and those left isolated by the pandemic, provided health and welfare information and created an audio archive of life under lockdown, *The Corona Chronicles*. It has not been alone in this. Many community radio stations likewise responded positively to the pandemic, combining resourcefulness with a powerful sense of mission. They delivered a trusted news and public information voice, rooted in a great sympathy with the stranded communities they served.

Kurt Barling

News:
Fact or fiction?

The modern world of gathering the news bears little resemblance to the world that first saw the emergence of the desire to share what might loosely be described as factual information with a willing audience. Facts and objectivity are now seen as key ingredients in presenting news to a mass audience. But these elements only emerged as sacrosanct after a long and often tortuous journey down the centuries.

n this chapter we look at five artefacts. Four barely resemble modern journalism and give a glimpse of how storytelling based on perceived real life has evolved since the 1600s. The fifth is an illustration from the present, of the challenges posed for the conventions of journalism in a world of contestable facts brought about by a deluge of digitally sourced information. It is a reminder that fact can still do battle with fiction in the news space.

Contemporary journalistic codes of ethics, adopted in many Western countries after the Second World War, owe a lot to a sense that newspapers fell prey to hoaxes and that these undermined the essential credibility of news operations to uphold certain standards of accuracy, verification and truth. In more recent times the advent of so-called 'spin-doctors' to assist in public messaging of difficult truths is, in this sense, just a modern exemplar of what editorial teams have had to wrestle with.

Although we think of regulation of the press as a modern phenomenon, the idea of an unruly press is actually several centuries old. So too is the idea that you should not believe everything you read in the newspapers. There is a journalistic adage, deployed often in jest but no doubt sometimes out of expediency, that 'you can't always let the facts get in the way of a good story.'

The broadsides produced by these printers and writers were not strictly purposed with telling the truth.

Psychologists have in recent years come to a view that we form our views of the world around us when we are quite young and then resist challenges to those beliefs. These cognitive biases present a 'variety of ways of thinking (indeed a variety of routine ways of thinking) that constrain one's perceptions and interpretations of the world'.[1] These biases can affect the way journalists interpret information. At the same time, what the media produces is often consumed through the prism of personal bias and a predilection to seek out and only acknowledge views that fit with those we already have. This suggests that as consumers of news we often seek out what we know and are sceptical of alternative narratives that challenge that understanding. Some argue this confirmation bias affects the way we interpret the news.

The theory may be modern, but the human behaviour it describes is unlikely to be something new. The question of authenticity and how readers (or listeners and viewers, in modern times) judge what is true and what is fictitious has been associated with literary forms of information dissemination that can be traced back to the earliest pamphleteers. The broadsides produced by these printers and writers and often posted on walls were not strictly purposed with telling the truth other than the truth as the news-maker wanted to present it.[2]

Literacy rates in the mid-1600s remained quite limited, estimated at around 30 per cent of men and 10 per cent of women, and therefore printed material other than the Bible had limited appeal to an overall population of a little over 5 million in what is now the United Kingdom.

THE WORLD IS RULED & GOVERNED BY OPINION (1641)

The World is Ruled & Governed by Opinion (1641) was published in the year before civil war broke out in England. This was a high point of public battles over religious tolerance and intolerance which ultimately cost the king his head. It was also an age in which printing presses were relatively easy to build, printing costs had become affordable and a class of literate activists was willing to soak up the new techniques in order to circulate information publicly.

It was already an age of political uncertainty, and rival broadsides fomented a febrile and panicky atmosphere. Fear of 'popish plots' and rumours that Irish rebels were landing to support the king abounded. The reporting of rumours that disorder was spreading across the kingdom led to open calls by conservative voices to limit the spread of opinion that stimulated open discord. At the same time, those who defended the expressions of dissent and their consequences challenged voices hostile to the freedom of expression. Here we get a sense of an early clash in public debates about the limits of the freedom of the press and the need for free expression.

In an illustration by the graphic artist Wenceslaus Hollar (1607–1677) to accompany a text by Henry Peacham (1578–1644) you can see Opinion (the blindfolded woman) crowned with the Tower of Babel. The globe is on her lap; a chameleon sits on her left arm and a staff is in her right hand. On the left a jester is watering the tree, and on the right an aristocratic figure is in debate with Opinion.

Fear of 'popish plots' and rumours that Irish rebels were landing to support the king abounded.

It is an example of views common at the time of the dangers of opinions being spread by printed news. Opinion is noticeably a parody of the figurative image of Justice and is watered by a fool. The message is clear: all that comes of this is confusion and a world turned upside down.

Indeed, in 1641 the Stationers' Company based in the City of London (which remains to this day the guild for journalists) petitioned Parliament to clamp down on an unruly press characterised by the emergence of these new and disruptive voices.[3]

If printing in England be not under good rule and government every libelling speritt will have libertie to traduce the proceedings of the state, every malicious spirit may then revile whomsoever he pleaseth to accompt his adversary, yea every pernicitious hereticke may have opportunity to poyson the minds of good mynded men of wicked errors and deplorable distractions which at this present doe soe much blemish and offend the glorious light of the reformed Religion hapily established amongst us.[4]

Within a year there was civil war in England.

THE WORLD IS RVLED & GOVERNED by OPINION.

Viator	Who art thou Ladie that aloft art set	*Viator.*	Cannot OPINION remedie the same.
	In state Maiestique this faire spredding	*Opinio*	Ah no then should I perish in the throng
	Vpon thine head a Towre-like Coronet,		Oth giddie Vulgar, without feare or shame
	The Worldes whole Compasse, resting on thy knee.		Who censure all thinges, bee they right or wrong
Opinio	I am OPINION who the world do swaie	*Viator*	But Ladie deare, whence came at first this fruite
	Wherefore, I beare it, on my head that Towr		Or why doth WISEDOME suffer it to grow
	Is BABELS: meaning my confused waie		And what's the reason its farre reaching roote
	The Tree so shaken, my vnsetled Bowre.		Is water'd by a sillie Foole below
Viator	What meaneth that Chameleon on thy fist	*Opinio*	Because that FOLLIE giveth life to these
	That can assume all Cullors saving white.		I but retaile the fruites of idle Aire
Opinio	OPINION thus can everie waie shee list,		Sith now all Humors utter what they please
	Transforme her self, save into TRVTH, the right		Toth loathing loading of each Mart and Faire.
Viator	And Ladie what's the Fruite, which from thy Tree	*Viator*	And why those saplings from the roote that rise
	Is shaken of with everie little wind		In such abundance of OPINIONS tree
	Like Bookes and papers this amuseth mee	*Opinio*	Cause one Opinion many doth devise
	Beside thou seemest (veiled) to bee blind		And propagate, till infinite they bee
Opinio	Tis true I cannot as cleare IVDGMENTS see	*Viator*	Adieu sweete Ladie till againe wee meete
	Through self CONCEIT and haughtie PRIDE,	*Opinio*	But when shall that againe bee, *Viator.* Ladie saie
	The fruite those idle bookes and libells bee	*Opinio*	Opinion's found in everie house and streete
	In everie streete, on everie stall you find		And going ever, never in her waie.

VIRO CLA.ᵐᵒ Dᵒ FRANCISCO PRVIEANO D: MEDICO, OMNIVM BONARVM AR:
tium et Elegantiarum, Fautori et Admiratori summo. D.D.D.   *Henricus Peachamus.*

Wenceslaus Hollar,
*The World is Ruled &
Governed by Opinion*
(London,1642). Satirical
broadside with verses
by Henry Peacham.
Opinion sits in a tree with
contrary pamphlets and
broadsides, anticipating
the divisions of the
English Civil War.

So, while we may baulk in the modern era at phone hacking and other such unethical practices and the need to regulate the misbehaviour of the press, Lord Leveson's inquiry in 2011 was in this sense a continuation of an age-old public debate about how we regard the behaviour of those news-makers who seek to inform us and what should be allowed to pass for public discourse: a debate, as we see, that can be traced back to the English Civil War.

THE FLYING SERPENT OF ESSEX (1669)

Of course, the debates were not always about politics and the stories were not necessarily guided by what we might now consider facts. A rather quaint, fantastical, almost mythical storybook encounter with *The Flying Serpent of Essex* (1669) – a sea-bound, dragon-like creature with extravagant gills, which was depicted along with the narrative text – demonstrates how news was afforded a very different meaning at the time: more about what was believable than what was observable fact.

People were still deeply superstitious, and the concepts of science and scientific understanding of life were deeply disputed. In the 1690s the overwhelming mass of information that circulated did so by word of mouth, and most people were not yet willing or able to challenge the veracity of mythology and folklore. There is scant regard for any evidence that the event was real or that anyone actually witnessed it. It is a reminder that when we look back across the centuries to understand news-making, we need to bear in mind the psychological, social and intellectual context in which these artefacts were being created. Let us not forget that some two centuries later the natural scientist Charles Darwin (1809–1882) had to fight a rearguard action against his book *The Origin of the Species* (1859) being judged heretical.

We need to bear in mind the psychological, social and intellectual context in which these artefacts were being created.

THE MARY TOFT HOAX (1726)

It is difficult to pinpoint precisely when the new and radical ideas of science and rationalism began to infiltrate the culture of news-making, or at least when the audience was willing to exercise scepticism and challenge the written word. One story that illustrates that readers were becoming unwilling to be taken for fools, even when a tall story gripped the

This case reflects the power of the press to present a tall story and for others to openly ridicule those who are credulous enough to believe it.

news-makers and public imagination, is the hoax surrounding the story of Mary Toft (*c.* 1701–1763).

Of course, hoaxes did not begin and end with Mary Toft, but in an age of enlightenment they began to risk shredding the reputations of respected men if they spread what were, empirically speaking, disprovable events. This case reflects the power of the press to present a tall story and for others to openly challenge it in other parts of the press, and even openly ridicule those who are credulous enough to believe the tall story in the first place. A concern for being truthful motivated the challengers; the ability to use truth to call out hoaxers is an issue we are still wrestling with.

To the modern eye, the story of Mary Toft looks faintly ridiculous, with the suggestion that a young pregnant woman from Godalming in Surrey had given birth to a litter of rabbits. The case became a sensation and was widely recirculated by newspapers and pamphlets. Toft was attended by at least six different doctors, including some members of the Royal College of Physicians, none of whom seemed to suspect Mary's story as a hoax.

From Guildford comes a strange, but well attested piece of News. That a poor woman who lives at Godalmin, near that town, who has a husband and two children now living with her; was, about a month past, delivered by Mr John Howard, an eminent surgeon and man-midwife living at Guildford, of a creature resembling a rabbit.[5]

In the early eighteenth century, midwifery was still largely outside the realm of medical practitioners. The practical work of assisting with the delivery of a baby lay with older women instead. These circumstances perhaps helped foster the hoax. It did not take long for pamphleteers such as Daniel Defoe (*c.* 1660–1731) and William Hogarth (1697–1764) to wade into the public conversation, heaping scorn on the physicians who appeared reluctant to call out the hoax, until Mary Toft herself confessed to it.

Although obviously dissimilar in character, in the sense that the alleged perpetrator always denied it, *The Sun*'s headline 'Freddie Starr Ate My Hamster' (13 March 1986) has something of the Mary Toft about it. In the comedian's view, the hoax came to overshadow a career as a public entertainer because so many people seemed to give the story credence. Many years after the alleged rodent

Mary Tofts [sic] *of Godelman the pretended Rabbit Breeder* (c.1726). Print of Mary Toft, who claimed to have given birth to rabbits.

lunch, the publicist Max Clifford (1943–2017) confessed that he encouraged the false story in a bid to raise publicity ahead of a new show for his client Freddie Starr (1943–2019). But it goes to show how a hoax only needs a grain of credibility to get traction if it can garner publicity.

THE PROTOCOLS OF THE ELDERS OF ZION (1903)

More sophisticated subjects of mythology and prejudice have on occasion been woven into a complex conspiratorial narrative. The willingness of readers to believe such a conspiracy can probably be accounted for by the psychological disposition we described earlier as confirmation bias, where readers are disposed to believe something if it confirms their own beliefs, however steeped they may be in ignorance or prejudice.

At the end of the nineteenth century a wave of anti-Semitism swept Europe, and the language and sentiment presented in arguments by the Zionist Theodor Herzl (1860–1904), who in his work *Der Judenstaat* (*The Jewish State*, 1896) outlined his case for a Jewish state, were distorted to make a case against the Jewish people. At the time Herzl's book was published, Alfred Dreyfus (1859–1935), a French Jewish military officer, was being accused of spying for the Germans.[6] This contributed to an outpouring of anti-Semitic prejudice across France. A number of anti-Semitic texts began to circulate, including what was initially passed off as a genuine Jewish text, *The Protocols of the Elders of Zion* (1903). This entirely fictional work purports to reveal a secret plan by the so called 'Elders of Zion' to achieve Jewish global domination.

The European and American press – both anti-Semitic and gullible – treated the work as an authentic tract. Indeed, it needed considerable effort to prove it was a fraud. It was finally exposed in 1921 by *The Times*, but not before the industrialist Henry Ford (1863–1947) had printed half a million copies for circulation and the respected journalist Carl W. Ackerman (1890–1970) had serialised his take on it in the *Public Ledger*.[7] Despite it being publicly evidenced as a hoax, it remains a potent conspiracy theory that still finds followers through digital distribution in parts of the Middle East and in extreme-right anti-Semitic circles.

The author Daniel Pipes describes the enduring power of this hoax:

> *The great importance of* The Protocols *lies in its permitting anti-Semites to reach beyond their traditional circles and find a large international audience, a process that continues to this day. The forgery poisoned public life wherever it appeared; it was self-generating; a blueprint that migrated from one conspiracy to another.*[8]

The propensity for readers to succumb to confirmation bias throws into sharp focus the need for news-makers to be subject to scrutiny.

The propensity for readers to succumb to confirmation bias, most grievously evidenced by outlandish conspiracy theories, throws into sharp focus the need for news-makers to be subject to scrutiny and for the press to have and uphold standards that are transparent and a basis for accountability. Of course, no honest publication would now entertain circulating *The Protocols of the Elders of Zion*, but as the internet repeatedly reminds us, other purveyors of untruths are not so scrupulous, and this and other conspiracies that circulate there can and will continue to do great harm.

PHOTOGRAPHING THE PRESIDENTIAL INAUGURATION (2017)

We might like to think of ourselves as more discriminating users of the news-makers' outpourings than our predecessors, but the urge to control the media narrative and tell the story in a way that the facts might belie remains an instinct that many cannot resist. Dispensing with conspiracy, hoax, myth and the cacophony of competing opinions still leaves us with spin.

President Barack Obama's (born 1961) inauguration in 2009 was as seminal a moment in US presidential history as President Trump's was controversial. Donald Trump (born 1946) had not won the popular vote in November 2016, but gained a healthy margin in the electoral college. Hillary Clinton (born 1947) polled several million votes more. So the election result remained a matter of intense media debate right up to the inauguration ceremony in January 2017 to swear in the 45th President of the United States. There was widespread speculation in the media that this would lead to an unpopular presidency. The first popularity test was to see how many people would make the effort to come to Washington to see the presidential swearing in.

Reuters dispatched the photographer Lucas Jackson to the top of the Washington monument to take an image looking down the National Mall. The same vantage point had been used for Obama's inauguration. Two images placed side by side, taken eight years apart at the moment of the presidential pledge to uphold the Constitution, show substantially different numbers of people in attendance. This juxtaposition of the two photos in the press the morning after the inauguration became the first media controversy of the Trump presidency. His detractors pointed to an absence of numbers; the White House spokesperson Sean Spicer (born 1971) confirmed the President's view, expressed in a Tweet, that it was the largest turnout ever.

The urge to control the media narrative remains an instinct that many cannot resist.

Spicer illustrated his point with false figures and doctored photographs. On 22 January 2017, during the NBC programme *Meet the Press*, Kellyanne Conway (then a counsellor to Trump) defended the president's press secretary and said in Spicer's defence that he was using 'alternative facts'. President Trump characterised the use of Jackson's photograph as an example of 'fake news', pointing out that many more people had followed the proceedings by livestreaming the event. Looking

Contrasting photographs of crowds at the inauguration ceremonies of Presidents Barack Obama in 2009 (left) and Donald Trump in 2017.

back across the four years of the Trump presidency, this can be seen as the start of a shift towards public officials actively sowing seeds of doubt in the minds of citizens that news-makers and their stories lacked veracity, and that news-makers were not trustworthy.

The stories discussed here are an important reminder of why news-makers need rules and ethical guidelines. Without these, prejudice and the psychological disposition towards bias can infect both the news-maker and the consumer. Thus begins the perilous journey towards misinformation and untruth. Facts are the foundation of robust journalism and allow that journalism to be tested. Allowing something other than facts to dictate the course of journalistic narrative leads in a different direction: towards propaganda, delusion and even conspiracy theories.

Rachel Beer

Profile by Beth Gaskell

Rachel Beer (1858–1927) was the first British woman to edit a national daily newspaper, working on *The Sunday Times* from 1894 to 1901, and *The Observer* from 1896 to 1901. Until recently Beer had been largely forgotten, appearing as only a footnote in the history of the British press.

Beer was a descendant of a prominent Jewish family, the Sassoons, who had held positions of authority in Iraq, and who later made a fortune trading opium from India to China. Her father settled in London, bringing his young family to join him. Rachel was afforded a liberal education, developing forward-thinking ideas about female education and employment. She worked for a time as a nurse, before marrying Frederick Beer in 1887, a love match that led Rachel's family to disown her as Beer, though of Jewish heritage, had been baptised into the Anglican faith.

The Beer family had owned *The Observer* since 1870, and Frederick gained sole ownership of the publication upon his father's death. Early in their marriage Rachel showed an interest in working on the newspaper, which Frederick encouraged, but her input was poorly received by the staff. As an alternative Frederick purchased *The Sunday Times* on her behalf, and she served as owner/editor for nearly a decade. When Frederick's health deteriorated, she also took over his editorship at *The Observer*.

Rachel's tenure on both newspapers was characterised by a progressive approach, and she championed workers' rights, female suffrage, political accountability and cheap international communications. One of her crowning achievements was a scoop for *The Observer*, with a confession proving that Captain Alfred Dreyfus, the only Jewish officer serving on the French military general staff, had been falsely prosecuted for treason by the French military authorities.

Frederick Beer died in 1901. Rachel suffered a breakdown shortly after, withdrawing from her social and journalistic duties. Her family intervened and she was certified as of 'unsound mind', judged unfit to manage her own affairs. By 1905 both newspapers had been sold, and Rachel Beer's death in 1927 was barely acknowledged by either publication. In 2020 *The Observer* and *The Sunday Times* paid for the restoration of Beer's grave and for a new grave marker that recognised her pioneering role as a female journalist, editor and newspaper proprietor.

Black Lives Matter: The fight for identity in the media

It is impossible to understand the Black Lives Matter movement and the media representation of it without understanding the power of language and the use of slogans in Black empowerment. To understand this the linguistic evolution, symbolism and subsequent mediation of the phrase 'Black Lives Matter' is revealing.

Activist Alicia Garza (born 1981) was awaiting the outcome of a widely followed court case in Los Angeles. A year earlier, Trayvon Martin (1995–2012), a seventeen-year-old, had been fatally shot by George Zimmerman (born 1983) when he was returning home from the shops with a bag of sweets. Zimmerman claimed he looked suspicious. When the jury returned its verdict of not guilty on 13 July 2013, there was disbelief, anger and frustration. Garza would write on her Facebook page what she called a 'Love letter to Black people':

Btw stop saying we are not surprised. that's a damn shame in itself. I continue to be surprised at how little Black lives matter. And I will continue that. stop giving up on black life.
black people, I will NEVER give up on us. NEVER.

Garza ended her letter with, 'Black people. I love you. I love us. Our lives matter.' Some 300 miles away in a motel in Susanville, Patrisse Cullors (born 1983), also an activist, read the Facebook postings. Cullors knew Garza from previous work in 2005 and exclaimed, pointing to three words on the screen, 'That's it'. She placed a hashtag in front of the words, much to Garza's bemusement, and feverishly started reposting the phrase on her own Facebook account. Some days later Opal Tometi (born 1984), a friend of Garza, known as a 'dedicated organiser', was called up to take the lead in creating the infrastructure around a website, and Facebook, Tumblr and Twitter accounts for a new movement.[1] The phrase Black Lives Matter (BLM) was born.

Today, as detailed by copious texts, conversations and scholars, BLM is, among many things, a global human rights movement, a totem offline and a meme online. It seeks to draw attention to systematic racism, police militarisation and brutality, mass incarceration and funding for community schemes. Its platform has become a greater collective shared consciousness between Black, brown and white people on the issue of race and power that has so divided the United States and other parts of the world. 'I live in a white suburban neighbourhood,' Eugene Robinson, a Pulitzer Prize-winning journalist told me, 'and there are Black Lives Matter signs everywhere. I have never seen that before.'[2] How could three words do that?

A cardboard photo-realistic figure of Trayvon Martin at a crowd gathered to protest his case in Union Square, Manhattan, 14 July 2013.

WE ARE ALL TRAYVON MARTIN

The news helps us make sense of the world by its narratives, configured from news values, such as events that elicit surprise or involve elite persons, and how the story is relevant to an audience. However, as James Curran and Jean Seaton note, 'the overall interpretation they [news] provide in the long run are those which are most preferred by, and least challenging to, those with economic power'.[3] The constraints and forces from state institutions, such as the police, politicians and the media, work to maintain a power order within societies. This is the ecosystem BLM occupies.

The constraints and forces from state institutions work to maintain a power order within societies.

SYMBOLISM

To historians and students of Black or African American studies, BLM embodies various signifiers drawn from a kaleidoscope of past movements, particularly in the 1950s and 1960s. They include Martin Luther King's (1929–1968) civil rights campaign, crystallised in its manifesto to end white supremacy and provide rights and economic empowerment to Black people. King's aspiration, endowed by those indomitable words 'I have a dream', is widely recognised as an exemplar of the power of language.[4]

In the 1960s, the phrase 'Black Power' emerged to symbolise a different theme from those espoused by King. Its first popular use was by Stokely Carmichael (Kwame Ture, 1941–1998) in response to the shooting of James Meredith (born 1933) during the 'March Against Fear' from Memphis to Jackson. Carmichael said:

> It is a call for black people in this country to unite, to recognize their heritage, to build a sense of community. It is a call for black people to define their own goals, to lead their own organizations.

The message found many advocates, such as the Black Panthers' founders Huey Newton (1942–1989) and Bobby Seale (born 1936) who, unlike Carmichael, were not in favour of Black separatism. Their appearance emphasised black leathers, berets and an open display of weapons. Behind this popular image was an organisation in which women played a prominent role, particularly in the Panthers' social programmes. Women's roles hitherto may have been overlooked, but it is no accident that BLM was conceived by three women.[5]

It was the Panthers' clenched-fist gesture – a strong visual image – that, captured by the media, caused disquiet among swathes of white suburban America. The FBI, under its director J. Edgar Hoover's (1895–1972) COINTELPRO programme, claimed the Panthers were a national threat. Almost sixty years later, explicit language would be used to frame BLM co-founder Patrisse Khan-Cullors when she was labelled a terrorist by commentators including Fox News' Bill O'Reilly (born 1949). She would seek counsel from many, including former Panthers member Angela Davis (born 1944).[6]

For Malcolm X (born Malcolm Little, 1925–1965), combating racism would be achieved 'by any means necessary' because alternative means for demanding what were the rights of Black and brown people were slow in progress. The daughter of Malcolm X, Ilyasah Shabazz (born 1962), likened the Black Lives Matter movement to the present generation of young people, whom she saw as 'much like' her father in being '"sick and tired" of racism'. Black power, she explains, isn't exclusionary: 'It's rooted in the understanding that freedom is total and no one should be left out. None of us are free until all of us are free.'[7] The Black Power scholar Peniel Joseph draws a nuanced analysis of how the visions of Malcolm X and Martin Luther King converge in BLM. He achieves this by considering what BLM are protesting, which is the twin ideal of radical Black dignity *and* citizenship. Dr Joseph says radical Black dignity examines structural racism, inequality and tackling white supremacy and its institutions – a core focus of Malcolm X. Citizenship of the kind King advocated focused on transforming democratic institutions, seeking the provision of universal income, healthcare and education.[8]

The 1960s was the era of the alliterative phrase 'Black is beautiful'. This movement sought to undo colourism, retire the word 'negro' and tackle supremacist ideologies that slated Black as ugly or threatening – something in which the media was complicit. For example, in films such as *Birth of a Nation* (1915) and *Gone with the Wind* (1939) the overweight mammy figure is depicted. Blackface and watermelon lips cartoons appeared in animations

For Malcolm X, combating racism would be achieved 'by any means necessary'.

Blackface and watermelon lips cartoons appeared in animations by Looney Tunes, Walt Disney and RKO Radio Pictures.

by Looney Tunes, Walt Disney and RKO Radio Pictures. In the cartoon sections of a number of newspapers can be found derogatory images of Black people. For example, Asbestos was a Black stablehand, a sidekick in a popular horse-betting comic strip, 'Joe and Asbestos' (originally called 'Joe Quince'). Asbestos's facial features are baboonish, with a white watermelon smile. The strip ran from 1923/4 to 1926 and then from 1932 in the *New York Daily Mirror* and later the *New York Daily News*.[9]

'In my neighbourhood, calling someone "black" was an insult, often the trigger to a fight,' writes Harvard law professor Randall Kennedy (born 1954). And what of the impact of the media reporting Black issues, particularly in the Southern United States in the 1960s? The journalist Mark I. Pinsky uncovered contrition among newspapers. Some sixty years on, he writes, some white-owned newspapers admit to siding with white supremacists in their racist coverage and now apologise for the harm this brought Black people.[10]

'Say it loud, I'm black and I'm proud,' sang the 'Godfather of Soul' James Brown (1933–2006) in the 1960s, in a bid to unify Black Americans and eliminate the constructed stigma of being Black. It garnered much support. Soon afterwards a new descriptor would emerge to situate Black Americans in relation to their roots: 'African American'. In creating BLM, co-founder Khan-Cullors states that there was an intentionality in the use of the word 'Black'. The movement was designed for all Black people and the marginalised, such as Palestinians, not just African Americans. 'African American Lives Matter' also sounded less memorable and powerful. Khan-Cullors writes that there were people she was close to who thought the term 'Black' 'too radical to use'.[11]

Collectively, BLM draws from a spectrum of influences – too many to name, but each has become known for their agency and power of language to address a problematic system. They include Ella Baker (who inspired the Student Nonviolent Coordinating Committee), Angela Davis, Harriet Tubman, James Baldwin,

W.E.B. Du Bois and Ida B. Wells. Fundamentally, unlike previous movements, in BLM three Black women are at the helm. There have been key women in leadership roles, such as Ella Baker (1903–1986), and Shirley Chisholm (1924–2005), who ran for US president, but in BLM, three Black feminists, two of whom (Cullors and Garza) identify as queer, challenged the trope of masculinity and movements.

BLACK LIVES MATTER: 2020, A PIVOTAL YEAR

BLM is a continuum of a heritage of anti-Black racism, resistance and liberation. Its implicit power is derived from history, yet its current status resides in the here and now. In the 1960s, attracting media with their film equipment to a news event was a logistical challenge. Today this has been supplanted by the immediacy of a mobile phone and a hashtag. To some extent this has challenged mainstream media's dominance in news coverage and shaping views.[12]

Whereas 2013 was the catalyst for BLM's formation, a year later the fatal shooting of eighteen-year-old Michael Brown (1996–2014) in the city of Ferguson by white police officer Darren Wilson (born 1986) yielded renewed media and social media focus. Brown's death caused deep and widespread anger. His body lay on the road for four and a half hours before it was removed. BLM took up this injustice on the streets and gained wide traction in the press. The use of its hashtag proved pivotal. It first gained a presence on Twitter in the second half of 2013, used around thirty times a day. Following the case of Michael Brown its use soared to an average 58,747 times per day three weeks after his death. In November 2014, when a grand jury dismissed an indictment of the police officer involved in Brown's death, the #BlackLivesMatter hashtag dramatically spiked, featuring 1.7 million times in three weeks. There were other peaks before and after Brown, for example around the death of Eric Garner (whose dying words, 'I can't breathe,' after being put in a chokehold by New York police, have become a powerful slogan) in 2014, but the potency of the hashtag for spreading news globally was yet to be realised. Paradoxically, traditional media coverage from major news sources was perceived to diminish, enough that Angela Davis would reference BLM in a London Southbank Centre talk as 'short-lived'.[13]

BLM is a continuum of a heritage of anti-Black racism, resistance and liberation.

And then came 2020. On 25 May, eight minutes and forty-six seconds turned humanity around. That was the time for which police officer Derek Chauvin (born 1976) held his knee on the neck of George Floyd (1973–2020). Floyd's death was traumatic and visceral, recorded unfiltered on mobile phone footage. Following the posting online of that video, approximately 218,000 tweets with the #BlackLivesMatter hashtag were used the day after his death. Two days later, with protests spreading out from Minneapolis, across the US and the world, that figure rose past one million. According to the Pew Center, the following day, almost 8.8 million tweets containing the #BlackLivesMatter hashtag were recorded. This was the highest number used for the Black Lives Matter hashtag in a single day since the Center started its tracking research.[14]

Floyd's death came on the heels of a list of Black people dying at the hands of police. That list is long and includes Philando Castile (1983–2016); Breonna Taylor (died 2020), shot in her home by a police officer; and Ahmaud Arbery (died 2020), gunned down by a father and son when he was out jogging. Then came the shocking shooting of Jacob S. Blake (born 1991) in Wisconsin by law enforcers, seven times at close range.[15]

In 2020 BLM became colossal. Placards were carried by millions of protestors, and the number of demonstrators was estimated between 15 and 26 million across all fifty US states, as well as 2,000 other cities in sixty countries. In Washington, DC its insignia, fifty feet tall, adorned the streets. Art critic Roger Storr called it one of the most significant pieces of public art.[16] Words as typography had assumed the power as stimulus, to be explicit as well as conceptual. BLM's surge came, too, during a period like no other in contemporary history: the COVID-19 pandemic, a deadly disease which disproportionately affected Black people and those with pre-existing conditions.

The powerful images and the language used in the nightly news invariably appeared skewed to violence and protestors clashing with militarised police, when studies showed 90 per cent of the protests were peaceful. Reflecting in her memoir, Khan-Cullors says of a peaceful march in Oakland in 2013 associated with Trayvon Martin's acquittal that the police set upon the marchers. The media ignored this: 'Instead they focus on the one or two who are not peaceful, and they wholly ignore law enforcement, who attack everyone.' Is it time the media changed the way it reported protests? asked a Nieman Lab report in 2020.[17]

Against the backdrop of BLM's growth emerged an insidious development, a call for 'All Lives Matter' which became visible in 2016 and increasingly prominent in 2020. Whether stirred by anti-BLM supporters or those who plead ignorance to the distress it causes anti-racists, as Garza explained in a video interview, 'When we say All Lives Matter, that's a given. Of course, we're all human beings – we all bleed red – but the fact of the matter is some human lives are valued more than others, and that's a problem.'[18]

Against the backdrop of BLM's growth emerged an insidious development, a call for 'All Lives Matter'.

Black Lives Matter has never claimed all life does not matter. That's implicit. History, however, has shown how comparatively less regard is given to Black lives.

BLACK LIVES MATTER UK

The revulsion arising from Floyd's death started a chain reaction of worldwide protests. In Britain mass gatherings and marches took place in around 150 locations. Critics questioned the relevance in

> '*Black Lives Matter has transformed debates about race more profoundly than any phenomenon I have known in my lifetime.*'
>
> David Olusoga

a country that bore no resemblance to the United States, while advocates reflexively pointed to British racism, media power and language that was prejudicial, as well as a catalogue of police brutality. Champa Patel of the think tank Chatham House warned that Britain 'should not feel complacent about institutional discrimination'.[19]

Significantly, racism and the heightened awareness of Black Lives Matter yielded multiple conversations, not all unified in support, but enough to focus attention on many related grievances. Take the television industry, for instance, whose primary commodity is visual representations, language and the crafting of narratives. Its culpability and lack of introspection, as it reports on other institutions' shortcomings, can easily go unnoticed. The historian David Olusoga (born 1970) placed television under the lens in a powerfully worded speech delivered in 2020. Olusoga argued:

Black Lives Matter has transformed debates about race more profoundly than any phenomenon I have known in my lifetime ... Among the ideas the movement has forced into public consciousness is that the work of confronting racism and racial injustice is not the task of black and brown people alone.

By this the historian was referring to, among others, institutions, society, its leader and the media. On the latter, Olusoga said that in his twenty years in television he had had amazing opportunities and been in high demand, but also been patronised and marginalised:

But at other times I've been so crushed by my experiences, so isolated and disempowered by the culture that exists within our industry, that I have had to seek medical treatment for clinical depression. I've come close to leaving this industry on several occasions. And I know many black and brown people who have similar stories to tell.[20]

In a 1970s ground-breaking community programme its producers observed another theme. *It Ain't Half Racist, Mum* saw cultural theorist Stuart Hall (1932–2014) and Maggie Steed (born 1946) decoding the language of television, including BBC news and current affairs programming. They found language that was at times insidious and skewed against Black and brown people. Many in broadcasting dismissed this, taking Hall's conclusion as a personal attack.[21]

Newspapers too have been found wanting. The footballer Raheem Sterling (born 1994) has been the target of racism, negative coverage and gaslighting from the press. On Instagram in 2018 he accused the press of being the ones who 'fuel racism' and 'aggressive behaviour'. His feed featured two *Daily Mail* headlines. One read: 'Young Manchester City footballer, 20, on £25,000 a week splashes out on mansion on market for £2.25 million despite having never started a Premier League match.' The other: 'Manchester City starlet Phil Foden buys new £2million home for his mum.' Tosin Adarabioyo (of Nigerian descent) and Foden were teammates. Sterling spelt out what separated them: 'I think this is unacceptable, both [are] innocent and have done nothing wrong but just by the way it is worded this young black player is looked at in a bad light which helps fuel racism and aggressive behaviour.' Football pundits such as Henry Winter of *The Times* sided with Sterling.[22]

Raheem Sterling, Instagram feed, 6 December 2018. Manchester City footballer Raheem Sterling's angry response on Instagram to a MailOnline story about colleague Tosin Adarabioyo.

Criticisms levelled at BLM's movement include its lack of leadership, clarity and coherency of

Daily **Mail**   MORE STORIES

Young Manchester City footballer, 20, on £25,000 a week splashes out on mansion on market for £2.25million despite having never started a Premier League match

By Anthony Joseph for MailOnline
08:48 10 Jan 2018, updated 10:51 11 Jan 2018

sterling7 ● • Follow

sterling7 ● Good morning I just want to say , I am not normally the person to talk a lot but when I think I need my point to heard I will speak up. Regarding what was said at the Chelsea game as you can see by my reaction I just had to laugh because I don't expect no better. For example you have two young players starting out there careers both play for the same team, both have done the right thing. Which is buy a new house for there mothers who have put in a lot of time and love into helping them get where they are, but look how the news papers get there message across for the young black player and then for the young white payer. I think this in unacceptable both innocent have not done a thing wrong but just by the way it has been worded. This young black

636,420 likes
DECEMBER 9, 2018

Log in to like or comment.

aims, while a UK Conservative politician, Tom Hunt (born 1988), took aim at its politics. The MP for Ipswich accused BLM of being a Marxist organisation fomenting militant race messages. Sajid Javid (born 1969), a former chancellor of the exchequer, called them 'neo-Marxists'. Another attack on BLM involved the environment secretary George Eustice (born 1971) commenting on a Millwall vs Derby football match in which players were booed for taking the knee – a practice the Football Association has adopted since Floyd's death. While Eustice said that he took racism very seriously, he refused to condemn the booing, stating:

Black Lives Matter, capital B, L and M, is actually a political movement that is different to what most of us believe in, which is standing up for racial equality. Each individual can take their own choices about how they reflect this. I know a number of people feel quite strongly and have taken that approach.[23]

BLM has invariably seen itself as a social movement. In the US an independent agency, the Office of Special Counsel, provided clarity to government employees fearful of violating the Hatch Act, which restricts them from supporting political organisations. According to the Special Counsel, whose head was appointed by President Donald Trump, supporting BLM was not tantamount to 'inherently political activity' and it was not 'a partisan political group'.[24]

BLM's core feature of being decentralised and the presence of several anti-racist activist groups aligned with, but not part of BLM, such as Black Lives Matter UK, sow confusion. Black Lives Matter UK gave its first interview to Channel 4 News, defending the £1 million in funding it had acquired from supporters, and its alleged lack of transparency. Whatever power BLM had to further its cause would be short lived, doomed to failure, critics chimed. Garza disputes all these claims and argues against the need for a leader 'who tells the masses where to go, rather than the masses understanding that we can catalyse a movement in our own community'.[25]

Three news snapshots. On their way home, British athletes Bianca Williams (born 1993) and Ricardo dos Santos (born 1994) are stopped and pulled out of their car to be handcuffed by police. Their three-month-old son lies in the back seat. A police officer is seen on social media detaining a man by pressing his knee on the suspect's neck. In

> *'Black Lives Matter, capital B, L and M, is actually a political movement that is different to what most of us believe in, which is standing up for racial equality.'*
>
> George Eustice

Hyde Park, Hollywood movie star John Boyega (born 1992) takes a megaphone and, unscripted, passionately addresses a crowd protesting at the death of George Floyd, exhorting them to seize the moment, while wondering whether he will have a career afterwards. In Bristol a statue of Edward Colston (1636–1721), a slave owner, whose continuing public presence had become the source of much disquiet over several years, is toppled.[26]

The psychologist and best-selling author John Amaechi (born 1970) says, 'Hope is a backpack too heavy to carry,' citing the false dawn when he was living in the US in the aftermath of the beating of Rodney King in 1991. But BLM feels different to other movements, according to Garza, who says that this time people are fed up.[27] More than fifty years ago Angela Davis, then a member of the Black Panthers, may have had similar thoughts. On Channel 4 News she concluded:

What we are seeing now are new demands: demands to demilitarize the police, demands to defund the police, demands to dismantle the police and envision different modes of public safety. We're asked now to consider how we might imagine justice in the future … This is a very exciting moment. I don't know if we have ever experienced this kind of global challenge to racism and to the consequences of slavery and colonialism.[28]

> *When historians look back on 2020, BLM should undoubtedly feature prominently.*

When historians look back on 2020, BLM should undoubtedly feature prominently. Since George Floyd's death, the protests and reinvigorated public debate over race and culture point to a resurgence in initiatives, in spite of a rise in nationalism. This does feel different. Meanwhile BLM's founders are developing a raft of new social and policy platforms.[29] The fight for equality which threads through history is enduring and has adapted to address the challenges ahead.

Doreen Lawrence

Profile by Beth Gaskell

Doreen Lawrence (born 1952) is the mother of teenager Stephen Lawrence (1974–1993), who was murdered in a racially motivated attack. After Stephen's death, Doreen Lawrence became a campaigner for police reform and racial equality.

Stephen Lawrence was murdered while waiting for a bus in south-east London on the night of 22 April 1993. It took nearly twenty years for some of those guilty of the murder to be successfully prosecuted, with two of the five suspects receiving custodial sentences in January 2012. The murder investigation conducted by the Metropolitan Police came under intense scrutiny, with questions about its handling raised by Lawrence's parents and taken up by the British press. This resulted in a number of investigations both into the case itself, and into the Metropolitan Police more generally, which exposed institutional racism and corruption.

Stephen's death threw Doreen Lawrence into the spotlight, and she used her position not only to fight for justice for her son, and to challenge the police's conduct of the investigation, but also to campaign for police reform in matters of race relations, and racial equality more generally. She became a media figurehead, actively soliciting media interest in the case, and giving interviews and briefings to a wide range of news outlets. Notably, the *Daily Mail* took up the campaign for justice. Doreen Lawrence also engaged with the media in a much wider range of ways: she and Stephen's father gave the Channel 4 Christmas Day address in 1999; she has spoken on the daytime TV chat show *Loose Women*; she has written a book about her experiences, and has been a guest on BBC Radio 4's *Desert Island Discs*. She was a flag-carrier for the 2012 Olympic Games opening ceremony. All of this has kept her campaigning work in the spotlight. By her presence and principles, she has had a profound influence on policing and media reporting.

In 2003 Doreen Lawrence was awarded an OBE for her services to community relations, and in 2013 she was elevated to a life peerage as Baroness Lawrence of Clarendon.

Luke McKernan

Truth, trust and story

There was a boy on the hospital floor. Jack Williment-Barr, aged four, had been rushed to Leeds General Infirmary on 3 December 2019, with suspected pneumonia. Initially he had been given a bed in the paediatric emergency department, but an emergency case had come in, so for over four hours Jack was placed on the floor in a clinical treatment room, with an oxygen mask and a pile of coats for comfort. His mother took a photograph and, after her son had left the hospital, sent it to the *Yorkshire Evening Post*. An incident became a story.

The story was established by the journalist Daniel Sheridan. He took care to verify the facts, obtaining a statement from the hospital, which confirmed that the family had been given an apology.[1] His report, with the photograph, appeared on the website of the *Yorkshire Evening Post*, five days after the incident, at 11.52 on Sunday 8 December, and in the print edition the following day. The photograph told it all: the headline of the online article read, '"It was chaos": Shocking photo shows Leeds four-year-old with suspected pneumonia forced to sleep on floor of LGI due to lack of beds.' The print version splashed the photograph over most of its front page, with the headline 'How could this be allowed to happen?'[2]

It was general election time in the UK. Taking place shortly before election day on 12 December, the story brought together funding of the National Health Service (NHS), the familiar trope of someone left in a hospital without a bed and the pathetic figure of a child. It was a potent combination, all bound up in one photograph. The national news media swiftly picked up on the story, with the *Daily Mirror* (a newspaper opposed to the Conservative government) leading with the same photograph, the headline 'Desperate' and the accompanying words 'Picture that shames the Tories'.[3]

The evening television news bulletins all led with it, by which point the story had evolved into how the government was responding. Prime minister Boris Johnson (born 1964), on a visit to Grimsby, was shown being confronted by ITV journalist Joe Pike, who held up his phone and asked, 'How do you feel looking at that photo?' Johnson, unbriefed and caught off his guard, originally refused to look at the photograph. He then agreed that it was a distressing image. He absent-mindedly pocketed the journalist's phone, before later returning it. Meanwhile, in the same broadcasts, opposition leader Jeremy Corbyn (born 1949) waved a copy of the *Mirror* front page for the cameras.[4]

The health secretary Matt Hancock (born 1978) was sent to Leeds General Infirmary the same day,

Labour leader Jeremy Corbyn in Bristol showing the *Daily Mirror* front page to television news cameras, 9 December 2019.

9 December. On leaving the hospital, he passed a vociferous group of Labour Party supporters. The political editors for the BBC and ITV, Laura Kuenssberg (born 1976) and Robert Peston (born 1960), neither of whom was present, reported swiftly on Twitter that scuffles had broken out and that someone had thrown a punch at Hancock's adviser ('whacked in the face as he tried to help Hancock into his car', as Peston colourfully put it). Both apologised for their reactions (and deleted the tweets) when video footage emerged that made it clear that no such scuffle had occurred.[5] Both were fiercely attacked in some quarters for their supposed support of the Conservative Party viewpoint.

The accusation of fakery turned it into a story about news truth.

The story took a further twist. A Facebook post was published that day from a woman, Sheree, who said she was a nurse and had a good friend who was a senior nursing sister at Leeds. She had been told that the mother of the boy had placed him on the floor solely for the purpose of taking a photograph, which she 'uploaded to media outlets' before he climbed back onto his trolley. She asked people to think of nurses and doctors instead of 'constantly slagging them off' and dismissed the story as 'Momentum Propaganda' (Momentum being a left-wing political group supportive of the Labour Party under Jeremy Corbyn).[6]

This accusation of fakery turned it into a story about news truth. Why should we believe this picture? Why should we be made to believe this picture? The Facebook post was widely shared, including by some Conservative MPs, prospective candidates and right-wing political commentators who welcomed such questioning.[7] It had not been verified anywhere, but for some a set-up was entirely credible, and just to query the photograph's provenance was a necessary means of fighting against the tone of the reporting. Copyist versions of the Facebook post appeared. The editor of *The Yorkshire Post*, James Mitchinson (born 1981), whose sister paper had uncovered the story, wrote on Twitter in dismay about a message from a long-standing reader who firmly believed the post and demanded that he published a retraction:

This is the net effect of the proliferation of absurdity by bots, saps & sock puppets. Someone who buys and trusts her newspaper. One that she has taken for years. One she can call or pop in to. One where the editor would be happy to meet her – discredited by a shoddy FB [Facebook] post.[8]

The story reached some sort of a conclusion on 10 December when *The Guardian* reported that the woman, Sheree, a medical secretary, on whose account the Facebook post appeared, denied that she was its author, asserting that her account had been hacked. 'I was hacked. I am not a nurse and I certainly don't know anyone in Leeds,' she said.[9] Mitchinson brought the matter to a close with a heartfelt open letter to readers, published on his newspaper's site the same day at 5.00 p.m. The greater part of it comprised his letter of reply to the loyal reader who had questioned the report.

You have no way of holding Sheree to account, nor checking her words. She's a stranger to you. You don't even know if it is a real person, so why do you trust her claim over the newspaper you've taken for years, in good faith? ... Sheree – robot or human – did not offer a credible source. The words a 'good friend of mine' adds warmth and humanity to the post in order to dupe others into believing her words are credible. They are not, as far as anyone can tell ... Whatever you do, do not believe a stranger on social media who disappears into the night.[10]

The story of the boy on the hospital floor was the product of the final days of a fevered general election campaign contested by two parties with very different views of the best direction for the country. In some ways it was quite trivial, the sort of story that tends to crop up in British elections once the health service becomes the topic – there are echoes of the controversy over claims made in a Labour Party election broadcast in 1992, the so-called 'War of Jennifer's Ear'.[11] Similar fleeting controversies have flared up in the past, where complex issues are reduced to the case of one individual and one particular point in time. Such stories tend only to be interesting for the heat that they generate, not the light.

But the 2019 story was rooted in the growing mistrust of 'mainstream' news reporting from those at either end of the political spectrum, the phenomenon of 'fake news' which had been turned by the Trump administration in the United States into a political weapon. News could be 'untrue' because it did not reflect the truths you recognised. Still deeper, the story was rooted in the uncertainties of an online world, where any claim might be held up to be true and any opinion could quickly find ardent supporters. This was not a story about a child or funding the NHS; it was one small battle in an ongoing war over news and truthfulness in an unstable digital world.

The boy on the hospital floor became a story about a news story and the conversation around it. Gossip has been the essential accompaniment to the published news, ever since the coffeehouses of Samuel Pepys's time were places as important for the discussion about the news as they were for reading news publications themselves.[12] News is only news if it spreads. However, what has become distinctive about the news process in the twenty-first century is

Twitter has changed the nature of news itself, by changing the news story and its relationship to truth.

A typical London coffee house of the 1690s, coffee-seller on the left, table with newspapers and newsletters on the right.

the intervention of social media, particularly Twitter, as news outlet, news source, commentary, critique and audience all in one. It has changed the nature of news itself, by changing the news story and its relationship to truth.

Twitter is an American social networking service, founded in 2006. It has risen to have more than 330 million monthly users worldwide, with more than 16 million in the UK.[13] Initially conceived of as an online space for gossip, it limited its users to 140 characters per message (in standard script), raising this number to 280 in 2017. It has acquired huge influence over the world of news, partly because the roots of news lie in gossip, alongside the need to know commercial and political information, and because it has been adopted by an older demographic than other social media platforms, which includes news producers, commentators and news subjects (particularly politicians) themselves. To this mixture have been added lobbyists, agitators and ordinary people with something to say about what is being told – or not being told, or misleadingly told – about the world around them. All have a voice, all are equal (though those with more followers tend to be more equal than others). All are involved in the creation of the news.

Twitter circulates the news, and it is often the source of the news. It can be exciting to follow a breaking news story live on Twitter, such as an explosion or some such unexpected dramatic incident. The first uncertain eyewitness accounts and images appear, information (of uncertain degree of reliability) is offered, the first reporters arrive, facts are asserted and confusion reduced, and finally links are provided to formal accounts from professional news services, as all is explained. Stories published by the traditional news media that originate in a Twitter conversation have become standard; quoting tweets in anything from a leading news issue to a tribute is regular practice. To have said something on Twitter, no matter who you might be, if it is pertinent to the news matter in hand, makes you someone with something to say.

To have said something on Twitter, no matter who you might be, if it is pertinent to the news matter in hand, makes you someone with something to say.

This is the key to its particular power as a news medium. Ostensibly, Twitter is not a news publisher itself – as is also the case with Facebook, it has no journalists, no newsroom, only heads of news partnerships – but rather a news platform. In the words of commentator Jeff Jarvis, 'Twitter is not *The New York Times*. It is Times Square.'[14] It is a generator of conversations. However, a story such as the boy on the hospital floor highlights how the conversation – as the expression of public sentiment, for good or ill – is an integral part of the news. Historically this has always been so, but perhaps never so overtly as in the age of social media.[15] In becoming a platform for news in which the public can actively engage in the shaping of a news story, Twitter has made itself a manufacturer of news.

Gossip, or conversation, may be part of the lifeblood of news, but news principles must remain. James Mitchinson's comments quoted above focus on trust and truth. Without these two principles there is no news worth publishing, but they cannot stand alone. The two need to work in combination.

In her 2006 book *News*, Jackie Harrison argues that 'news can be understood through orientation towards the truth and contemporary events'.[16] This need not mean that news journalism must always and only be concerned with establishing the truth, 'since this would require tellers of an event to know everything about it, and to remove any element of subjectivity from their story'. But the orientation, or aspiration, towards truthfulness, is fundamental. It is a beautiful summary of the news's best intentions.

News is, or should be, a fundamentally virtuous activity.

Harrison's thinking was inspired by the philosopher Bernard Williams (1929–2003), author of *Truth and Truthfulness* (2002). Williams argues that 'truthfulness implies a respect for the truth', whose qualities lie in two basic virtues, sincerity and accuracy. Sincerity, for Williams, 'consists in a disposition to make sure that one's assertion expresses what one actually believes'; accuracy entails an 'investigative investment', establishing the balance between the value of possible information and the means to acquire it. The two virtues must necessarily work co-operatively, each feeding off the other. An element that binds them together is trust, for that which is relayed sincerely and accurately must be accepted as such by the party receiving such information.[17]

News is, or should be, a fundamentally virtuous activity. Its purveyors should inspire trust in those who recognise in them the necessary conditions for relaying that which is truthful, or tends that way. There are many who may place their trust in that which is objectively untruthful because to them it appears to have the quality of truth, but that is not news – or at least not news in any journalistic sense.

The boy on the hospital floor exemplifies these requirements for news, and the dangers inherent in people losing trust or understanding of how a news organisation must operate. The arguments the British print newspaper industry has been making to government in recent years, faced with the threat of internet platforms that have taken away the advertising money on which it depends, while presenting readers with, as it asserts, an indiscriminate, untrustworthy news environment, are based on these dangers.[18] James Mitchinson articulates them powerfully. Show good faith in those you can trust; do not believe in strangers.

Yet perhaps things are not so clear cut. Harrison defines how news may be understood, but takes care not to say what news is, or rather, she defines news through what it does. For something as complex and contested as news (for anything, ultimately, can be 'news') this is a sensible approach, particularly if one needs to understand the function of journalism, or the production of news. It is something to do with contemporary events, though it can encompass past events if they are of interest to us now. It needs to have an audience for whom such news is meaningful. It needs to be understood as news.

But there may be more to news and its relationship with truth. The story of the boy on the hospital floor may point to it, because it is a story. The function of news is to provide us with stories, because stories are what we as humans need for getting to the truth.

We know that the news is composed of stories, but it is only recently that neurological studies have shown how fundamental stories are to how we all live. Will Storr, in *The Science of Storytelling*, usefully sums up the unsettling conclusions that neuroscience is telling us:

In order to tell the story of your life, your brain needs to conjure up a world for you to live inside, with all its colours and movements and objects and sounds. Just as characters in fiction exist in a reality that's been actively created, so do we. But that's not how it feels to be a living, conscious human. It feels as if we're looking out of our skulls, observing reality directly and without impediment. But this is not the case. The world we experience as 'out there' is actually a reconstruction of reality that is built inside our heads. It's an act of creation by the storytelling brain.[19]

To find our place in the meaningless void in which we find ourselves, we create stories. They have cause and effect, dilemma and escape, conflict and resolution, a moral core that satisfies our sense of how the world should be if we are to survive in it. Fiction exists to serve this need of ours (and is the focus of Storr's interest). News stories are more complicated, if no less fictional in how they are constructed. Although, as with regular fiction, we may look for them to confirm our sense of what is right, and hence confirm the sense we have of ourselves, they are subject to how things in real life turn out. In news stories, 'good is not always rewarded, resolution is not always attained, wars do not end, wealth comes to the undeserving, and the wrong people win elections'.[20]

There is a profound relationship between story and truth. John Yorke, in a celebrated study of the philosophical and psychological basis of dramatic structure, *Into the Woods*, says: 'All stories at some

The function of news is to provide us with stories, because stories are what we as humans need for getting to the truth.

level are about a search for the truth of the subject they are exploring. Just as the act of perception involves seeking out the "truth" of the thing perceived, so storytelling mimics that process.'[21]

We need stories because we need things to be true. This is how the news story must work. The fact that we disagree with the story – how it has been composed, what it leaves out, what bias it betrays – is irrelevant to the function of news, if not to its journalistic principles. The fact that we use it constantly to test our assumptions and to understand our place in the world shows that news works. It exists to remind us who we are.

Jack Williment-Barr on the floor of a hospital was not a story. What was made of it was. It was originally crafted into a story by a *Yorkshire Evening Post* journalist as evidence of government failings over the NHS, but it rapidly grew into a story about news reporting, ideology, the social media, truth and trust. Everyone, from Jack's mother to journalists, to politicians, to the real or unreal Sheree, to thousands of sharers, re-tweeters and silent readers, contributed to and enriched the story. It is good that the truth of the matter was made clear. It is good that trusted journalists establish such truths (and apologise when occasionally they get things wrong). But no one owns our news stories. They have a life of their own, the moment they are released into the consciousness of an audience. Social media has made understanding the news more challenging at times, yet it has also enriched how news stories are told, by involving anyone who cares in the process.[22] We can all play our part in establishing a news truth.

Our news stories have a life of their own, the moment they are released into the consciousness of an audience.

Afterword:
The future of news

'There is a future for news.
We just don't know what it is yet.'

his observation, made in 2021 by Jeff Jarvis, Leonard Tow Chair for Journalism Innovation at the City University of New York, could no doubt have been made at any time in the last 150 years. While news has been an intrinsic element of the human experience for millennia, it has constantly evolved in ways that suggest both threat and opportunity. The generation and consumption of news have been shaped by emerging technologies – including the shift from scribal newsletters to the first printed newspaper in Germany in 1609 and the transformative effects of mass media publications, broadcasts, and now the internet and social media. Each technological innovation has brought with it the possibility of sharing information ever more widely and catering for an increasingly diverse range of needs and desires on a global scale. Innovation has also created moral and social panics: how will the masses process and cope with the deluge of information they are now confronted with? How, in all the white noise of the overcrowded infosphere, can facts and common narratives be established? Who will regulate the increasingly complex informational ecosystem and ensure that it serves rather than destroys society? The modern world has struggled to resolve these questions satisfactorily while continuing to recognise the critical function of news. There has always been a future for news – and it has always been uncertain.

New methods of consumption are undoubtedly driving change and forcing a new business model. The Reuters Institute Digital News Report 2021 highlighted the sharp decline in print media, hastened, no doubt, by the effects of the COVID-19 pandemic and widespread lockdowns on distribution and access: 73 per cent of respondents across all countries report accessing news via a smartphone,[1] and increasingly people receive breaking news through wearables, such as smart watches. The shift to online content will undoubtedly further force a consideration of new ways to generate profit, or indeed determine whether certain outlets remain sustainable. The future of traditional local news outlets, with an increasingly narrow focus, appears particularly doubtful.[2] Yet, perhaps now more than ever, we need to feel connected to and understand our local environment. As a BBC report on the future of the news in 2015 noted, in not supporting local journalism, news is failing where it may be needed most.[3]

Concerns around the shift to online news content are not confined to profitability. The exponential growth of the internet has created a veritable wild west of 'news' content. How much of this content is of genuine value, however, is disputable. The COVID-19 pandemic has shone a harsh light on the damaging effects of mis- and disinformation, and understandably demand has increased for reliable and accurate news. History repeatedly demonstrates the strange paradox that, at times of crisis, we both seek out any information to make sense of an uncertain world (including outlandish theories and rumours) and turn to more authoritative sources for reliable news. This is a very human reaction to incomprehensible, fast-moving events.[4] If we experience a period of political, economic and social stabilisation in the coming years, combined with a collective exposure of and assault on 'fake news', it is possible that we will see mainstream news regain its position as a trusted, impartial arbiter. Even if we do not experience stability (and this is looking unlikely from a geopolitical, economic and environmental perspective), there is

> *The COVID-19 pandemic has shone a harsh light on the damaging effects of mis- and disinformation, and understandably demand has increased for reliable and accurate news.*

It may well be that in an increasingly chaotic and unstable world reliable information could prove an important anchor.

still hope. 'Truth is hard, expensive and frequently boring,' as Amol Rajan, journalist and former editor of *The Independent*, has lamented,[5] but it is remarkable the premium truth may command when there is no access to it at all. Even under the threat of the death penalty, the people of Nazi Germany still tuned into foreign radio to glean information on the war effort – information they knew was not being provided by their leaders.[6] It may well be that in an increasingly chaotic and unstable world – a world made all the more overwhelming by 'data overload' – channelled, accurate and reliable information could prove an important anchor. The American journalist Walter Lippmann suggested much the same thing in the 1920s in response to post-war turbulence and the boom in media content.[7]

Where will technology take us next? We are already seeing greater use of personalised news, with algorithms filtering the stories we receive based on our own browsing history and interests. While this may seem convenient, it can also be limiting, confining us to our already sealed echo chambers, closing our horizons, and making us less exposed to worlds we do not know and to things we might discover serendipitously.

If our content is automated, will journalism go the same way, with auto-generated content becoming the norm, our news teams a vast phalanx of 'robojournalists' fronted by an AI-generated news reader, such as that recently created by the Chinese Xinhua news agency?[8] I doubt very much that this is what we want or what we need. While news may be broken in real time on social media by anyone with a smartphone, journalism remains a skilled profession, delivering stories with empathy and providing expert analysis, interpretation and context. News – at its most hard-hitting – is and should always be inherently human. The news reports I recall most clearly in my mind's eye captured both what I needed to know and the human dimensions of the story: famine in Ethiopia, 9/11, the death of Diana, Princess of Wales, the fall of the Berlin Wall. We will all have our own recollections. But these memories underscore the importance of journalists conveying news in impactful and very human ways, ways that explain and help us to feel, understand and make up our own minds on the key issues of the day. This cannot – and should not – change, whatever the future of news may hold.

Camera operator Mohamed Amin and BBC reporter Michael Buerk documenting the Ethiopian famine, 1984.

Notes

Websites accessed 23 November 2021.

CONFLICT AND THE PRESS

1 [*Hereafter ensue the trewe encountre or ... batayle lately don betwene. Engla[n]de and: Scotlande*], England, R. Faques, 1513, British Library, c.123.d.33.
2 George Veseler and Peter van Der Keere, *Corrant out of Italie etc.*, Amsterdam, 23 December 1620, British Library, C.55.l.2.
3 *Corante, or, Newes from Italy, Germany, Hungarie, Spaine and France*, London, 23 September 1621, British Library, C.55.l.2.
4 Marchmont Needham, *Mercurius Britannicus*, xcii, 21 July 1645.
5 *The Morning Post*, 22 June 1815, p. 3.
6 Charles Gruneisen, *Sketches of Spain and the Spaniards during the Carlist Civil War* (London: Robert Hardwicke, 1874), p. 14.
7 'From Our Special Correspondent' [William Howard Russell], 'The War in the Crimea', *The Times*, 14 November 1854, p. 7.
8 'Evacuation of the BEF', *Pathé Gazette*, issue 40/46, 6 June 1940 [newsreel].
9 Robert Dunner, 'Force Afloat', dispatch No. 1 H 02026 18:00, 5 June 1944, reproduced at https://www.bbc.co.uk/news/magazine-27701206.
10 Choire Sicha, 'The Only British Newspaper Reporter in Syria Killed,' *The Awl*, 22 February 2012, https://www.theawl.com/2012/02/the-only-british-newspaper-reporter-in-syria-killed/.
11 Marie Colvin, '"We Live in Fear of a Massacre"', *The Sunday Times*, 19 February 2012, pp. 18–19.
12 Dominic Ponsford and Charlotte Tobitt, 'The UK Journalists Killed Covering Conflicts of the 21st Century', *Press Gazette*, 23 April 2019, https://www.pressgazette.co.uk/uk-journalists-who-lost-their-lives-covering-conflict-2000; Committee to Protect Journalists, https://cpj.org/data/killed.

SENSATIONALISM'S SHOCKING SECRETS

1 Sandra Clark, *Women and Crime in the Street Literature of Early Modern England* (Basingstoke: Palgrave Macmillan, 2003), p. 21.
2 Mitchell Stephens, *A History of News* (Oxford: Oxford University Press, 2007), p. 80.
3 *The Araignement & Burning of Margaret Ferne-seede* (London, 1608), British Library, C.21.b.5.
4 Clark, *Women and Crime*, p. 20.
5 Peter Lake, 'Deeds against Nature: Cheap Print, Protestantism and Murder in Early 17th Century England', in Kevin Sharpe and Peter Lake (eds), *Culture and Politics in Early Stuart England* (London: Macmillan, 1994), p. 262.
6 *The Most Cruell and Bloody Murther Committed by an Inkeepers Wife, Called Annis Dell [...]* (London: Printed by T. Purfoot for William Firebrand and Iohn Wright, 1606), British Library, C.27.c.28.
7 *Morning Herald*, 9 April 1790, held in [*A collection of broadsides, cuttings from newspapers, engravings, etc., of various dates, formed by Miss S. S. Banks. Bound in nine volumes*], British Library, L.R.301.h.3.

8 *Mr Angerstein Informs the Public* (Printed by J. Moore, 1790), British Library, L.R.301.h.3.
9 *The Monster*, British Library, L.R.301.h.3.
10 *One Hundred Pounds Reward. Public Office, Bow-Street. April, 1790* (Printed by J. Moore, 1790), British Library, L.R.301.h.3.
11 'The Illustrated Police News: "The Worst Newspaper in England"', British Newspaper Archive blog, 19 April 2016, https://blog.britishnewspaperarchive.co.uk/2016/04/19/the-illustrated-police-news-the-worst-newspaper-in-england.
12 'The Murder in Whitechapel', *The Illustrated Police News*, 8 September 1888, p. 2.
13 *The Illustrated Police News*, 6 October 1888, pp. 1, 2.
14 W. T. Stead, 'Wanted A Court of Conscience', *The Pall Mall Gazette*, 5 October 1888, p. 1.

DEVOURING SCANDAL

1 William Shakespeare, *The Rape of Lucrece* (1594), l. 1006.
2 Oscar Wilde, *De Profundis*, ed. Robert Ross (New York: Putnam, 1910), p. 106.
3 *The Sun*, 6 February 1992, p. 1.
4 Richard Dowden, 'I Implored Him to Tell Thatcher', *The Times*, 14 October 1983, p. 1.
5 *The Complete Works of William Hazlitt*, ed. P.P. Howe (London and Toronto: Dent, 1930–4), vol. 20, p. 136.
6 Petition from Godalming, Surrey, No. 42, p. 28, HC/CL/JO/6/148, Parliamentary Archives, cited in https://archives.blog.parliament.uk/2020/10/29/protest-and-petitions-part-2-after-the-trial.
7 Petition from Cockermouth, Cumberland, no. 8, p. 7, HC/CL/JO/6/148, Parliamentary Archives, cited in https://archives.blog.parliament.uk/2020/10/29/protest-and-petitions-part-2-after-the-trial.
8 E.P. Thompson, *The Making of the English Working Class* (Harmondsworth: Penguin, 1968), p. 794.

CELEBRITY NEWS

1 WAG is an acronym referring to the wives and girlfriends of high-profile footballers, popularised during the 2006 FIFA World Cup.
2 BBC Radio 4 *Today*, 10 October 2019, at 2:24:58.
3 Greg Jenner, *Dead Famous: An Unexpected History of Celebrity* (London: Weidenfeld & Nicolson, 2020), 'Chapter 2: Fame Thrust Upon Them', sub-heading 'Rage against the machine?', paragraph 1. Kindle Edition.
4 Brian Cowan, 'Histories of Celebrity in Post-Revolutionary England', *Historical Social Research/Historische Sozialforschung*, supplement no. 32 (2019), pp. 83–98.
5 'Lord Byron's Poems on His Own Domestic Circumstances', *The Champion*, 14 April 1816, p. 117.
6 Reproduced at https://www.britishmuseum.org/collection/object/P_1868-0808-8316.
7 Fiona MacCarthy, *Byron: Life and Legend* (London: John Murray, 2014), p. 274.
8 [William Rees-Mogg], 'Who breaks a butterfly on a wheel?', *The Times*, 1 July 1967, p. 11.
9 Quoted in https://www.express.co.uk/news/uk/90610/Jade-Tributes-flood-in-from-around-world.

REPORTING DISASTERS

1 Iain McLean and Martin Johnes, *Aberfan: Government and Disaster* (Cardiff: Welsh Academic Press, 2019), p. 3.
2 Ashleigh O'Collaghan, 'Aberfan 50 Years On: How the Press Covered the Disaster and the Aftermath', *Wales Online*, 17 October 2016, https://www.walesonline.co.uk/news/wales-news/aberfan-50-years-on-how-11973335.
3 McLean and Johnes, *Aberfan*, pp. 58, 22, 16, 16.
4 *London Gazette*, 85 (3–10 September 1666).
5 Alexandra Walsham, '"The Fatal Vesper": Providentialism and Anti-Popery in Late Jacobean London', *Past & Present*, 144 (1994), pp. 36–87.
6 Joad Raymond, *Making The News: An Anthology of the Newsbooks of Revolutionary England 1641–1660* (Moreton-in-Marsh: Windrush Press, 1993), ch. 4; Ottavia Niccoli, *Profeti e popolo nell'Italia del Rinascimento* (Rome and Bari: Laterza, 1987); Joad Raymond (ed.), *The Oxford History of Popular Print Culture*, vol. 1: *Cheap Print in Britain and Ireland to 1660* (Oxford: Oxford University Press, 2011).
7 Anne Saada and Jean Sgard, 'Tremblements Dans la Presse', in Theodore E.D. Braun and John B. Radner (eds), *The Lisbon Earthquake of 1755: Representations and Reactions* (Oxford: Voltaire Foundation, 2005), pp. 208–24; Hans-Jürgen Lüsebrink, 'Le tremblement de terre de Lisbonne dans les périodiques français et allemands du XVIIIe siècle', in Henri Duranton et Pierre Rétat (eds), *Gazettes et information politique sous l'Ancien Régime* (Saint-Étienne: Publications de l'Université de Saint-Étienne, 1999), pp. 301–11; Helena Murteira, 'Between Despair and Hope: The 1755 Earthquake in Lisbon', in Deborah Simonton and Hannu Salmi (eds), *Catastrophe, Gender and Urban Experience, 1648–1920* (New York and London: Routledge, 2017), pp. 42–63.
8 Quoted in Murteira, 'Between Despair and Hope', p. 49.
9 Agustín Udías and Alfonso López Arroyo, 'The Lisbon Earthquake of 1755 in Spanish Contemporary Authors', in Luiz A. Mendes-Victor, Carlos Sousa Oliveira, João Azevedo and António Ribeiro (eds), *The 1755 Lisbon Earthquake: Revisited* (Berlin: Springer, 2009), pp. 7–24.
10 Matthias Georgi, 'The Lisbon Earthquake and Scientific Knowledge in the British Public Sphere', in Braun and Radner (eds), *The Lisbon Earthquake of 1755*, pp. 81–96; Robert G. Ingram, '"The Trembling Earth is God's Herald": Earthquakes, Religion and Public Life in Britain During the 1750s', in Braun and Radner (eds), *The Lisbon Earthquake of 1755*, 97–115.
11 Jake Soll, 'The Long and Brutal History of Fake News', *Politico*, 18 December 2016; Carmen Espejo Cala, 'Spanish News Pamphlets on the 1755 Earthquake: Trade Strategies of the Printers of Seville', in Braun and Radner (eds), *The Lisbon Earthquake of 1755*, pp. 66–80.
12 Johan Galtung and Mari Holmboe Ruge, 'The Structure of Foreign News', *Journal of Peace Research*, 2.1 (1965), pp. 64–91.
13 James Curran and Jean Seaton, *Power Without Responsibility* (London: Routledge, 1997).

POLITICAL THEATRE

1 Matthew Parris, 'The Lady Sails Proudly Away', *The Times*, 17 March 1992, p. 18.
2 Andrew Marr, *My Trade: A Short History of British Journalism* (London: Macmillan, 2004), pp. 145–51.
3 *Thatcher: The Downing Street Years*, episode 4, BBC One tx. 10 November 1993.
4 *Daily Express*, 23 November 1990, p. 5.
5 Ibid, p. 3.

6 Colin Welch, 'The Moment It Sunk In: What Have We Done?', *Daily Mail*, 23 November 1990, p. 8.
7 Stephen Goodwin and Judy Jones, 'Thatcher Makes Spirited Defence of Record', *The Independent*, 23 November 1990, p. 8.
8 Andrew Rawnsley, 'Dying Swan Gives Commons a Command Performance', *The Guardian*, 23 November 1990, p. 1.
9 Philip Johnston, 'Final Defence a Fitting Testimony', *The Daily Telegraph*, 23 November 1990, pp. 1–2.
10 *The Independent*, 23 November 1990, p. 8.
11 Matthew Parris, 'Only Two Dead as the Final Curtain Closes', *The Times*, 28 November 1990, p. 1.

THE NEWS AND CELEBRATION

1 The original photograph is reproduced at https://oldnycphotos.com/products/fitzgeralds-bar-downtown-574-atlantic-ave-1941. The paper has the words 'Brooklyn Eagle' beneath the headline. There is sufficient text visible to indicate that what is being celebrated is the Brooklyn Dodgers winning the pennant on 13 September 1941. No such front page is in the regular issues of the *Brooklyn Eagle*, suggesting that what is held up is a Saturday evening special, produced to mark the victory, and not a full newspaper.
2 'The Great Pugilists of England', *Illustrated Sporting News and Theatrical and Musical Review*, 14 February 1863, pp. 447–8.
3 Kevin R. Smith, *Black Genesis: The History of the Black Prizefighter 1760–1870* (Lincoln, NE: iUniverse, 2003), pp. 145–61; 'Boxing: Death of Bob Travers, a Famous Old-Timer', *Sport*, 26 December 1918, p. 11.
4 Adapted from Luke McKernan, 'The Black Wonder', https://blogs.bl.uk/thenewsroom/2019/02/the-black-wonder.html.
5 *British Paralympic Association Guide to Reporting on Paralympic Sport* (2012), p. 5, https://paralympics.org.uk/footer-pages/media.
6 Episode one broadcast Channel 4, tx. 30 August 2012.
7 Hugo Rifkind, 'How Alex Brooker Made Political Interviews Interesting Again', *The Spectator*, 7 February 2015, https://www.spectator.co.uk/article/how-alex-brooker-made-political-interviews-interesting-again. The interview can be seen at https://youtu.be/BLGjPuaEgyw.
8 Andrew Chaikin, *A Man on the Moon: The Voyages of the Apollo Astronauts* (London: Michael Joseph, 1994), p. 204.
9 Michael Allen, *Live from the Moon: Film, Television and the Space Race* (London: I.B. Tauris, 2009), pp. 149–56.
10 Although most of the NASA footage survives, almost all of the BBC and ITV coverage, a combination of studio presentation, discussions, variety acts and poetry readings, is now lost, the tapes having been wiped or subsequently mislaid.
11 Joe Moran, *Armchair Nation: An Intimate History of Britain in Front of the TV* (London: Profile Books, 2013), pp. 182–4; James Jeffery, 'Apollo 11: "The greatest single broadcast in television history"', BBC News, 10 July 2019, https://www.bbc.co.uk/news/world-us-canada-48857752.

SUPPRESSING THE NEWS

1 *Press Gazette* daily news briefing email, 7 September 2020.
2 Stephen Coleman, *Stilled Tongues: From Soapbox to Soundbite* (London: Porcupine Press, 1997), p. 5.
3 Henry Wickham Steed, *The Press* (Harmondsworth: Penguin, 1938), p. 110.

4 Quoted in Granville Williams, *Milton and the Modern Media* (Accrington: B&D Publishing, 2005), pp. 65–106.
5 Andrew Pettegree, *The Invention of News: How the World Came to Know about Itself* (New Haven, CT/London: Yale University Press, 2015), p. 237.
6 Quoted in David Keir, *Newspapers* (London: Edward Arnold, 1948), p. 23.
7 Keir, *Newspapers*, pp. 22–3.
8 Anna Beer, *Milton: Poet, Pamphleteer and Patriot* (London: Bloomsbury, 2008), p. 292.
9 Dorothy Turner, 'Roger L'Estrange's Deferential Politics in the Public Sphere', *The Seventeenth Century*, 13.1 (1998), p. 95.
10 *Observator*, 13 April 1681; see Pettegree, *The Invention of News*, p. 244.
11 Binakuromo Ogbebor, *British Media Coverage of the Press Reform Debate: Journalists Reporting Journalism* (Cham: Palgrave Macmillan, 2020); Gordon Ramsay, *How Newspapers Covered Press Regulation After Leveson* (London: Media Standards Trust, 2014), http://mediastandardstrust.org/wp-content/uploads/2014/09/Final-Draft-v1-040914.pdf.
12 Stanley Harrison, *Poor Men's Guardians: A Survey of the Struggles for a Democratic Newspaper Press, 1763–1973* (London: Lawrence & Wishart, 1974), p. 13.
13 Pettegree, *The Invention of News*, p. 245.
14 Newspaper Stamp Duties Bill debate, House of Lords, 29 December 1819, https://hansard.parliament.uk/Lords/1819-12-29/debates/75a29bb0-c8b2-4ccc-8aee-3fdd5c507df5/NewspaperStampDutiesBill.
15 Kevin Williams, *Get Me a Murder a Day! A History of Mass Communication in Britain* (London: Arnold, 1998), p. 44.
16 Mark Hanna and Mike Dodd, *McNae's Essential Law for Journalists*, 25th edn (Oxford: Oxford University Press, 2020), p. 3.
17 David Widgery, 'Gay was Good', *New Society*, 12 May 1983, p. 227.
18 Peter Tatchell, 'Blasphemy Law is Dead', *New Humanist*, 11 July 2002, https://www.petertatchell.net/religion/blasphemy.
19 Cheryl R. Jorgensen-Earp, *Discourse and Defiance Under Nazi Occupation: Guernsey, Channel Islands, 1940–1945* (East Lansing: Michigan State University Press, 2013), p. 206; Gillian Carr, 'The Archaeology of Occupation and the V-sign Campaign in the Occupied British Channel Islands', *International Journal of Historical Archaeology*, 14 (2010), pp. 575–92.
20 Jorgensen-Earp, *Discourse and Defiance*, p. 206.

THE PARTISAN PRESS

1 Caroline Shaw, 'Freedom of Expression and the Palladium of British Liberties, 1650–2000: A Review Essay', *History Compass* (2020), DOI: 10.1111/hic3.12629.
2 Mark Hampton, 'The Fourth Estate Ideal in Journalism History', in Stuart Allan (ed.), *The Routledge Companion to News and Journalism* (Abingdon: Routledge, 2010), pp. 3–12.
3 *The North Briton*, 5 June 1762, p. 7.
4 W.T. Stead, *The Maiden Tribute of Modern Babylon*, ed. Antony E. Simpson (Lambertville, NJ: True Bill Press, 2007).
5 *The Times*, 30 August 1914, p. 1.
6 Adrian Gregory, *The Last Great War: British Society and the First World War* (Cambridge: Cambridge University Press, 2008), p. 32.
7 'The Tragedy of the Shells', *Daily Mail*, 21 May 1915, p. 4.
8 'The Limpets', *Daily Mail*, 2 December 1916, p. 4.

9 Stephen Koss, *The Rise and Fall of the Political Press*, vol. 1, *The Nineteenth Century* (London: Hamish Hamilton, 1981).
10 Huw Richards, *The Bloody Circus: The Daily Herald and the Left* (London: Pluto Press, 1997).
11 'Civil War Plot by Socialists' Masters', *Daily Mail*, 25 October 1924, p. 9.
12 *Daily Mirror*, 25 October 1951, p. 1; Roy Greenslade, *Press Gang: How Newspapers Make Profits from Propaganda* (London: Macmillan, 2003), pp. 84–5.
13 James Thomas, *Popular Newspapers, the Labour Party and British Politics* (Abingdon: Routledge, 2005), ch. 4.
14 Kevin Williams, *Read All About It! A History of the British Newspaper* (Abingdon: Routledge, 2010), pp. 87–8.
15 Michelle Tusan, *Women Making News: Gender and Journalism in Modern Britain* (Urbana: University of Illinois Press, 2005).
16 Bill Schwarz, 'Claudia Jones and the West Indian Gazette: Reflections on the Emergence of Post-Colonial Britain', *Twentieth Century British History*, 14.3 (2003), pp. 264–85.
17 Central Office of Information, *Britain 1987: An Official Handbook* (London: HMSO, 1987), p. 414.

VISUAL SATIRE

1 Colin Seymour-Ure and Jim Schoff, *David Low* (London: Secker & Warburg, 1985), p. 96.
2 Kevin Williams, *Read All About It! A History of the British Newspaper* (Abingdon: Routledge, 2010), p. 154.
3 *Daily Express*, 6 January 1939, pp. 8, 6.
4 Osbert Lancaster, *With an Eye to the Future* (London: John Murray, 1967), p. 152.
5 Ibid.
6 *Daily Express*, 14 January 1939, p. 6; *Daily Express*, 19 May 1939, p. 6.
7 *Daily Express*, 19 December 1939, p. 4.
8 *Evening Standard*, 14 May 1940.
9 *Daily Express*, 20 March 1944, p. 3.
10 Quoted in James Knox, *Cartoons and Coronets: The Genius of Osbert Lancaster* (London: Frances Lincoln, 2008), p. 203.
11 *The Manchester Guardian*, 14 September 1945, p. 5.

IN THE PUBLIC INTEREST

1 Thomas Jefferson, letter to Charles Yancey, 6 January 1816. See https://founders.archives.gov/documents/Jefferson/03-09-02-0209.
2 BBC Editorial Guidelines, 1.3. See https://www.bbc.co.uk/editorialguidelines/guidelines/editorial-standards.
3 Leveson Inquiry, *An Inquiry into the Culture, Practices and Ethics of the Press* (London: HMSO, 2012), pp. 9–11.
4 Ibid.
5 Lynette Sheridan Burns and Benjamin J. Matthews, *Understanding Journalism*, third edition (London: Sage, 2018), pp. 5–6.
6 These guidelines act as a kind of BBC production 'bible' that runs to 355 pages and forms the bedrock of ethical thinking underpinning the production of BBC content.
7 Ronald Harker, a reporter for the Bradford local *Telegraph and Argus*, filed the story with the Press Association. From there it made the national front pages on 3 December 1936.
8 The bishop later claimed that he had no knowledge of Wallis Simpson and was merely expressing concern over the lack of church attendance by the head of the Church.
9 A fuller account of this can be found in Réda Hassaïne

and Kurt Barling, *Abu Hamza Guilty: The Fight against Radical Islam* (London: Redshank, 2014).

10 Kurt Barling, *Investigation of Lakanal House Fire* (2017), http://lakanalhousefire.co.uk.

11 Quoted in Glenn Greenwald, 'Edward Snowden: The Whistleblower behind the NSA Surveillance Revelations', *The Guardian*, 9 June 2013, https://www.theguardian.com/world/2013/jun/09/edward-snowden-nsa-whistleblower-surveillance.

12 Alan Rusbridger, *The Remaking of Journalism: And Why It Matters Now* (Edinburgh: Canongate, 2018), pp. 301–13.

13 See, for example, the mission and values statement (2020) of digital news platform Knowhere News, https://knowherenews.com.

CROSSING THE LINE

1 News International changed its title several times in this period: until June 2002: News International plc; until 31 May 2011: News International ltd; until 26 June 2013: NI Group Ltd; until present: News UK. For more on secret commissions, see Stephen Donovan and Matthew Rubery (eds), *Secret Commissions: An Anthology of Victorian Investigative Journalism* (London: Broadview Press/Eurospan, 2012), in which Stead's investigation features among many others. For more on the 'Maiden Tribute' see Gretchen Sonderland, *Sex Trafficking, Scandal, and the Transformation of Journalism* (Chicago: University of Chicago Press, 2013), especially pp. 24–67. For more on Stead, see Laurel Brake, Ed King, Roger Luckhurst and James Mussell (eds), *W.T. Stead: Newspaper Revolutionary* (London: British Library, 2012) and the W. T. Stead Resource Site (https://attackingthedevil.co.uk/); on Mahmood, *Panorama*, BBC One, tx. 12 November 2014, BBC (https://youtu.be/59WI8q5SK1c) and Wikipedia. On Snowden, see *citizenfour*, dir. Laura Poitras, Praxis Films, 2014 (Archive.org), and *Snowden*, dir. Oliver Stone, 2016 (You Tube), as well as Edward Snowden, *Permanent Record* (New York: Metropolitan, 2019).

2 The *NOTW* was closed by its proprietors in July 2011. Snowden has escaped imprisonment, having been charged by the US government under the Espionage Act in June 2013 soon after the story broke, and in a civil lawsuit on 17 September 2019 for information included in *Permanent Record*, his memoir. Although an arrest warrant has been issued, the US has not apprehended him, as he fled to Russia, where he has become a citizen.

3 The attempt of the British government to limit the circulation of Snowden's files was rendered ineffectual by his distribution of copies to several sites in different countries and legal jurisdictions. The physical destruction of *The Guardian*'s computer was understood by all witnesses including *The Guardian* and GCHQ to be in vain.

4 In 1999, Mahmood was Reporter of the Year, and in 2011 he won Scoop of the Year and was honoured by the Sports Journalists' Association.

5 *citizenfour*, 2014.

6 *Heroes and Hero Worship* (1840/1). Burke used the phrase 'the fourth estate' in 1787 in a Parliamentary debate.

7 W.T. Stead, 'Government by Journalism', *Contemporary Review*, 49 (May 1886), pp. 653–74.

8 'New Journalism' is a term used to describe marked developments in the nineteenth-century press. Coined in 1888 by Mathew Arnold and Stead, it referred to a gradual transformation of the press from the 1850s to make it more accessible and attractive to a wider readership. It involved shorter articles, in brighter prose; cheaper prices; and radical changes of layout to enhance readability, e.g. the introduction of headings, headlines and sections; more personal journalism such as 'interviews'; illustration; entertainment such as puzzles, riddles and prizes; fashion and sports; sensation and celebrity. For more on the 'new journalism', see Joel Wiener (ed.), *Papers for the Millions: The New Journalism in Britain, 1850s to 1914* (Westport, CT/London: Greenwood, 1988).

9 *The Guardian* and *The Washington Post* were awarded a Pulitzer Prize in 2014 for their reports on the NSA surveillance that Snowden documented.

10 Among these examples, Stead's 'Maiden Tribute' is uniquely 'one-off' in that, although it appeared serially, the report of the Secret Commission was finite, beginning and ending within a week. By contrast, the *NOTW* stories and attempts to probe them spread over years, even decades. The immediate coverage of the Snowden leak proved to be the seed of its recurrence, as various national figures and institutions – private and governmental – explore the implications for themselves in the NSA data.

11 While the proprietor of the *PMG* may have permitted his editor to investigate and publish 'The Maiden Tribute', he soon expressed his discomfort at the mismatch between his upmarket newspaper and the sordid story, his editor's trial and imprisonment and what he judged to be the ensuing disrepute of his paper. That Stead was forced to publish two articles in 1886 on his resulting vision of journalism not in his own paper but in a monthly magazine suggests his proprietor's immediate misgivings. In 1888 Stead's sub-editor staged a coup in his absence and proprietor Yates Thompson reduced his salary, and in late 1889 Stead's resignation was accepted. For a detailed account of Stead's fortunes after 'The Maiden Tribute', see Grace Eckley, *Maiden Tribute: A Life of W.T. Stead* (Philadelphia: Xlibris, 2007), pp. 103–45.

12 'Slave Trade in English Girls', *Northern Echo*, 13 October 1880, p. 3. This first leader was occasioned by a new pamphlet on the topic by Alfred S. Dyer, whose description of his own investigation of English 'slaves' in Brussels may well have inspired Stead's five years later. With Benjamin Scott, Dyer was co-chair of the London Committee for Suppressing the Traffic of British Girls for Purposes of Continental Prostitution (1879) and a member of the Gospel Purity Association (1885). It was Scott who approached Stead in 1885 to revive the Criminal Law Amendment bill and whose visit prompted Stead's investigation for 'The Maiden Tribute'.

13 For the history of the *NOTW*, see Laurel Brake, Chandrika Kaul and Mark W. Turner (eds), *The News of the World and the British Press, 1843–2011: 'Journalism for the Rich, Journalism for the Poor'* (Basingstoke: Palgrave Macmillan, 2016).

14 See Nick Davies, *Hack Attack: How the Truth Caught Up with Rupert Murdoch* (London: Chatto and Windus, 2014) and Snowden, *Permanent Record*.

15 See the account of demand outstripping supply: 'The Maiden Tribute' part four, *The Pall Mall Gazette*, 10 July 1885, p. 1.

16 Davies, *Hack Attack*.

17 See 'The Government Prosecution of Mr Stead', *The Pall Mall Gazette*, 1 October 1885, p. 8.

18 See advertisement for a penny pamphlet published by the *PMG*, *The Eliza Armstrong Case: Mr Stead's Defence*

with Notes and Elucidations Printed, *The Pall Mall Gazette*, 1 October 1885.

19 *The Life of Mr W.T. Stead, Editor of the 'Pall Mall Gazette'* (London: John Kensit, n.d.).

20 'The Government Prosecution of Mr Stead', p. 8.

21 Emily Pennink, 'Scores of Cases Set to Be Reviewed or Dropped after Collapse of Tulisa Trial', *The Independent*, 6 October 2016.

22 Katie Forster, 'Mazher Mahmood sentence: "Fake Sheikh" Jailed for 15 Months for Tampering with Tulisa Case Evidence', *The Independent*, 21 October 2016.

23 Impress, Max Mosley's model for a new regulatory body, operating within the remit of a Royal Charter, was adopted by the government's Press Recognition Panel in principle. It remains unacceptable to most titles, and has not been realised, due to the government's refusal to activate section 40 of the Crime Courts Act 2013. Instead, a new regulator, the Independent Press Standards Organisation (IPSO), organised and managed by the press, has been formed. Most British titles subscribe to it, but *The Guardian*, *The Financial Times* and *The Independent* do not; they have formed their own body.

24 Snowden called himself 'citizenfour' in his first communications with journalists to whom he would deliver the files. In his self-characterisation, citizens one, two and three were others within the NSA who had spoken out publicly before him, whose lead he followed.

SEEING IS BELIEVING

1 Susan Sontag, *On Photography* (New York: Farrar, Straus and Giroux, 1977), p. 175.

2 Ibid, p. 175.

3 Daniel Cornu, *Journalisme et vérité: L'éthique de l'information au défi du changement médiatique* (Geneva: Labor et Fides, 2009).

4 http://100photos.time.com/photos/kevin-carter-starving-child-vulture.

5 The AFPU were the providers of visual material from Bergen-Belsen to all the British newspapers and the newsreel companies that showed their bulletins in cinemas.

6 Quoted in Hannah Caven, 'Horror in our Time: Images of the Concentration Camps in the British Media, 1945', *Historical Journal of Film, Radio and Television*, 21.3 (2001), pp. 205–53.

7 Pierre Bourdieu, *Photography: A Middle-brow Art*, trans. Shaun Whiteside (Cambridge: Polity, 1990).

8 Onora O'Neill, *A Question of Trust: The BBC Reith Lectures* 2002, Lecture 5: Licence to Deceive (Cambridge: Cambridge University Press, 2002), p. 5.

9 This phrase occurred in *Picture Post*'s own explanation for publishing the story. The images had an enduring impact on the causes associated with LGBT rights.

10 The narrator for the 1945 Sidney Bernstein film, quoted in *Night Will Fall* (2014), a documentary by André Singer.

STAYING ALERT

1 Professor David Hunter, quoted in Virginia Berridge, *Public Health: A Very Short Introduction* (Oxford: Oxford University Press, 2016), p. 19.

2 Neil Henderson, 'TELEGRAPH BUSINESS: £119m Covid ad deal struck in early March #TomorrowsPapersToday' [Twitter post], 22.34, 25 October 2020, https://twitter.com/hendopolis/status/1320494033177874434.

3 Hugh Pym, 'Chris Whitty: The Man with our Lives in His Hands', BBC News, 17 March 2020, https://www.bbc.co.uk/news/health-51924796.

4 'First TV Ad for Coronavirus Public Information Campaign', uploaded 18 March 2020, https://www.youtube.com/watch?v=PBpjOIXlnUE; Greg Heffer, 'Coronavirus: Government to Air First TV Adverts with Advice for Britons', Sky News, 18 March 2020 (edited 20 March 2020), https://news.sky.com/story/coronavirus-government-to-air-first-tv-adverts-with-advice-for-britons-11959840.

5 Bryony Dixon, 'Silent Film and the Great Pandemic of 1918', 3 June 2020, https://www.bfi.org.uk/news-opinion/news-bfi/features/silent-film-great-pandemic-1918; *Dr Wise on Influenza* (1919), https://player.bfi.org.uk/free/film/watch-dr-wise-on-influenza-1919-online.

6 'Let Us Spray!', *Gaumont Graphic*, no. 1652, 20 January 1927, https://youtu.be/HbszpwutKNo; 'La Grande Gargle!', *Gaumont Graphic*, no. 1868, 14 February 1929, https://www.britishpathe.com/video/VLVA20XSAT7DZ32ENPTSQHA11AULE-FRANCE-HEALTH-WARSPITE-BOYS-GARGLING-AND-OTHER-EXAMPLES-OF-ANTI.

7 *The Careless Sneezer* (1942), https://www.youtube.com/watch?v=inE7D_YEOjM.

8 'Land Club', *New Series Pictorial*, no. 291, 27 October 1941, https://youtu.be/VdYl8_vfiCY; *A-Tish-oo* (1941), https://player.bfi.org.uk/free/film/watch-a-tish-oo-1941-online; 'Germ-Masks for Crowds', *Pathé Gazette*, no. 41/12, 2 February 1941, https://youtu.be/EMNElX229lU.

9 Grace E. Stephenson, 'British Newsreels at War, 1939–45: Significant Source for Scholars', *British Journal for Military History*, 6.3 (2020), pp. 148–54.

10 Imogen Watson, 'Government Imposes Stricter Measures with Third Phase of Coronavirus Campaign', *The Drum*, 24 March 2020, https://www.thedrum.com/news/2020/03/24/government-imposes-stricter-measures-with-third-phase-coronavirus-campaign.

11 Libby Brooks and Stephen Morris, 'Millions of Britons Clap for Carers on Coronavirus Frontline', *The Guardian*, 26 March 2020, https://www.theguardian.com/world/2020/mar/26/millions-of-britons-clap-for-carers-on-coronavirus-frontline.

12 'All In, All Together: Gallery', *Newsworks*, 17 April 2020, https://www.newsworks.org.uk/All-in-news/all-in-all-together-cover-wraps.

13 Virginia Berridge, *AIDS in the UK: The Making of Policy, 1981–1994* (Oxford: Oxford University Press, 1996), pp. 113–15.

14 The National Archives (TNA): HO 256/1160, 'After the 19 hour warning, the 5 second warning', public information advert; 'AIDS – The Facts', BBC1, 21.30, tx. 27 February 1987, *Radio Times* listing data, https://genome.ch.bbc.co.uk/schedules/bbcone/london/1987-02-27.

15 *Coronavirus: How Do I Know if I'm Infected and What Happens Next?*, 20 March 2020, https://www.youtube.com/watch?v=2JsWf-2nN1Y.

16 'Live Blog UK Coronavirus: 12,000 Former NHS Workers to Return and Emergency Hospital to Open as Death Toll Rises – As It Happened', *The Guardian*, 24 March 2020, https://www.theguardian.com/politics/live/2020/mar/24/uk-coronavirus-live-news-lockdown-boris-johnson-sports-direct-abandons-talk-of-opening-stores-as-gove-clarifies-scope-of-lockdown-rules.

17 Edward Malnick, 'Stay alert: Boris Johnson's new message to the nation, as he unveils Covid-19 warning system' [Twitter post], 21.30, 9 May 2020, https://twitter.com/edwardmalnick/status/1259219157754806273.

18 Adam Bienkov, 'Downing Street have just sent out this 137-word explanation of their new coronavirus slogan' [Twitter post], 12.33, 10 May 2020, https://twitter.com/AdamBienkov/status/1259446479183392768.

19 YouGov, 'Brits Split on Changes to Coronavirus Lockdown Measures', https://yougov.co.uk/topics/health/articles-reports/2020/05/11/brits-split-changes-coronavirus-lockdown-measures; Matt Chorley, 'Most people think "stay at home" is clearer. Downing Street source tells me: "It's a very nuanced message so will make more sense as we move forward"' [Twitter post], 09.07, 11 May 2020, https://twitter.com/MattChorley/status/1259757018711314433; Emily Maitlis, *Newsnight*, BBC Two, 22.45, tx. 11 May 2020; Charlie Cooper, 'Boris Johnson Turns to Polling and "Common Sense"', 13 March 2020 (edited 15 March 2020), https://www.politico.eu/article/boris-johnsons-coronavirus-fudge.

20 David Welch, *Protecting the People* (London: British Library, 2019), pp. 205–10, 221.

21 *The Finishing Line* (1977), https://player.bfi.org.uk/free/film/watch-the-finishing-line-1977-online; Patrick Russell, 'Finishing Line, The (1977)', http://www.screenonline.org.uk/film/id/1077210/index.html; *Nationwide*, BBC1, 17.55, tx. 2 September 1977; TNA: AN111/784 *Radio Times* press cutting.

22 TNA: AN111/784 'Safety First', *Welwyn Times and Hatfield Advertiser*, 23 July 1976 press cutting; Cyril Heath, 'Shock Film to Fight Vandalism', *Hertfordshire Mercury*, 30 July 1976 press cutting; 'British Rail's Film Frightener', *Daily Express*, 5 August 1976 press cutting.

FACT OR FICTION

1 S. Holly Stocking and Paget H. Gross, *How Do Journalists Think? A Proposal for the Study of Cognitive Bias in Newsmaking* (Bloomington, IN: ERIC Clearinghouse on Reading and Communication Skills, 1989).

2 A broadside was a printed sheet of paper with words, often on both sides, distributed by pamphleteers.

3 The Worshipful Company of Stationers (and Newspaper Makers from 1937) was formed in 1403 and received a royal charter in 1557. It held a monopoly over the publishing industry until the Copyright Act of 1710.

4 Quoted in Joad Raymond, *Pamphlets and Pamphleteering in Early Modern Britain* (Cambridge: Cambridge University Press, 2003), p. 257.

5 Quoted in K. Harvey, 'What Mary Toft Felt: Women's Voices, Pain, Power and the Body', *History Workshop Journal*, 80.1 (2015), pp. 33–51.

6 Dreyfus was initially imprisoned on Devil's Island off the coast of Guiana and then rehabilitated after being pardoned in 1906.

7 This journalistic error of judgment did not prevent Ackerman becoming the first dean of the Columbia School of Journalism. The forgery was exposed in a series of articles by *The Times* journalist Philip Graves on 16–18 August 1921.

8 Daniel Pipes, *Conspiracy: How the Paranoid Style Flourishes and Where It Comes From* (New York: Simon & Schuster, 1997), p. 85.

BLACK LIVES MATTER

1 Richard Luscombe, 'George Zimmerman Acquitted in Trayvon Martin case', *The Guardian*, 14 July 2013, https://www.theguardian.com/world/2013/jul/14/zimmerman-acquitted-killing-trayvon-martin; Patrisse Khan-Cullors and Asha Bandele, *When They Call You a Terrorist: A Black Lives Matter Memoir* (New York: St Martin's Press, 2018), p. 180; Jamilah King, 'How Three

Friends Turned a Spontaneous Facebook Post into a Global Phenomenon', *The California Sunday Magazine*, 1 March 2015, https://stories.californiasunday.com/2015-03-01/black-lives-matter; Patrisse Khan-Cullors and Asha Bandele; 'Black Lives Matter: Trayvon Martin, the Verdict that Changed Everything', *The Sydney Morning Herald*, 16 February 2018, https://www.smh.com.au/world/black-lives-matter-trayvon-martin-the-verdict-that-changed-everything-20180206-h0ur4c.html; Bioneers conference, *Patrisse Cullors: Women of the #BlackLivesMatter Movement* (2018), https://youtu.be/_YyDrKS8kAo.

2 Darren Sands, 'What Happened to Black Lives Matter?', *Buzzfeed*, 21 June 2017, https://www.buzzfeednews.com/article/darrensands/what-happened-to-black-lives-matter; David Dunkley Gyimah, interview with Eugene Robinson, 2020.

3 Tony Harcup and Deirdre O'Neill, 'What is News?: News Values Revisited (Again)', *Journalism Studies*, 18.12 (2017), pp. 1470–88; James Curran and Jean Seaton, *Power Without Responsibility: Press, Broadcasting and the Internet in Britain* (London: Routledge, 2018), p. 340.

4 'Martin Luther King Jr. Saw Three Evils in the World: Racism Was only the First', *The Atlantic*, February 2018, https://www.theatlantic.com/magazine/archive/2018/02/martin-luther-king-hungry-club-forum/552533; Gary Younge, 'Martin Luther King: The Story behind His "I Have a Dream" Speech', *The Guardian*, 9 August 2013, https://www.theguardian.com/world/2013/aug/09/martin-luther-king-dream-speech-history.

5 Stokely Carmichael, *The King Encyclopedia*, https://kinginstitute.stanford.edu/encyclopedia/carmichael-stokely; Stokely Carmichael and Charles V. Hamilton, *Black Power: The Politics of Liberation in America* (New York: Vintage, 1967); Bobby Seale, *Seize the Time: The Story of the Black Panther Party and Huey P. Newton* (New York: Black Classic Press, 1996); Robyn C. Spencer, *The Revolution Has Come: Black Power, Gender, and the Black Panther Party in Oakland* (Durham, NC: Duke University Press, 2016); Stanley Nelson, *The Black Panthers: Vanguard of the Revolution*, 2015 [film].

6 Rob Warden, 'Hoover Rated Carmichael as "Black Messiah"', *Chicago Daily News*, 10 February 1976, p. 25; Young Turks, *Black Lives Matter Labelled A Hate Group By Fox News* (2015), https://youtu.be/uHzgW09ddb0.

7 'Black Lives Matter: Malcolm X's Daughter Says Young Protesters are "Much Like" Her Father', Sky News, 15 June 2020, https://news.sky.com/story/black-lives-matter-malcolm-xs-daughter-says-young-protesters-are-much-like-her-father-12005548; Keith Nelson Jr, 'Malcolm X's Daughter on BLM, Sports Activism, and the "Right" Way to Protest', *Momentum*, 14 September 2020, https://momentum.medium.com/malcolm-xs-daughter-on-blm-sports-activism-and-the-right-way-to-protest-224abc5c71cd.

8 Terry Gross, 'Black Power Scholar Illustrates How MLK And Malcolm X Influenced Each Other', 12 August 2020, https://wamu.org/story/20/08/12/black-power-scholar-illustrates-how-mlk-and-malcolm-x-influenced-each-other.

9 'Black is Beautiful: The Emergence of Black Culture and Identity in the 60s and 70s', National Museum of African American History and Culture, https://nmaahc.si.edu/blog-post/black-beautiful-emergence-black-culture-and-identity-60s-and-70s; Bayer Mack, *No Lye: An American Beauty Story* (2019) [film]; Steve

Loring Jones, 'From "Under Cork" to Overcoming: Black Images in the Comics', Ferris State University: Jim Crow Museum of Racist Memorabilia, https://www.ferris.edu/HTMLS/news/jimcrow.

10 Randall Kennedy, 'How James Brown Made Black Pride a Hit', *The New York Times*, 20 July 2018, https://www.nytimes.com/2018/07/20/opinion/sunday/james-brown-say-it-loud-50-years.html; Mark I. Pinsky, 'Maligned in Black and White: Southern Newspapers Played a Major Role in Racial Violence. Do They Owe Their Communities an Apology?', *Poynter*, 8 May 2019, https://www.poynter.org/maligned-in-black-white.

11 Zoë Mitchell and Meghna Chakrabarti, '"Say It Loud": 50 Years Ago, James Brown Redefined Black Pride', 24 July 2018, https://www.wbur.org/radioboston/2018/07/24/james-brown-black-pride; Khan-Cullors, *When They Call You a Terrorist*, p. 197. The Black Panthers likewise supported the Palestinian people.

12 Bijan Stephen, 'Get Up Stand Up', *Wired*, October 2015, https://www.wired.com/2015/10/how-black-lives-matter-uses-social-media-to-fight-the-power.

13 Dhrumil Mehta, 'National Media Coverage of Black Lives Matter Had Fallen During the Trump Era – Until Now', *FiveThirtyEight*, 2020, https://fivethirtyeight.com/features/national-media-coverage-of-black-lives-matter-had-fallen-during-the-trump-era-until-now; Monica Anderson, 'The Hashtag #BlackLivesMatter Emerges: Social Activism on Twitter', Pew Research Center, 15 August 2016, https://www.pewresearch.org/internet/2016/08/15/the-hashtag-blacklivesmatter-emerges-social-activism-on-twitter; Khadija Jones, 'Angela Davis in Conversation at Southbank Centre London', *I Am HipHop*, https://www.iamhiphopmagazine.com/angela-davis-conversation-southbank-centre-london.

14 Monica Anderson, Michael Barthel, Andrew Perrin and Emily A. Vogels, '#BlackLivesMatter Surges on Twitter after George Floyd's Death', Pew Research Center, 10 June 2020, https://www.pewresearch.org/fact-tank/2020/06/10/blacklivesmatter-surges-on-twitter-after-george-floyds-death.

15 'Jacob Blake: What We Know about Wisconsin Police Shooting', BBC News, 31 August 2020, https://www.bbc.co.uk/news/world-us-canada-53909766.

16 Larry Buchanan, Quoctrung Bui and Jugal K. Patel, 'Black Lives Matter May Be the Largest Movement in US History', *The New York Times*, 3 July 2020, https://www.nytimes.com/interactive/2020/07/03/us/george-floyd-protests-crowd-size.html; Gyimah, interview with Eugene Robinson.

17 Mehta, 'National Media Coverage Of Black Lives Matter Had Fallen'; Khan-Cullors, *When They Call You a Terrorist*, p. 197; Kendra Pierre-Louis, 'It's Time to Change the Way the Media Reports on Protests. Here Are Some Ideas', Nieman Lab, 24 June 2020, https://www.niemanlab.org/2020/06/its-time-to-change-the-way-the-media-reports-on-protests-here-are-some-ideas.

18 Laura Flanders, 'Building Movements Without Shedding Differences: Alicia Garza of #BlackLivesMatter', *Truthout*, 24 March 2015, https://truthout.org/video/building-movements-without-shedding-differences-alicia-garza.

19 Rachell Eborall, 'Over 150 UK Towns join BLM protests', *rs21*, 8 June 2020, https://www.rs21.org.uk/2020/06/08/over-150-uk-towns-join-blm-protests; Champa Patel, 'Tackling Police Racism', Chatham House, https://www.chathamhouse.org/publications/the-world-today/2020-08/tackling-police-racism.

20 David Olusoga, MacTaggart lecture (2020), transcript at *Broadcast Now*, https://www.broadcastnow.co.uk/home/david-olusoga-mactaggart-lecture-in-full/5152544.article.

21 Rianna Jade Parker, 'How Stuart Hall Exposed the Racist Agenda Behind "Harmless" British Humour', *Frieze*, 7 February 2019, https://www.frieze.com/article/how-stuart-hall-exposed-racist-agenda-behind-harmless-british-humour.

22 John Jewell, 'Shocking not Shocked', *Jomec*, 13 December 2018, https://www.jomec.co.uk/blog/shocking-not-shocked; Raheem Sterling, Instagram feed, 6 December 2018, https://www.instagram.com/p/BrKYvF3gH9e; James Walker, 'Journalists Support Footballer Raheem Sterling's Claim Press Coverage "Fuels Racism" Following Alleged Abuse from Fan', *Press Gazette*, 10 December 2018, https://www.pressgazette.co.uk/journalists-support-footballer-raheem-sterlings-claim-press-coverage-fuels-racism-following-alleged-abuse-from-fan.

23 Daniel Trilling, 'Why is the UK Government Suddenly Targeting "Critical Race Theory"?', *The Guardian*, 23 October 2020, https://www.theguardian.com/commentisfree/2020/oct/23/uk-critical-race-theory-trump-conservatives-structural-inequality; Jon Stone, 'Black Lives Matter is "Not Force for Good" says Tory MP Sajid Javid', *The Independent*, 5 October 2020, https://www.independent.co.uk/news/uk/politics/sajid-javid-black-live-matter-blm-racism-tory-mp-b806336.html; Joe Evans, 'Why is Black Lives Matter Being Described as a "Political Movement"?', *This Week*, 7 December 2020, https://www.theweek.co.uk/108897/why-people-describe-black-lives-matter-political-movement.

24 Michael Levenson, 'Federal Employees Can Express Support for Black Lives Matter, Watchdog Says', *New York Times*, 16 July 2020, https://www.nytimes.com/2020/07/16/us/federal-employees-black-lives-matter.html.

25 Symeon Brown, 'Black Lives Matter UK Gain Legal Status and Access to £1m for the Cause', Channel 4 News, tx. 29 October 2020, https://www.channel4.com/news/black-lives-matter-uk-gain-legal-status-and-access-to-1m-for-the-cause; Jelani Cobb, 'The Matter of Black Lives', *The New Yorker*, 14 March 2016, https://www.newyorker.com/magazine/2016/03/14/where-is-black-lives-matter-headed.

26 Haroon Siddique, 'Athlete Stopped by Met Police Says It Feels Like "Being Black is a Crime"', *The Guardian*, 6 July 2020, https://www.theguardian.com/uk-news/2020/jul/06/bianca-williams-athlete-stopped-by-met-police-being-black-is-a-crime; Vikram Dodd, 'Get Off My Neck: London Police Officer Suspended after Arrest Incident', *The Guardian*, 17 July 2020, https://www.theguardian.com/uk-news/2020/jul/17/get-off-my-neck-london-police-officer-suspended-after-arrest-incident; 'John Boyega George Floyd Protest London Speech in Full: Star Wars Actor's Powerful Hyde Park Message', 3 June 2020, https://www.youtube.com/watch?v=GGXEB25WdyQ.

27 Isaac Chortiner, 'A Black Lives Matter Co-Founder Explains Why This Time Is Different', *The New Yorker*, 3 June 2020, https://www.newyorker.com/news/q-and-a/a-black-lives-matter-co-founder-explains-why-this-time-is-different.

28 Channel 4 News, tx. 2 June 2020, extract at https://www.channel4.com/news/this-moment-holds-possibilities-for-change-we-have-never-before-experienced-in-this-country-activist-and-writer-angela-davis.

29 M4BL, 'End the War on Black Communities', https://
    m4bl.org/policy-platforms/end-the-war-on-black-
    communities.

TRUTH, TRUST AND STORY

1   Daniel Sheridan, 'I feel the need to clarify a few things
    about this story after seeing some tweets/accounts
    doubting the basis of it' [Twitter post], 20.46, 9
    December 2019, https://twitter.com/DSheridanYEP/
    status/1204140196909977602. My thanks to Tamara
    Tubb at the British Library for her documentation of
    the timeline of this news story.
2   '"It was chaos": Shocking photo shows Leeds
    four-year-old with suspected pneumonia forced to
    sleep on floor of LGI due to lack of beds', Yorkshire
    Evening Post [website], 8 December 2019, https://www.
    yorkshireeveningpost.co.uk/news/people/it-was-
    chaos-shocking-photo-shows-leeds-four-year-old-
    suspected-pneumonia-forced-sleep-floor-lgi-due-lack-
    beds-1334909; 'How could this be allowed to happen?',
    Yorkshire Evening Post [print newspaper], 9 December
    2019, p. 1.
3   'Desperate', Daily Mirror, 9 December 2019, p. 1. The
    Mirror was the only national to carry the story on 9
    December, but the following day The Guardian and The
    Independent (digital only) featured the story on their
    front pages, while the Conservative-leaning nationals
    pointedly did not. On 10 December the Daily Mirror led
    with another photograph of a baby lying in a chair at
    a hospital A&E department, but this failed to have the
    same impact. 'Here's another picture you won't want to
    look at, Mr Johnson', Daily Mirror, 10 December 2019,
    p. 1.
4   ITV Evening News, tx. 9 December 2019.
5   Laura Kuenssberg, 'Happy to apologiSe [sic] for
    earlier confusion about the punch that wasn't a
    punch outside Leeds General – 2 sources suggested it
    had happened but clear from video that was wrong'
    [Twitter post], 18.48, 9 December 2019, https://twitter.
    com/bbclaurak/status/1204110491242643457; Robert
    Peston, 'It is completely clear from video footage
    that @MattHancock's adviser was not whacked by
    a protestor, as I was told by senior Tories, but that
    he inadvertently walked into a protestor's hand.
    I apologise for getting this wrong' [Twitter post],
    18.09, 9 December 2019, https://twitter.com/Peston/
    status/1204100056762265600. The original tweets
    by Kuenssberg and Peston are no longer available on
    Twitter but are reproduced in Peter Jukes, 'Trolls, Sock
    Puppets and Useful Idiots: An Anatomy of an Election
    Disinformation Campaign', Byline Times, 10 December
    2019, https://bylinetimes.com/2019/12/10/trolls-sock-
    puppets-and-useful-idiots-an-anatomy-of-an-election-
    disinformation-campaign.
6   The original Facebook posting and the account have
    been deleted but there are links to screenshots at
    https://fullfact.org/online/LGI-photo-boy-facebook.
7   Will Taylor, '"Monstrous" Accusation that Photo of
    Sick Boy on Hospital Floor was Staged Refuted', Yahoo
    News, 10 December 2019, https://uk.news.yahoo.com/
    sick-boy-leeds-hospital-nhs-101427982.html.
8   James Mitchinson, 'This is the net effect of the
    proliferation of absurdity by bots, saps & sock
    puppets ...' [Twitter post], 07.50, 10 December
    2019, https://twitter.com/JayMitchinson/
    status/1204307425597239296.
9   Alex Hern and Kate Proctor, '"I Was Hacked," Says
    Woman Whose Account Claimed Hospital Boy Photo
    Was Staged', The Guardian, 10 December 2019, https://
    www.theguardian.com/media/2019/dec/10/woman-
    says-account-hacked-to-post-fake-story-about-
    hospital-boy. The newspaper did not give her name
    because she said she had been the subject of death
    threats.
10 James Mitchinson, '"Do not Believe a Stranger on
    Social Media who Disappears into the Night" – An
    Open Letter from our Editor to You', The Yorkshire
    Post, 10 December 2019, https://www.yorkshirepost.
    co.uk/news/politics/do-not-believe-stranger-social-
    media-who-disappears-night-open-letter-our-editor-
    you-1746000.
11 Peter Riddell, 'The War of Jennifer's Ear', The Times, 28
    March 1992, p. 16.
12 Matthew White, 'Newspapers, Gossip and Coffee-
    House Culture', Discovering Literature, https://www.
    bl.uk/restoration-18th-century-literature/articles/
    newspapers-gossip-and-coffee-house-culture.
13 Figures as of October 2020 from Statista, https://www.
    statista.com/topics/737/twitter.
14 Jeff Jarvis, 'Platforms Are Not Publishers', The Atlantic,
    10 August 2018, https://www.theatlantic.com/ideas/
    archive/2018/08/the-messy-democratizing-beauty-of-
    the-internet/567194.
15 On news and the public sphere, see Jackie Harrison,
    News (Abingdon: Routledge, 2006), pp. 108–15.
16 Ibid, p. 2.
17 Bernard Williams, Truth and Truthfulness (Princeton,
    NJ: Princeton University Press, 2002), pp. 11, 87–8, 96.
18 For a summary of UK news industry campaigning
    issues, see the News Media Association, http://www.
    newsmediauk.org/Current-Topics.
19 Will Storr, The Science of Storytelling (London: William
    Collins, 2019), pp. 20–1.
20 Luke McKernan, 'News and the Storytelling Brain',
    19 July 2020, https://lukemckernan.com/2020/07/19/
    news-and-the-storytelling-brain.
21 John Yorke, Into the Woods: A Five-Act Journey into
    Story (New York: Overlook Press, 2014), p. 71.
22 Bernard Williams would have disagreed with such
    an analysis. Writing four years before Twitter was
    invented, he said of the internet and news, 'It
    constructs proliferating meeting places for the free
    and unstructured exchange of messages which bear
    a variety of claims, fancies, and suspicions ... The
    chances that many of these messages will be true is
    low' (Williams, Truth and Truthfulness, p. 216).

AFTERWORD

1   Reuters Institute Digital News Report 2021, https://
    reutersinstitute.politics.ox.ac.uk/sites/default/
    files/2021-06/Digital_News_Report_2021_FINAL.pdf,
    p. 26.
2   Ibid, p. 11.
3   'Future of News', http://newsimg.bbc.co.uk/1/shared/
    bsp/hi/pdfs/29_01_15future_of_news.pdf, p. 21.
4   See, for example, Tamotsu Shibutani, Improvised News:
    A Sociological Study of Rumor (Indianapolis: Bobbs-
    Merrill, 1966).
5   Amol Rajan, tweet of 5 November 2019, https://twitter.
    com/amolrajan/status/1191829175876894723.
6   Robert Gellately, Backing Hitler: Consent and Coercion
    in Nazi Germany (Oxford: Oxford University Press,
    2001), p. 186.
7   Walter Lippmann, Public Opinion (New York: Harcourt,
    Brace and Company, 1922).
8   'China's "AI newsreader": Which of these isn't real?',
    BBC News, 8 November 2018, https://www.bbc.co.uk/
    news/av/world-asia-china-46135116.

Timeline

Luke McKernan

1476 The first printing press in Britain is set up by William Caxton

1500 Wynkyn de Worde establishes his press in Fleet Street

1513 Earliest surviving printed news report in Britain, on the Battle of Flodden

1557 Royal charter granted to the Stationers' Company of London, giving it regulatory control over publishing

1586 Star Chamber decree on government regulation of printing

1620 *Corrant out of Italy, Germany, etc*: first coranto, or newspaper, in English, published in Amsterdam

1621 First newspaper to be published in Britain, *Corante, or, Newes from Italy, Germany, Hungarie, Spaine and France*

1626 Ben Jonson's play *The Staple of News* satirises newspapers

1641 Abolition of Star Chamber brings some measure of press freedom

1641 *The Heads of several proceedings in this present parliament*: first official printed reporting of Parliament

1643 Civil War rivalry between Royalist and Parliamentarian newspapers, such as the Royalist *Mercurius Aulicus* and the Parliamentarian *Mercurius Britannicus*

1644 John Milton's *Areopagitica* published, on the principle of a free press

1652 Possible date of the first London coffeehouse. Coffeehouses become important venues for the exchange and discussion of news

1655 Oliver Cromwell restores the licensing system and suppresses all newspapers except official publications

1662 Following the Restoration, the Licensing of the Press Act brings in stringent press control

1663 Roger L'Estrange becomes Surveyor and Licensor of the press, suppressing dissent and producing the only two permitted newspaper titles himself, *The Public Intelligencer* and *The News*

1665 *Oxford Gazette* founded, becoming *London Gazette* in February 1666. The world's oldest surviving periodical

1679 Lapse of the Licensing Act brings a flood of unlicensed newspapers, later suppressed

1693 *Ladies Mercury* published, the first women's magazine. Lasts for four weekly issues only

1695 Parliament decides against renewing the Licensing Act, clearing the way for a free press

1701 *The Norwich Post* (1701–12) founded, probably the first provincial newspaper

1702 *The Daily Courant* founded, the first daily paper

1711 Joseph Addison and Richard Steele found *The Spectator*, a highly influential daily publication (runs to 1712; current British journal *The Spectator* borrows its name)

1712 Stamp duty imposed on newspapers and advertisements

1731 Edward Cave founds *The Gentleman's Magazine*

1738 Complete ban imposed on reporting Parliament

1763 John Wilkes is prosecuted for seditious libel for an edition of *The North Briton* (no. 45) attacking a speech given by King George III

1771 Press wins the right to report parliamentary proceedings

1780 First Sunday newspaper published by Elizabeth Johnson, *E. Johnson's British Gazette & Sunday Monitor*

1781 *The Observer* founded, the world's oldest surviving Sunday newspaper

1785 *The Daily Universal Register* founded by John Walter. Becomes *The Times* on 1 January 1788

1802 *Cobbett's Annual Register* founded, later *Cobbett's Weekly Political Register*

1814 First issue of a newspaper, *The Times*, printed on a Koenig steam press

1817 Three politically motivated trials of journalist and bookseller William Hone for libel; he was acquitted each time

1819 Peterloo massacre at St Peter's Field, Manchester, when cavalry charges into a crowd calling for reform of parliamentary representation

1819 'Six Acts' introduced following Peterloo, with the goal of controlling protest including Blasphemous and Seditious Libels Act and Newspaper and Stamp Duties Act (extending taxes on news publications)

1821 *Manchester Guardian* founded by John Edward Taylor. Becomes *The Guardian* in 1959

1822 Stamp Office begins sending copies of stamped newspapers to the British Museum

1830 Liverpool and Manchester Railway, the first inter-city railway line and first operated entirely by steam power. Agreement to convey newspapers to newsagents made in 1831, leading to the end of stage coaches as means of distribution

1837 Isaac Pitman introduces his shorthand system

1837 Cooke and Wheatstone electric telegraph, first commercial telegraph service

1839 Daguerreotypes and collotypes, early types of photograph, demonstrated

1842 *Illustrated London News* first published

1843 *News of the World* founded by John Browne Bell, priced 3d, the cheapest newspaper of its time

1843 Rotary printing press invented by American Richard March Hoe

1844 Newsprint invented by Charles Fenerty in Canada, a paper that could be produced in great quantities at low cost, transforming the newspaper industry

1844 First story based on telegraphed news printed in *The Times* on 6 August, on birth of Queen Victoria's son at Windsor

1848 W.H. Smith opens its first railway station news-stand, at Euston

1850 First submarine cable between Britain and France

1850 Public Libraries Act, giving local boroughs power to establish free public libraries, including free newsrooms

1851 Reuters News Agency opens in London

1854 William Howard Russell's ground-breaking reports of the Crimean War expose mismanagement and contribute to the fall of the government; Robert Fenton's photographs of the war exhibited

1855 Repeal of the Stamp Act opens the way for cheap, mass-circulation newspapers

1855 *Daily Telegraph & Courier* founded, becomes *The Daily Telegraph* in 1856

1861 Paper duty abolished

1865 First successful transatlantic cable

1869 Newspapers received at British Museum Library through legal deposit

1876 Alexander Graham Bell invents the first successful telephone

1880 W.T. Stead becomes editor of the *Pall Mall Gazette* and introduces the 'new journalism', including the interview, the gossip column and the use of undercover reporting, into Britain

1885 W.T. Stead imprisoned after 'Maiden Tribute of Babylon' articles on child prostitution

1886 Eastman Kodak hand camera

1891 Rachel Beer becomes first woman editor of a British national newspaper when she takes over *The Observer*; in 1893 she becomes editor of *The Sunday Times* as well

1896 First public exhibition of projected film in Britain held in January by Birt Acres

1896 *Daily Mail* launched by Alfred Harmsworth (later Lord Northcliffe)

1900 *Daily Express* founded by Arthur Pearson

1901 Guglielmo Marconi demonstrates transatlantic radio telegraphy

1904 Alfred Harmsworth launches the *Daily Mirror*, initially as a newspaper for women produced by women. It is changed to a pictorial newspaper with broader focus in 1904

1910 First British newsreel, *Pathé's Animated Gazette*

1911 Aviator Gustav Hamel delivers the first airmail, flying from Hendon to Windsor, with postcards and some newspapers

1914 UK cuts German undersea cables at the outset of the First World War

1916 Max Aitken (later Lord Beaverbrook) takes a controlling share in *Daily Express*

1917 *War Office Official Topical Budget* propaganda newsreel issued, runs to 1919

1918 Ministry of Information propaganda body formed, headed by Lord Beaverbrook

1922 British Broadcasting Company formed, later the British Broadcasting Corporation (BBC)

1926 Most newspapers suspended during the General Strike. Government publishes *The British Gazette*; Trades Union Congress publishes *The British Worker*

1926 John Logie Baird demonstrates television

1929 First sound newsreels in Britain

1930 First newsreel theatre in Britain opens, the G.B. Movietone and News Theatre on Shaftesbury Avenue, London

1932 BBC Empire Service radio broadcasting begins. Becomes BBC Overseas Service in 1939 and BBC World Service in 1965

1936 BBC Television Service starts from Alexandra Palace, London

1938 First British radio broadcasts in a foreign language (Arabic)

1938 *Picture Post* launched by Edward Hulton

1939 Ministry of Information re-formed

1939 BBC Monitoring established to select and analyse foreign media and propaganda

1946 British government's communications body, the Central Office of Information, formed (closed 2011)

1948 *BBC Television Newsreel*, first BBC-produced television news series

1953 *Panorama* first broadcast on the BBC – now the longest-running British television news programme

1955 On-screen newsreaders introduced by the BBC, ahead of ITN newsreaders when ITV service launches in September

1957 *Today* radio programme launched on BBC Home Service

1958 Claudia Jones founds the *West Indian Gazette* in Brixton, London

1961 *Private Eye* satirical magazine launched

1962 *That Was the Week That Was* satirical television series broadcast by the BBC, hosted by David Frost. Closed in 1963, ostensibly because a general election was imminent

1963 Tim Hewat at Granada Television creates investigative current affairs series *World in Action*

1967 First BBC local radio station, BBC Radio Leicester

1967 *News at Ten* first broadcast by ITV

1969 *The Sun* relaunched as a tabloid by Rupert Murdoch

1971 Teletext invented – a system for displaying text and rudimentary graphics on TV. Used by BBC to provide Ceefax news service 1974–2014 and by ITV for ORACLE news service 1978–1992

1973 Independent local radio introduced; first contracts issued to LBC and Capital Radio

1977 Apple II personal computer goes on sale

1979 The last British newsreel closes (*British Movietone News*)

1981 Rupert Murdoch buys *The Times* and *Sunday Times*

1982 Betacam videocassettes developed by Sony, widely used in broadcast news industry

1982 *The Voice* newspaper launched, for British Afro-Caribbean audience

1982 Channel 4 television service

1984 The first free daily newspaper in the UK, *The Birmingham Daily News*, is launched

1986 News International moves all national titles to its new plant at Wapping, enabling a change from traditional printing processes to computerised newspaper production

1986 *Today* launched by Eddy Shah, first national newspaper with colour photography

1988 'Death on the Rock', part of Thames Television's *This Week* current affairs series, causes political furore with evidence of government shoot-to-kill policy for IRA operatives

1989 First transatlantic fibre optic cable

1989 *Sky News* launched, first twenty-four-hour news TV channel in UK

1990 First episode of BBC satirical news review programme *Have I Got News For You*

1994 *The Telegraph* launches the UK's first newspaper website, *Electronic Telegraph*

1996 Internet Archive founded by Brewster Kahle

1997 Google search

1997 BBC website, bbc.co.uk

1998 *Se1* (May) and *Rochdale Online* (June), arguably the UK's first hyperlocal websites

1999 RIM launches the first Blackberry (as an email pager)

1999 RSS web feed application released by Netscape, leading to the development of news aggregators

2003 First release of Wordpress blogging software

2005 Launch of social news aggregator Reddit

2005 First video uploaded to YouTube

2006 Google News app officially launched

2006 First message on Twitter

2006 Facebook, founded in 2004, opens to anyone aged over thirteen with a valid email address

2006 Wikileaks founded

2007 Apple introduces the iPhone

2009 The London *Evening Standard* becomes a free newspaper, after 150 years as a paid-for title

2010 First iPad

2010 Image-sharing social network Instagram launched

2011 British Newspaper Archive website launched

2011 Leveson inquiry into the culture, practices and ethics of the press; *News of the World* closes as consequence of phone hacking scandal

2013 CIA employee Edward Snowden leaks leaked highly classified information on global surveillance operations from the National Security Agency

2013 National Library of Wales launches Welsh Newspapers Online

2013 Legal Deposit Libraries (Non-Print Works) Regulations lead to formal archiving of UK websites

2014 MailOnline becomes the most visited English-language newspaper website

2014 Bellingcat open-source investigative journalism site founded

2016 *The Independent* national newspaper goes online only

2016 The last two journalists leave Fleet Street

2020 COVID-19 pandemic sees many local newspapers close or go online only; community radio flourishes in response to local needs

2020 Black Lives Matter movement (founded 2013) gains high-profile news presence worldwide after the killing of George Floyd by US police

2021 Twitter permanently suspends President Donald Trump's account

Beth Gaskell and Luke McKernan

British Library news collection

The British Library collects the nation's news. Our earliest printed news publication dates from 1513 (a report on the Battle of Flodden); our earliest British newspaper dates from 1621 (*Corante, or, Newes from Italy, Germany, Hungarie, Spaine and France*).

The bedrock of the collection is newspapers, but since 2010 we have been building up extensive radio and television news archives, and since 2013 we have collected the UK web news. Each week we take in more than 3,500 different news publications, in print, digital and audiovisual forms. Our news collections are accessible to researchers at our reading rooms in St Pancras, London and Boston Spa, Yorkshire, with a rapidly growing percentage of digitised newspapers also available via the British Newspaper Archive (https://www.britishnewspaperarchive.co.uk).

NEWSPAPERS

The British Library's newspaper collection comprises more than 36,000 titles from the UK and overseas, or 60 million individual issues, from 1619 to the present day. This includes newspapers from the earliest printed in English through to the ongoing collection of UK and Irish newspapers, which are received under legal deposit: the legal requirement that a copy of a publication is submitted to a designated repository. The collection is made up of printed newspapers (around 450 million pages), microfilm copies of one-third of these and digital copies (nearly 50 million digitised pages, and growing at a rate of over 5 million a year).

The newspaper collection was founded on two special collections of early English newspapers: the Thomason Tracts, which contain newspapers and newsbooks from the English Civil War period (1642–51) collected by the printer George Thomason (c. 1602–1666); and the Burney Collection of newspapers and related news publications from 1603 to 1818, collected by Charles Burney (1757–1817). From 1822 the British Museum Library began systematically collecting British newspapers, deposited via the Stamp Office, and from 1869 British and Irish newspapers were received through legal deposit.

The collection includes full runs of the main London edition of all the British national daily and Sunday newspapers. Most daily and weekly provincial newspapers are also held, including some from the early eighteenth century onwards. Newspapers are acquired selectively from overseas, in English and some other languages. This includes an extensive collection of newspapers from Commonwealth countries which were formerly received through colonial copyright deposit. Currently around 1200 UK and Irish newspaper titles are received on a daily or weekly basis, and nearly 100 titles from overseas. There are historic newspapers in the collection from more than 190 countries.

The Library's holdings of early printed newspapers include a number covering the period of the Civil War, the Commonwealth and the Restoration, as well as the *London Gazette*, the world's longest-running active newspaper title, from its earliest issue (as the *Oxford Gazette*) in 1665.

The collection of eighteenth-century newspapers is particularly strong for London-based titles, but also contains English provincial, Irish and Scottish papers, and a few examples from the American colonies, France and the Netherlands. Important titles included are *The British Journal, The Daily Courant, The Daily Gazetteer, Lloyd's Evening Post and British Chronicle, The London Chronicle, The Morning Chronicle and London Advertiser, The St James's Chronicle or British Evening Post* and *Whitehall Evening Post or London Intelligencer*.

The Library's nineteenth-century collection is

The Library's holdings of early printed newspapers include the London Gazette, *the world's longest-running active newspaper title, from its earliest issue in 1665.*

more comprehensive, including early illustrated titles, political and special-interest newspapers and provincial newspapers from around the country. There are complete runs of well-known titles such as *The Times*, the *Morning Herald* and the *Daily Mail*, but also less familiar but significant specialist titles such as *The Poor Man's Guardian*, *The Illustrated Police News* and *The Lady's Newspaper*. The collection covers all the key events of the century, from Queen Victoria's coronation to the Crimean War, from the 1832 Reform Act to the first sailing of the SS *Great Eastern*.

The twentieth- and twenty-first-century newspaper holdings include all the UK's national daily and weekly newspapers, as well as provincial and local publications. The Library has all the major titles in hard copy, with copies held also on microfilm and/or via digital subscriptions. As well as titles familiar from today, there are newspaper titles once famous that are no longer published (*The Daily Sketch*, *Reynold's News*, *Today*) and titles that reflect the country's rich diversity *(Al-Arab, Daily Jang, The Voice)*. They provide an incomparable resource for all the events of the period, including the two World Wars, the sinking of the *Titanic* and the women's suffrage movement, right up to the fall of the Berlin Wall, 9/11 and COVID-19, as well as being a rich source for family history research.

Currently the British Library acquires most British newspapers in print form, but is planning to have the capability to take many in digital form only.

The twentieth- and twenty-first-century newspaper holdings include all the UK's national daily and weekly newspapers, as well as provincial and local publications.

OTHER MEDIA

Since 2010 the British Library has been recording selected television news programmes broadcast in the UK. Programmes have been acquired not only from the BBC, ITV, Channel 4 and Sky News, but also from global channels such as Al Jazeera English, CNN, RT (formerly Russia Today) and Turkey's TRT World, all of which are licensed to broadcast in the UK. The collection includes documentaries, interviews, debates, party political broadcasts and news satire. There are special collections on topics such as the UK riots of 2011, the Olympic and Paralympic Games, general elections, the Scottish independence referendum, COVID-19 and Black Lives Matter. There is a small but growing collection of news-based podcasts.

Our extensive radio collections go back to the 1920s and includes many news programmes. As with television, we have made a special feature of recording programmes as they are broadcast. At the start of 2020 we launched a National Radio Archive pilot, which has recorded selected programmes from more than sixty UK radio stations, with a particular focus on community radio, including enterprising stations such as BCB 106.6fm (Bradford Community Broadcasting) and Ujima Radio. Radio and television in the UK are not covered by legal deposit legislation, but are collected by the Library for their essential research value and to complement the print news holdings.

In 2013, legal deposit was extended to cover electronic publications. The number of UK web pages collected by the British Library since then runs into the billions. Among these are news websites, which are collected on a daily or weekly basis. The web news collection comprises more than 2,500 titles, from the online versions of established print titles to many web-only publications, with a particular focus on the 'hyperlocal' sector of community-focused news sites, such as *A Little Bit of Stone*, *South Leeds Life* and *On the Wight*. The social media platforms strongly associated with news, such as Facebook and Twitter, are based in the United States and consequently lie outside British legal deposit obligations. A few Twitter accounts with a strong news focus are nevertheless collected by the British Library.

The number of UK web pages collected by the British Library runs into the billions.

As the ways in which news is published change, so must the British Library adapt to ensure that we continue to preserve and make available the nation's news. As well as being alert to how news publications are changing, we will look to ways in which to link together these different media in an integrated form that reflects appropriately the world of news, yesterday and today.

http://www.bl.uk/subjects/news-media

Further reading

General

Jill Abrahamson, *Merchants of Truth: Inside the News Revolution* (London: Bodley Head, 2019)

Asa Briggs and Peter Burke, *A Social History of the Media: From Gutenberg to the Internet*, second edition (Cambridge/Malden, MA: Polity Press, 2005)

George Brock, *Out of Print: Newspapers, Journalism and the Business of News in the Digital Age* (London: Kogan Page, 2013)

Martin Conboy, *Journalism in Britain: A Historical Introduction* (London: Sage, 2011)

James Curran and Jean Seaton, *Power Without Responsibility: Press, Broadcasting and the Internet in Britain*, eighth edition (London: Routledge, 2018)

Tony Harcup, *Journalism: Principles and Practice*, third edition (London: Sage, 2015)

Jackie Harrison, *News* (Abingdon: Routledge, 2006)

———, *The Civil Power of the News* (Basingstoke: Palgrave Macmillan, 2019)

Richard Hoggart, *Mass Media in a Mass Society: Myth and Reality* (London/New York: Continuum, 2004)

Phillip Knightley, *The First Casualty: The War Correspondent as Hero and Myth-Maker from the Crimea to Iraq*, third edition (Baltimore, MD: Johns Hopkins University Press, 2004 [orig. 1975])

Andrew Marr, *My Trade: A Short History of British Journalism* (London: Macmillan, 2004)

Lionel Morrison, *A Century of Black Journalism in Britain: A Kaleidoscopic View of Race and the Media (1893–2003)* (London: Truebay, 2007)

Alan Rusbridger, *The Remaking of Journalism: And Why it Matters Now* (Edinburgh: Canongate, 2018)

Michael Schudson, *The Sociology of News*, second edition (New York/London: W.W. Norton, 2011)

Andrew Sparrow, *Obscure Scribblers: A History of Parliamentary Journalism* (London: Politico's, 2003)

Kevin Williams, *Get Me a Murder a Day! A History of Mass Communication in Britain* (London/New York: Arnold, 1998)

Newspapers

Richard D. Altick, *The English Common Reader: A Social History of the Mass Reading Public, 1800–1900* (Chicago/London: University of Chicago Press, 1957)

Laurel Brake and Marysa Demoor (eds), *Dictionary of Nineteenth-Century Journalism* (Ghent/London: British Library/Academia Press, 2009)

Laurel Brake, Ed King, Roger Luckhurst and James Mussell (eds), *W.T. Stead, Newspaper Revolutionary* (London: British Library, 2012)

Paul Brighton, *Original Spin: Downing Street and the Press in Victorian Britain* (London/New York: I.B. Tauris, 2016)

Peter Chippindale and Chris Horrie, *Stick It up Your Punter! The Uncut Story of the Sun Newspaper* (London: Heinemann, 1990)

Bob Clarke, *From Grub Street to Fleet Street: An Illustrated History of English Newspapers to 1899* (Brighton: Revel Barker, 2010)

Martin Conboy and Daniel Finkelstein (series eds), *The Edinburgh History of the British and Irish Press*, 3 vols (Edinburgh: Edinburgh University Press, 2020–)

Hugh Cudlipp, *Publish and be Damned! The Astonishing Story of the Daily Mirror* (London: Andrew Dakers, 1953)

Nick Davies, *Hack Attack: How the Truth Caught Up with Rupert Murdoch* (London: Chatto & Windus, 2014)

Matthew Engel, *Tickle the Public: One Hundred Years of the Popular Press* (London: Gollancz, 1996)

Harold Evans, *My Paper Chase: True Stories of Vanished Times – An Autobiography* (London: Little, Brown, 2009)

Harold Evans (in association with Edwin Taylor), *Pictures on a Page: Photo-Journalism, Graphics and Picture Editing* (London: Pimlico, 1997 [orig. 1978])

Roy Greenslade, *Press Gang: How Newspapers Make Profits from Propaganda* (London: Macmillan, 2003)

Stanley Harrison, *Poor Men's Guardians: A Survey of the Struggles for a Democratic Newspaper Press, 1763–1973* (London: Lawrence and Wishart, 1974)

Ruth Herman, *Grub Street: The Origins of the British Press* (Stroud: Amberley, 2020)

Martin Hewitt, *The Dawn of the Cheap Press in Victorian Britain: The End of the 'Taxes on Knowledge', 1849–1869* (London: Bloomsbury, 2014)

Andrew Hobbs, *A Fleet Street in Every Town: The Provincial Press in England, 1855–1900* (Cambridge: Open Book Publishers, 2018)

Leveson Inquiry, *An Inquiry into the Culture, Practices and Ethics of the Press* (London: HMSO, 2012)

Mass-Observation, *The Press and Its Readers* (London: Art & Technics, 1949)

Rachel Matthews *The History of the Provincial Press in England* (London: Bloomsbury, 2017)

Eilat Negev and Yehuda Koren, *First Lady of Fleet Street: The Life, Fortune and Tragedy of Rachel Beer* (London: JR Books, 2011)

Andrew Pettegree, *The Invention of News: How the World Came to Know About Itself* (New Haven, CT/London: Yale University Press, 2014)

Joad Raymond, *The Invention of the Newspaper: English Newsbooks, 1641–1649* (Oxford: Clarendon Press, 2005 [orig. 1996])

Matthew J. Shaw, *An Inky Business: A History of Newspapers from the English Civil Wars to the American Civil War* (London: Reaktion Books, 2021)

A.J.P. Taylor, *Beaverbrook* (London: Hamish Hamilton, 1972)

Julie Welch, *The Fleet Street Girls: The Women Who Broke Down the Doors of the Gentlemen's Club* (London: Trapeze, 2020)

Kevin Williams, *Read All About It! A History of the British Newspaper* (Abingdon: Routledge, 2010)

Ben Wilson, *The Laughter of Triumph: William Hone and the Fight for the Free Press* (London: Faber and Faber, 2005)

Newsreels

Ciara Chambers, Mats Jönsson and Roel Vande Winkel (eds), *Researching Newsreels: Local, National and Transnational Case Studies* (Cham: Palgrave Macmillan, 2018)

Luke McKernan (ed.), *Yesterday's News: The British Cinema Newsreel Reader* (London: British Universities Film and Video Council, 2002)

Radio

Hugh Chignell, *Public Issue Radio: Talks, News and Current Affairs in the Twentieth Century* (London: Palgrave Macmillan, 2011)

John Humphrys, *A Day Like Today* (London: William Collins, 2019)

Television

Michael Cockerell, *Live from Number 10: The Inside Story of Prime Ministers and Television* (London: Faber and Faber, 1988)

Geoffrey Cox, *Pioneering Television News: A First Hand Report on a Revolution in Journalism* (London: John Libbey, 1995)

Stephen Cushion and Richard Sambrook (eds), *The Future of 24-Hour News: New Directions, New Challenges* (New York: Peter Lang, 2016)

Grace Wyndham Goldie, *Facing the Nation: Television and Politics, 1936–76* (London: Bodley Head, 1977)

Emily Maitlis, *Airhead: The Imperfect Art of Making News* (London: Michael Joseph, 2019)

New media

Nicholas Diakopoulos, *Automating the News: How Algorithms are Rewriting the Media* (Cambridge, MA: Harvard University Press, 2019)

Andrew Duffy, *Smartphones and the News* (Abingdon/New York: Routledge, 2021)

David Harte, Rachel Howells and Andy Williams, *Hyperlocal Journalism: The Decline of Local Newspapers and the Rise of Online Community News* (Abingdon/New York: Routledge, 2019)

Eliot Higgins, *We Are Bellingcat: An Intelligence Agency for the People* (London: Bloomsbury, 2021)

Francesco Marconi, *Newsmakers: Artificial Intelligence and the Future of Journalism* (New York: Columbia University Press, 2020)

Rasmus Kleis Nielsen (ed.), *Local Journalism: The Decline of Newspapers and the Rise of Digital Media* (London/New York: I.B. Tauris, 2015)

David Patrikarakos, *War in 140 Characters: How Social Media is Reshaping Conflict in the Twenty-First Century* (New York: Basic Books, 2017)

Edward Snowden, *Permanent Record* (London: Macmillan, 2019)

Illustration sources

All images from the collections of the British Library except the following:

cover (mobile phone and layered newspapers) Shutterstock; **20–1** Shutterstock; **29** The Times/News Licensing; **31** Library of Congress, Washington, D.C.; **40** CC-BY-4.0 © European Union 2020 – Source: EP; **44** The Daily Telegraph; **50** From Alex Mitchell's *Come the Revolution*, NewSouth Publishing, Sydney 2011; **57** The Sun/News Licensing; **68** The Mohamed Amin Foundation; **71** Parliamentary Recording Unit; **76** Photo by Louise Kennerley/Fairfax Media via Getty Images; **84** © Donal F. Holway/ NYT; **86–7** Shutterstock; **98** Courtesy of the Priaulx Library, Guernsey; **99** © The Voice newspaper; **108** Modern Records Centre, University Library, University of Warwick; **110** The Sun/News Licensing; **112** National Portrait Gallery, London; **115** © Solo Syndication; **117** © Steve Bell 2019 – All Rights Reserved; **122–3** seraficus/iStock; **134** Copyright Guardian News & Media Ltd 2021; **137** The Bristol Cable; **142** PA Images/Alamy Stock Photo; **147** The Sun/News Licensing; **149** Courtesy Carole Cadwalladr; **154** Pathé News; **162** Photo by John Davidson/ Liverpool Echo/Mirrorpix/Getty Images; **164–5** Shutterstock; **170** BFI; **172** Department of Health and Social Care; **178** Bradford Community Broadcasting; **182** Trustees of the British Museum; **188 left:** Photo by Jewel Samad/AFP via Getty Images, **right:** Photo by Lucas Jackson-Pool/Getty Images; **189** National Portrait Gallery, London; **191** Shutterstock; **196** PA Images/Alamy Stock Photo; **199** © Raheem Stirling/Instagram. Photo by Sam Bagnall – AMA/Getty Images; **202** Photo by Jeff Spicer/Getty Images; **204** Photo by Finnbarr Webster/Getty Images; **207** Trustees of the British Museum; **215** The Mohamed Amin Foundation.

Index

BACK-BENCH LABOUR MPs AIM FOR STORM

DEAD

sleep

Daily Mirror

The time

July 20, A

MAN ON

'My wife was misled'

FINAL NIGHT

SHIRTS.

Crowds stampede at St. Peter's

FERRARI TALKS WITH B.M.C.

AND THE MESSAGE FROM EARTH WE'RE